谢新洲◎主编

竞争情报进展 (2012)

Progress in Competitive Intelligence

华夏出版社
HUAXIA PUBLISHING HOUSE

竞争情报进展(2012)编委会

主　任：丁　辉
副主任：李永进　谢新洲
编　委：(按姓氏拼音排序)
　　　　Henri Dou　Martin Grothe　霍国庆　李　纲　刘细文
　　　　卢小宾　陆　伟　Rainer Michaeli　John E. Prescott
　　　　Alan L. Porter　Jean-Marie Rousseau　沈固朝
　　　　Sheila Wright　Yoshio Sugasawa　孙建军　王知津
　　　　时艳琴　Fumiyuki Takahashi　陶庆久　王　强
　　　　吴晨生　夏立新　谢新洲　夏勇其　肖雪葵　查先进
　　　　张士运　赵　刚　赵升祥　郑彦宁
主　编：谢新洲
副主编：王　强　刘细文

序

竞争情报已逐渐成为企业参与竞争、开展科技创新、获取竞争优势的重要支撑,同时外部环境的快速变化对竞争情报提出了新的要求。首先,大数据时代的到来极大拓展了数据获取的渠道,快速增长的海量、异构大数据给竞争情报研究和服务带来了前所未有的挑战。其次,社会化媒体近两年迅速普及,已经渗透到社会的各个角落,为人际网络情报的获取提供了新的数据源,如何通过社会化媒体平台获取人际网络情报成为了竞争情报研究的新课题。越来越多有价值的情报内容不断出现在包括社会化媒体在内的各种信息平台,并通过信息媒介快速传播,随后迅速淹没在大数据的汪洋之中。如何在低价值密度的大数据中快速挖掘有价值的情报,既是决策的需要,也是竞争情报面临的新任务,对竞争情报的发展提出了新的挑战,同时也为竞争情报方法和应用的创新提供了新的机遇。

为此,北京大学竞争情报与竞争力中心和北京市科学技术研究院竞争情报与创新评估重点实验室从2010年开始,汇聚国内外竞争情报权威研究专家和资深从业人员,系统地分析梳理国内外竞争情报发展过程、最新进展及未来趋势,为竞争情报最新理论、方法和应用成果搭建展示平台。在首卷本《竞争情报进展(2010)》中,二十余位国内外竞争情报权威专家系统地追溯了中、英、法等国的竞争情报发展历程,并对未来竞争情报所面临的机遇与挑战进行了总结和展望,同时就产业竞争情报、专利情报研究方法、观点挖掘与情报分析、技术竞争情报等专门问题展开了深入研究。《竞争情报进展(2012)》是《竞争情报进展(2010)》的延续和深化,我们再次集结来自中、美、法、日等国竞争情报界的专家学者,凝结他们的智慧和心血,或从整体或从局部,或从方法或从应用,探究竞争情报发展规律,以期推动国内外竞争情报研究更上一个台阶。

本书在内容上聚焦于竞争情报的方法、技术和应用。在竞争情报方法方面,北京大学谢新洲教授等在竞争情报方法体系搭建的基础上,阐述了竞争情报在获取、分析、可视化及工具软件等方面的最新进展;美国匹兹堡大学教授John E. Prescott等提出了一个产业融合过程中的预警框架;武汉大学李纲教授等梳理了国内外人际情报网络研究现状;武汉大学查先进教授采用文献计量方法,对近25年来国内竞争情报研究进展进行了系统梳理总结。

在信息技术与软件工具方面,法国马赛三大教授Henri Dou等通过专利自动分析技术来揭示技术战略依赖关系;美国詹姆斯·麦迪逊大学陶庆久博士提出了竞争情报软件选用的方法和标准;德国Complexium公司总裁Martin Grothe教授等针对社会化媒体信息,研究了运用计算语言学和语义分析工具来挖掘竞争情报的方法;武汉大学陆伟教授等通过文章句子中的词汇、词性标注和词汇之间的距离关系实现了观点指示动词识别和观点持有者识别,从而达到网络人物观点识别的目标。

在应用方面,中国科学院文献情报中心刘细文研究员以管理目标、关注内容、情报任务等三大要素为内容,以面向管理决策、目标性、稳定性等为原则,实现了面向企业技术创新的关键竞争情报课题构建;日本经济大学Yoshio Sugasawa教授和日本静冈大学Fumiyuki Takahashi博士深入阐述了情景分析、技术信号理论在技术创新和技术挖掘中的应用;日本仙台Waste Management公司Yoshinari Noboru等介绍了日本大地震恢复重建过程中Waste Mangement公司的竞争情报实施;来自法国的区域竞争情报专家Jean-Marie Rousseau等探讨了竞争情报方法和技术在中国经济增长方式转变中的应用。

本书是继《竞争情报进展(2010)》后,国内外竞争情报领域权威专家又一次先进思想大集结。他们从更高的视角为竞争情报研究及从业者展现了竞争情报方法、技术和应用在新环境下的发展,对竞争情报领域的研究者和实践者具有参考价值和启发意义,同时为企业和政府决策过程中竞争情报新方法和新技术的应用提供了新思路。

在此,感谢"北京市科学技术研究院科技创新工程项目"专项资金的支持,并再次感谢参与本书写作的各位同仁诚恳而辛勤的付出!

谢新洲

2013年6月26日

目　录

竞争情报方法与工具的新进展 ………… 谢新洲　王强　金学慧（1）

Early Warning during the Industry Convergence Process
　………… Sean Tsu–Hsiang Hsu　John E. Prescott（16）

近25年我国竞争情报研究进展 …………………… 查先进　刘莉（51）

Waste Management Data Collection during Disaster Recovery
　…… Yoshinari Noboru　Ohuchi Azuma　Sugasawa Yoshio（74）

人际情报网络研究进展 ……………………… 李纲　王忠义（107）

Technological Innovation and Scenario Analysis seen from Competitive technical Intelligence … Sugasawa Yoshio　Fumiyuki Takahashi（130）

Evaluation and Selection of Competitive Intelligence Software
　…………………………………………………………… 陶庆久（142）

网络人物观点识别研究 ……………… 陆伟　雷声伟　张晓娟（152）

Exploring the Unknown Unknows – Advanced Computer – Linguistic Methods for Social Media Analysis
　………………………… Martin Grothe　Hanna Huber（162）

Automatic Patent Analysis – Technological Strategic Dependence
…Henri Dou　Jean Marie Dou J　Getachew Mengistie Alemu（173）

面向企业技术创新的关键竞争情报课题构建 ……… 刘细文　熊瑞（193）

Study on Signaling Theory and the Practice of High – Tech Information Exploring ……………… Fumiyuki Takahashi　Jiang Dianchun
　　　　　　　　　　　　　　　　　　　　　Xian Guoming（236）

The applications of Method and Technology of Competitive Intelligence ………… Jean – Marie Rousseau　Wen Hongjian（251）

竞争情报方法与工具的新进展

谢新洲[①] 王强[②] 金学慧[③]

[**摘要**] 方法研究与创新是竞争情报研究的核心问题之一,软件工具是提高方法应用效率和效果的有效途径,因此,对竞争情报方法与工具最新进展情况进行梳理和总结,对指导竞争情报事业发展具有先导和启示作用。本文首先从不同的角度分析了竞争情报方法体系的构成,然后根据方法体系,介绍了情报获取、分析和可视化的新方法,并结合目前主流竞争情报软件工具的比较分析,总结了竞争情报工具的发展现状和趋势。

[**关键词**] 竞争情报 方法 软件工具 最新进展

Development of the Methods and Tools of Competitive Intelligence

[**Abstract**] The methodological development and innovation is one of the core issues of CI research. Software is effective route for improving the efficiency and effect of the application of CI. So it will play a leading role in guiding the development of CI to systematically research. Firstly this paper introduce the new method of CI acquisition, CI analysis and visualization based on the analyzing the composition of CI method system. Then the status and trends of the development of CI tools are summarized by comparison of the main CI software and tools.

[**Keywords**] Competitive Intelligence, Methods, Software and Tools, the

---

① 谢新洲,教授,博士生导师,北京大学竞争情报与竞争力研究中心,xzxie@pku.edu.cn
② 王强,博士研究生,北京大学新闻与传播学院,北京市科学技术情报研究所,wq971120@163.com
③ 金学慧,助理研究员,北京市科学技术情报研究所,jinxuehui@126.com

Latest Development

1 引　言

　　方法研究的目的在于指导实践、改造世界,因此方法较之纯理论对实践具有更为直接的推动作用,而实践是竞争情报价值得以真正实现的唯一途径。以为企业创造竞争优势为使命的现代竞争情报兴起于二战后的欧美国家。二战后的全球经济恢复及市场竞争激化,催生了美国、日本等发达国家企业竞争情报实践,在实践发展的推动下,同时伴随着20世纪现代竞争理论的诞生,尤其是迈克尔·波特"竞争三部曲"的发表,国外的竞争情报理论研究逐渐兴起。与我国竞争情报事业发展截然不同,在成熟和发达的市场经济推动下,在欧美国家,竞争情报实践发展先于竞争情报理论总结,由此也造就了欧美国家竞争情报研究更加注重实践的传统。与此同时,由于方法操作性强,方法研究与实践应用有着密不可分的联系,因此方法研究与工具开发一直以来都是竞争情报专家和从业者执着的重点方向。

　　本文首先从不同的角度分析了竞争情报方法体系的构成,然后根据方法体系,介绍了情报获取、分析和可视化的新方法,并结合对目前主流竞争情报软件工具的比较分析,总结了竞争情报工具的发展现状和趋势。

2　竞争情报方法体系

　　根据包昌火研究员对竞争情报的定义:"竞争情报既是一种过程,又是一种产品。过程,是指对竞争情报的收集和分析;产品,是指由此形成情报或策略。"[1]竞争情报作为一个过程,人类通过竞争情报收集信息、分析信息得到情报,从而认识客观世界;作为一种产品,人类通过竞争情报制定策略从而改造客观世界。而方法是人类认识客观世界和改造客观世界应遵循的某种方式、途径和程序的总和。从竞争情报的定义和本质来说,方法构成了竞争情报的核心,它贯穿于竞争情报工作的始终,在竞争情报研究、管理、评估等各个环节发挥着至关重要的作用。

2.1 从竞争情报循环看竞争情报方法体系

典型的竞争情报循环包括情报计划、信息收集、信息组织、情报分析、形成报告并提交、情报评估等各个环节。从竞争情报研究过程看,竞争情报方法包括研究课题的选择方法、情报信息的获取方法、情报信息的整序方法、情报信息的抽象方法、情报研究成果的表达方法和情报研究成果的评价方法(图1)。[2]

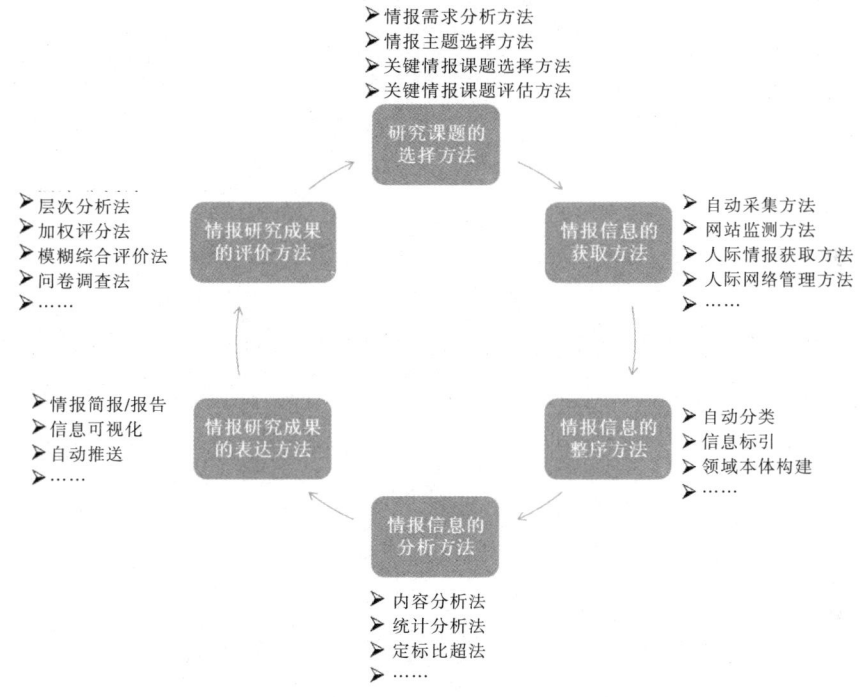

图1 从竞争情报循环看竞争情报方法体系

2.2 从竞争情报构成要素看竞争情报方法体系

竞争情报工作的落脚点是支撑企业管理和企业决策,作为企业管理的一项完整内容,竞争情报由信息资源、人力资源、组织机构等多种管理要素共同构成。[3]因此,从竞争情报构成的要素来看,竞争情报方法包括竞争情报项目管理方法、竞争情报机构管理方法、竞争情报人员培训方法和反竞争情报方法(图2)。

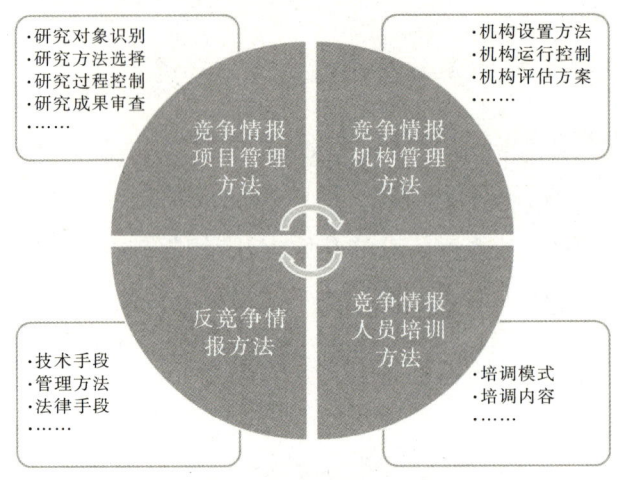

图 2　从竞争情报要素看竞争情报方法体系

2.3　从方法来源看竞争情报方法体系

竞争情报作为情报学同经济学、管理学以及现代竞争理论相互交叉、渗透的结果,其方法体系由经济学方法、管理学方法、情报学方法、社会学方法、统计学方法、数学方法和系统科学方法等多个学科的方法相互渗透发展而成[4],所以在竞争情报的方法体系中,不可避免地保留了以上方法的内容,这些方法也成为竞争情报方法的主体(图 3)。

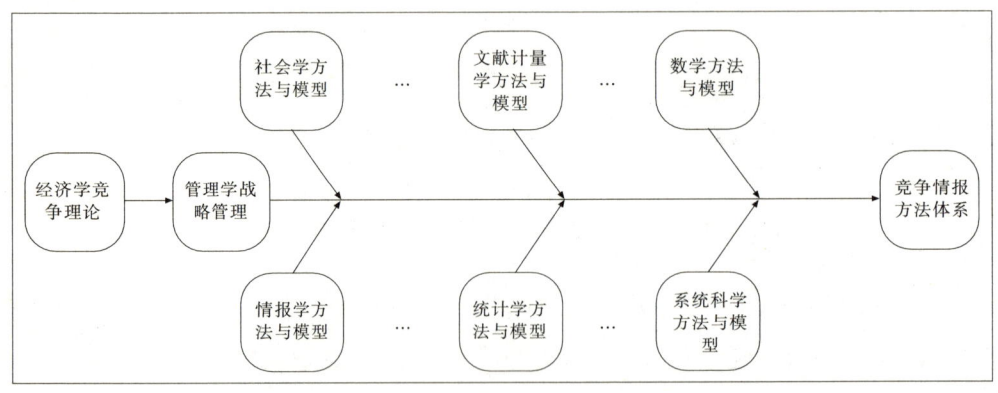

图 3　从形成过程看竞争情报方法体系

经过国内外竞争情报学者和从业者的共同努力,竞争情报已经形成了比较稳定的方法体系,然而方法问题作为竞争情报的核心问题一直是竞争情报研究的热点,一些新的方法仍然层出不穷。本文就情报获取、情报分析和情报展现三个环节中的一些新方法进行介绍。

3 情报获取的新方法

情报获取是竞争情报的基础环节,随着竞争情报的发展,情报获取的方法和手段也不断革新,互联网及数据库检索、市场调查、专利分析、人际网络分析等方法一直在沿用,同时还出现了感官营销情报、财务情报、展会情报等情报搜集、获取的新方法。

3.1 感官营销情报

感官营销是企业通过不同的感官策略和感官表达,以客户的五官感觉为中心,来建立与客户身份、生活方式和个性相关的品牌意识和品牌形象。[5]通过对企业感官营销策略的分析,能够得到企业的营销战略和客户关系信息。

感官营销情报(Sensory Marketing Intelligence)来源于营销管理,以感官营销理论为基础,以感官营销模型为分析框架(图4),是一种隶属于市场情报的新的竞争情报方法。[6]感官营销情报主要是根据五官进行情报工作划分,例如收集手机产品的情报,需要从竞争对手产品的外观(视觉)、触感(触觉)、音效(听觉)等方面进行分析和比较,获知不同的手机在产品定位、用户体验和销售策略方面的特点,依据感官营销情报分析的结果,制定或调整手机的营销策略及经营战略。

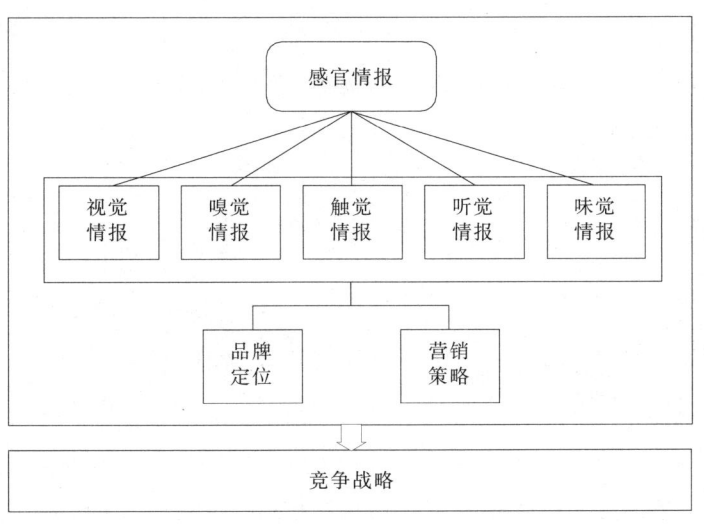

图 4 感官营销情报分析框架

3.2 XBRL 与财务情报

可扩展商业报告语言(eXtensible Business Reporting Language,XBRL)是一种基于 XML 的标记语言,自 1998 年起,XBRL 就获得了迅速发展,成为财务信息处理的最新标准和技术。XBRL 的出现,让公众可以更为简单、翔实地了解公司财务信息,同时极大地提高了对财务信息的处理效率和能力。随着 XBRL 研究领域发生的巨大进步,XBRL 成为商业报告数据和信息交换的新标准,并受到全球工商界的青睐。

XBRL 的工作原理是将财务信息化为 XBRL 格式的文件,输入差异性的组合参数便可以显示各个财务项目间的关系以及不同层次的财务数据,同时由于 XBRL 的互通性,可以使得会计系统及任何系统中的财务相关资料以不同的模式输出。对于情报需求者来说,可以按需提取适当格式的文件,做到文件互通。财务报告中所包含的报表种类繁多,如财务状况报表、信用报表、税率报表等,这些不同内容的报表,也可从同一份 XBRL 文件中产出。[7]

XBRL 在财务信息处理领域确实有着得天独厚的优越性,将 XBRL 引入情报分析中来,为财务情报的收集提供了更好的方法,是经济学方法在竞争情报工作中的应用。但由于财务信息的专业性较强,这也就对情报人员提出了更高的要求。XBRL 的使用必须结合相应的财务信息知识,情报人员必须首先了解到哪些财务信息可以从中得到,同时还要将不同的财务信息进行组合利用,相互比较,只有这样才能充分发挥 XBRL 的作用,以达到从财务报表中抽取情报这一目的。可以说,通过 XBRL 获取财务情报的方式,情报人员的相关知识素养将成为关键因素。

3.3 展会情报

展会是企业为了宣传产品、技术进行的一种宣传活动,对于企业来说,有拓展渠道、促进销售、传播品牌等作用。由于展会具有低成本、快速、直接和互动等特征,使之成为产品供需双方信息交流的集中场所,同时也为竞争情报的获取提供了平台。展会情报(Trade Show Intelligence,TCI)正是利用了展会信息密集的特性,通过展会接触竞争对手,了解其相关产品、技术或服务,进行竞争情报的搜集。一手信息的获取对于竞争情报来说至关重要,这些信息约 80% 具有情报价值[8],而与竞争对手及其员工直接接触是获取一手情报的重要方式[9],展会因而成为了竞争情报获取一手信息的重要途径。

展会情报要达到预期效果,首先必须明确以下情报相关人员对展会情报收集的意图:情报使用者和情报收集者。情报使用者希望了解到展会情报的可靠性、真实性、时效性以及展会的档次、规模和参会成本。而展会情报收集者则必须明确展会情报收集行动的目标。目标的制定可以通过头脑风暴法提出,再根据实际情况进行筛选并最终确定。其次,将展会的参与对象进行分类锁定。明确行业内的供应商、客户,以及政府官员、新闻媒体、行业专家、领域学者等其他对象,按照以上划分进行归类。在此之后,展会情报收集进入了关键情报课题(KITs)分类阶段,这一阶段包括对本次展会情报行动的服务对象、任务要求、难易程度、时间控制、收集类型等 KITs 类别进行识别。至此,展会情报行动即将开始。Andreas Vesper 将展会情报收集分为三个阶段:展会情报准备阶段、展会情报收集阶段以及展会情报整理阶段。[10](三个阶段所需完成的具体工作内容见图5)最终得到的展会情报再与人际网络情报等其他情报内容相结合,便能将其价值发挥到最大化。同时通过不同情报间的相互对比,可以对展会情报的真实性和有效性做出判断。

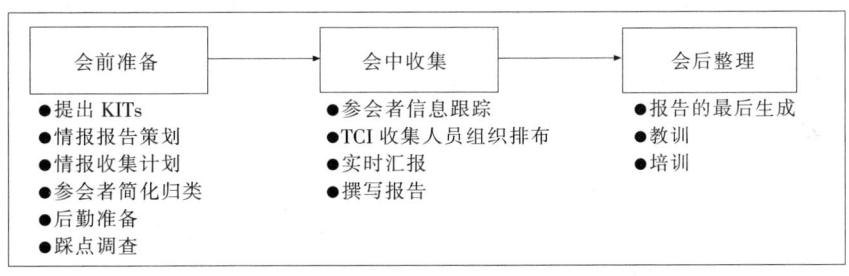

图 5 展会情报三阶段模型

4 竞争情报分析的新方法

情报分析是实现信息向情报转变的关键,竞争情报分析方法历来是竞争情报从业人员研究的重点,而方法上的创新突破又是其中之重中之重。一直以来,情报分析主要从方法来源中寻求创新。通过广泛考察,国内外竞争情报分析方法最新研究成果涉及的主题主要包括协同金字塔及协同观察、国际项目竞争情报分析方法、社会化媒体分析方法、潜在情报要素识别等方法。

4.1 协同金字塔及协同观察

日益复杂的竞争环境对竞争情报工作提出了越来越高的要求,个别情报人员甚至少数人组成的情报小组已经难以应对竞争环境复杂化带来的挑战,竞争情报工作需要一定规模的团队和外脑,随之而来的问题便是如何将这些人进行有效组织、协同工作。协同金字塔由协同小组构建、问题理解分享、成员知识交换、小组认识与共识和人员分配构成(见图6),并使用协同工具,完成大型、复杂的竞争情报项目。[11]对于任何一个成功的竞争情报项目来说,人是其中的核心和关键,并且必须发挥集体的智慧,而协同观察(Collaborate Watch)是建立在协同金字塔全过程的信息共享机制。协同观察不止是在一个企业或一个用户社区内部发布和共享信息,也不止是在企业内部个别员工之间分享信息,它应该是指成员之间彼此交换各自的信息和知识,分享彼此对某一问题的理解和看法。而要想提高协同观察的效率,借助一定的手段和工具是不可避免的,这类工具包括 Xwiki、KB Crawl 4、Zotero 等系统和软件,还包括 RSS 订阅、tag 标签等小工具。

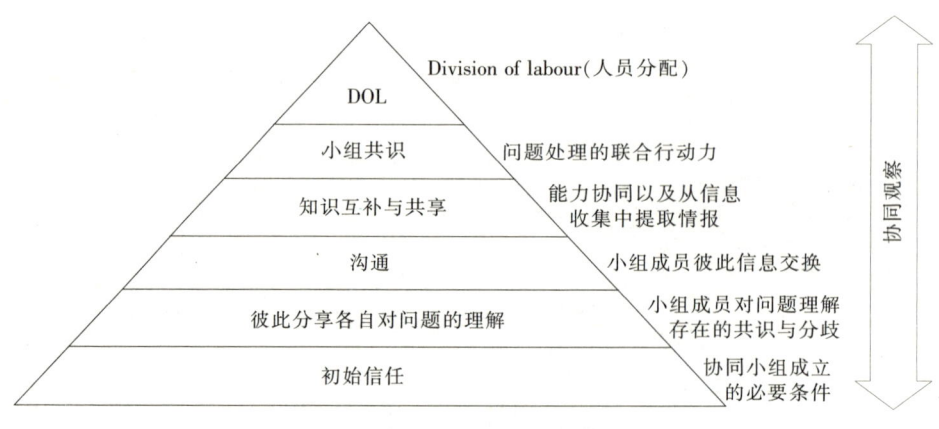

图6 协同金字塔及协同观察

4.2 国际项目竞争情报分析方法

全球化是竞争环境复杂化的一个重要影响因素,随着企业国际化程度的不断提高,以及竞争全球化的加剧,竞争情报面临全球统一协作的挑战。除了竞争情报各要素的影响外,竞争情报工作还受到不同国家文化、政策、利益等复杂因素的影响,项目管理的复杂化对竞争情报方法提出了新的挑战。

国际项目竞争情报分析方法从项目参与人员所属国别的文化、项目利益相关方形成的关系网络等角度,对项目所处的环境进行微观分解,并运用 SWOT 方法,给出了一张影响因素与项目问题之间因果关系的鱼骨图(图7)。[12]该方法以竞争情报问题为导向,从国际项目中竞争情报工作面临的环境变化和管理差异入手,提出竞争情报工作进行所必需的物质基础和人员保障,并结合文化和环境的差异,制定特定的竞争情报管理制度和评估标准,应用面向不同语言和文化的分析方法,对竞争情报课题进行解答。

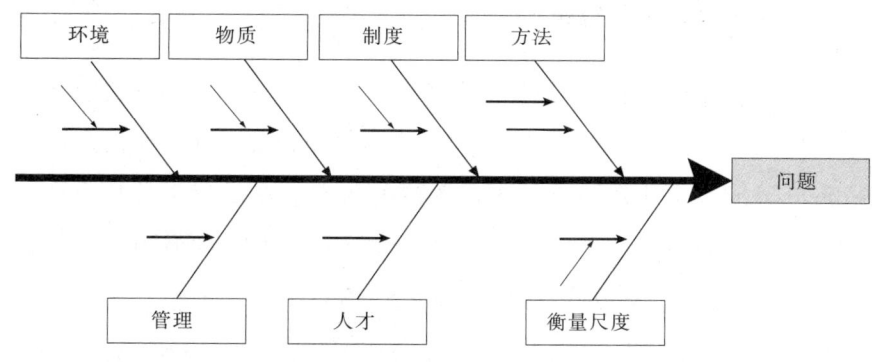

图 7 国际项目影响因素鱼骨图

4.3 社会化媒体分析

在竞争企业群体当中可以侦查到红后效应(Red Queen Effect)[13],这意味着企业必须努力实践竞争情报活动,以保持其竞争力。如果某个企业的竞争对手能够高效地获得竞争环境以及该企业的即时信息,而该企业自身却不能做到这一点,那么这家企业就有随时被挤出该行业的危险。有关即时信息的源头往往蕴藏在一些社交网络当中。当前借助 Web 及日益发达的移动互联技术,各种社会化媒体日益兴盛,使互联网的终端用户由信息的接收者转换成了接收者与提供者的双重角色,这种变化为竞争情报提供了新的机会,无论是对于情报获取还是人际网络情报的实施,都提供了新思路。对于论坛、博客、微博等社交网站所产生的即时信息进行实时信息跟踪和收集,是社会化媒体时代企业竞争情报收集工作所面临的紧迫任务。

社会化媒体中蕴含着一个更加"真实的世界"(real world),一方面对竞争情报的信息处理能力提出了巨大挑战,同时,信息源的进一步增多也给竞争情报工作带来了机遇,社会化媒体无疑将成为竞争情报工作的一大重要工具,而twitter等社会化媒体的出现,使互联网成为了一手数据的重要来源。[14]面对社交网络制造出来的庞杂信息,社会化媒体分析的对象和范围包括市场洞察、企业社交洞察和业主洞察三个维度。[15]社会化媒体分析应围绕企业最核心任务彼此交流协作,从监控对象、社会化媒体用户行为和竞争情报服务内容三个维度收集、分析社会化媒体信息,使用YAMMER、ENGAGE等社会化媒体分析工具建立全球社交网络,开展竞争情报工作。[16]

4.4 潜在情报要素的识别方法

显性情报由于其可获取性,已经越来越难以适应当前经济和社会的发展,怎样通过已知的信息去获取未知的情报,从而尽早制定应对策略,及时做出正确的决策,已经成为企业竞争情报人员关注的焦点。竞争对手分析是竞争情报工作的典型内容,对一个企业的竞争情报工作而言,竞争对手的情报跟踪和研究工作并不仅仅限定于自己直接的、当下的竞争对手——那些与本企业分享市场份额或者客户的企业和个人,还要挖掘潜在竞争对手,从而形成针对潜在竞争对手的预警能力。Ralf Anders[17]从潜在竞争者的定义入手,对潜在竞争者的特征和可能采取的行动进行了深入分析,提出一个通过持续的市场监测来发现潜在竞争者的监控框架。所谓潜在竞争对手是指那些对你现有的商业模式可能有着重大威胁的公司,与显性竞争对手相比,他们具有较强的隐蔽性,往往身处你的监测范围之外。

潜在情报要素识别过程将人们对一个事物或问题的发觉和认知状态抽象为三种类型:知道你所知道的(known knowns)、知道你所不知道的(known unknowns)和不知道你所不知道的(unknown unknowns),而对于商业情报分析的终极挑战就在于挖掘出"你不知道你所不知道的"信息和问题。潜在情报要素识别方法借鉴乔哈里资讯窗(Johari Window)理论,构建一个企业战略规划层面的已知和未知矩阵(图8)[18],通过该矩阵分析依靠领域专家的决策所固有的缺陷以及管理中的盲点,从概念模型和具体方法两个角度应对战略计划制定过程中的终极挑战——Unknown Unknowns。

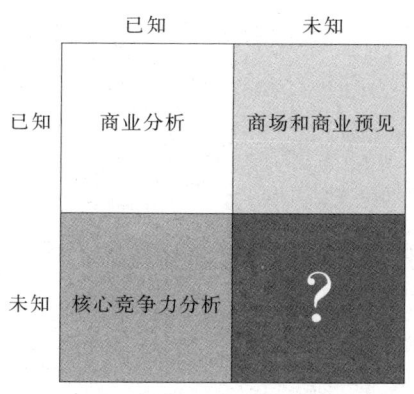

图 8　战略规划中的已知未知矩阵

5　竞争情报可视化新方法

可视化是情报结果展现的有效途径,借助当前信息可视化技术的发展和移动互联网应用的普及,可视化方法由于其直观、动态的优势,越来越受到情报用户的青睐,其中,战争模拟的可视化方法成为了研究的新课题。

战争模拟也称战争游戏,起源于军事,指用各种方法对实际作战环境、军事行动和作战过程的描述和模仿。战争模拟能够有效检验军队战略和策略有效性,同时可以降低成本,特别是在 IT 技术的帮助下,战争模拟已经广泛应用于军队的演习和训练中。经济全球化下,随着商业竞争的加剧以及竞争环境的日益复杂多变,如果在竞争情报中引入有效的模拟方法,那么潜在情报要素的识别就可以更加简单、高效,同时会有效降低竞争情报工作的成本。已经为越来越多的企业所借鉴的战争游戏法,通俗来说就是一种"商业竞争模拟工具,通过各种角色的扮演模拟过程,在预演竞争对手和市场环境的各种战略可能性的基础上,制定并评估本企业战略,根据模拟过程中获取的数据,分析成败得失,对决策或行动计划进行评价或选择,并对未来竞争态势做出预期"。[19]

"竞争情报作战室"、"战争游戏"等竞争情报中的分析方法,在国内外已有研究和应用,然而怎样将模拟的结果通过更加直观的方式进行展现,却鲜有涉及。Stephane Goria[20]认为行销战争(Marketing Warfare)是一个以市场和竞争对手为导向而不是以客户为导向的概念,它好比一场军事演示,需要更多地权衡市场环境和竞争对手。借鉴军事战争相关理论,Stephane Goria 详细设计了一个可操作的模拟步骤:目标消费者选择——消费者经验行为的过程分解——

消费者兴趣参数确立——信息收集——对抗者及地图绘制——对抗者在地图中对号入座——行动方案,并以 Nintedo 和 Sony 的家庭视频游戏机为例,模拟了二者竞争的发展。

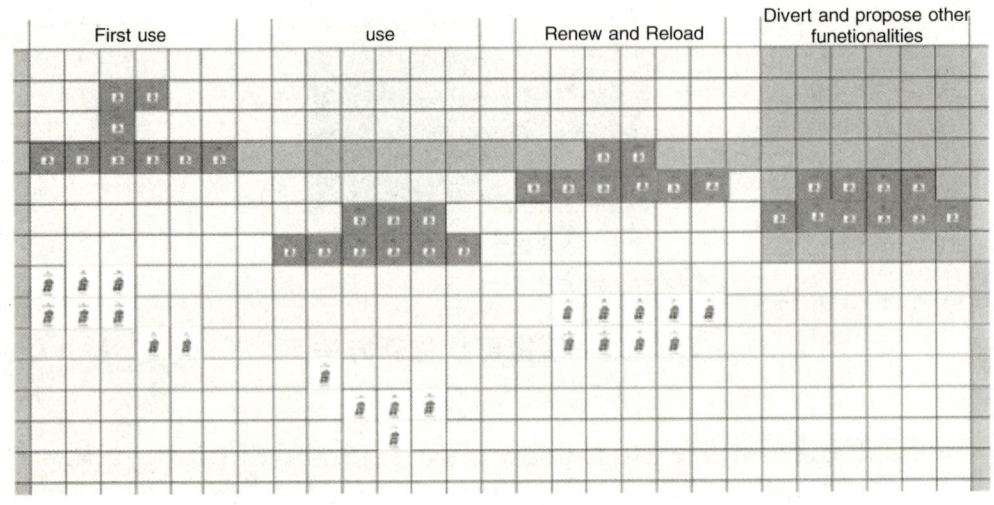

图 9　战争模拟可视化效果

6　竞争情报软件工具发展的新趋势

大数据时代的到来对竞争情报提出了新的挑战,面对海量的非结构化信息,面对跨领域、跨行业、跨地区的竞争情报协作,竞争情报需要更加规范化的工作流程、更加智能的信息分析方法和更加流畅的信息共享机制。作为竞争情报系统和竞争情报工作流程的载体,竞争情报软件的性能和效率等已经成为制约企业竞争情报工作的重要工具因素。竞争情报软件供应商在新的形势下对产品和服务进行了优化,竞争情报软件工具的发展呈现出新的趋势。[21-24]

6.1　知识共享成为软件工具的必备功能

竞争情报工作已经不是一个部门和少数人能够完成的工作,它已经渗透到了企业的多个部门,这就要求来自不同部门、不同背景、对竞争情报有着不同理解的人共同参与到竞争情报的工作中,分享情报内容和分析结果。因此,知识共享成为了竞争情报工作必不可少的环节,也成为竞争情报软件必备的一项功能。

6.2 软件的集成应用成为竞争情报工作的新模式

竞争情报工作的复杂性和协作性也决定了并非单一的软件就可以解决所有问题,在软件工具繁多的情况下,同时,出于应用成本的考虑,如何选择最适合自己的软件工具就成为竞争情报从业人员必须要面对的问题。在实际的竞争情报项目中,可以通过构建软件工具评价指标、整合多个软件工具,并针对特定竞争情报目标使用不同软件工具协同工作,以达到最优的分析效果。[25]

6.3 非结构化信息处理技术不断进步

对于竞争情报分析来说,更多的数据属于非结构化的文本数据,甚至是图片、音频、视频等多媒体数据,这些数据不仅没有特定结构,而且数量巨大,为竞争情报的获取和分析带来了很大的难度,很多情报研究人员也致力于非结构化信息的处理技术。从调研的软件来看,几乎所有的软件都具备了非结构化信息处理的功能,尽管仍然存在较大的改善空间,但较之早期版本,在功能和性能方面都有了极大的提升,为竞争情报工作提供了越来越有力的技术支撑。

6.4 社会化媒体分析功能逐渐强大

很多竞争情报软件及时跟上了社会化媒体飞速发展的脚步,情感分析和观点挖掘等语义分析技术已经开始用于社会化网络分析,以此来对互联网进行监控,进而实时有效地监控媒体的信息,以便对公众观点和自身形象做出及时的反应,同时对企业面临的威胁和风险进行评估、预测和预警。

7 结 语

大数据时代的到来,一方面为情报工作提供了海量的数据,另一方面过量和无序的海量数据也为情报人员从中获取有价值的情报带来了困扰,如何准确高效的收集和分析信息成了情报工作的一大挑战。

从本文对竞争情报新方法和工具的阐述可以看出,竞争情报方法和工具正在向更加智能化、协同化、精细化的方向发展,以应对大数据带来的诸多挑战,从而更加有效、准确地挖掘大数据蕴含的巨大价值,更加有效地将竞争情报应用于企业的决策当中,同时,社会化媒体的发展和普及也为竞争情报的未来发展提供了更加广阔的空间,也提出了新的挑战。

参考文献

[1] 包昌火,谢新洲. 竞争情报与企业竞争力[M]. 北京:华夏出版社,2001.

[2] 包昌火. 情报研究方法论[M]. 北京:科学技术文献出版社,1990.

[3] 王延飞. 竞争情报方法[M]. 北京:北京大学出版社,2007.

[4] 吴晓,宋文官,徐福缘. 企业竞争情报分析方法来源及发展[J]. 情报杂志,2006(4):2-6.

[5] B Hultén, N Broweus, M Van Dijk. *Sensory marketing*[M]. *Palgrave Macmillan*, 2009:6.

[6] Luis Madureira. *Sensory Marketing Intelligence* [C]. *Institute of Competitive Intelligence*, AT-ELIS. *International Competitive Intelligence Conference* 2011. *Bad Nauheim, Germany*: Institute of Competitive Intelligence, 2011:47-60.

[7] Robert Pinsker, Shaomin Li. *Costs and Benefits of XBRL Adoption: Early Evidence*[J]. *Communications of the ACM*, 2008,51(3):47-50.

[8] R. Michaeli. *Competitive intelligence: strategische Wettbewerbsvorteile erzielen durch systematische Konkurrenz-, Markt- und Technologieanalysen. Springer-Verlag, Berlin. Heidelberg*, 2006.

[9] Calof J, Hohhof B. *Conference and trade show intelligence. Topics in CI Volume 2 of Competitive Intelligence Foundation. Alexandria. SCIP*, 2007:91.

[10] Andreas Vesper. *Trade Show Intelligence*[C]. *Institute of Competitive Intelligence*, ATELIS. *International Competitive Intelligence Conference* 2011. *Bad Nauheim, Germany*: Institute of Competitive Intelligence, 2011:135.

[11] Victor Odumuyiwa. *Collaborative Watch: towards an effective intelligence gathering* [C]. *Institute of Competitive Intelligence*, ATELIS. *International Competitive Intelligence Conference* 2011 (Conference handout Day 1). *Bad Nauheim, Germany*: Institute of Competitive Intelligence, 2011:147-157.

[12] Marco Benkert. *CI capabilities and methods within the implementation of complex international projects* [C]. *Institute of Competitive Intelligence*, ATELIS. *International Competitive Intelligence Conference* 2011 (Conference handout Day 1). *Bad Nauheim, Germany*: Institute of Competitive Intelligence, 2011:29-40.

[13] Peltoniemi M, Vuori E. *Competitive Intelligence as a Driver of Co-Evolution within an Organization Population*[J]. *Journal of Competitive Intelligence and Management*, 2008,4(3):50-62.

[14] Dabrowska Dominika. *Internet evolved : from secondary to primary competitive intelligence*

data[EB/OL]. http://opus.bsz-bw.de/fhhv/volltexte/2011/354/pdf/Dabrowska_Internet_evolved_primary_competitive_intelligence_data.pdf. [2011-4-5].

[15] Martin Grothe. *Social Media Analysis for Competitive Intelligence*[EB/OL]. http://www.institute-for-competitive-intelligence.com/channel-ici-conference-2011/social-media-analysis-for-competitive-intelligence. [2011-06-01].

[16] Alexandra Nelles. *Competitive Intelligence and Web2.0 - Experiences at a global player*[C]. *Institute of Competitive Intelligence, ATELIS. International Competitive Intelligence Conference* 2011 (Conference handout Day 1). Bad Nauheim, Germany: Institute of Competitive Intelligence, 2011:47-60.

[17] Ralf Anders. *Be aware of your game - changing Hidden Competitors*[C]. *Institute of Competitive Intelligence, ATELIS. International Competitive Intelligence Conference* 2011 (Conference handout Day 2). Bad Nauheim, Germany: Institute of Competitive Intelligence, 2011:83.

[18] Klaus Heinzelbecker. *Unknown Unknowns: The ultimate challenge for Business Intelligence*[C]. *Institute of Competitive Intelligence, ATELIS. International Competitive Intelligence Conference* 2011 (Conference handout Day 1). Bad Nauheim, Germany: Institute of Competitive Intelligence, 2011:125-144

[19] Kurtz J. *Business Wargaming: Simulations Guide Crucial Strategy Decisions*[J]. Strategy & Leadership, 2003, 31(6): 12-16.

[20] Stephane Goria. *Board wargame presentation for marketing strategy identification*[C]. *Institute of Competitive Intelligence, ATELIS. International Competitive Intelligence Conference* 2011 (Conference handout Day 1). Bad Nauheim, Germany: Institute of Competitive Intelligence, 2011:187-203.

[21] Cipher Systems. *Cipher Systems Competitive Intelligence: Helping You Make Better Decisions*[EB/OL]. http://www.cipher-sys.com/. [2012-11-7].

[22] LexisNexis. Product & Service[EB/OL]. https://www.lexisnexis.com/en-us/home.page. [2012-11-7].

[23] Digimind. WHAT WE DO[EB/OL]. http://www.digimind.com/category/solutions/. [2012-11-7].

[24] TRS. 竞争情报系统白皮书[EB/OL]. http://www.trs.com.cn/servpport/pdf/trsciswhite.pdf. [2012-11-7].

[25] Muriel Séménéri. *Competitive Technical Intelligence: How to Boost Innovation and Knowledge Sharing*[C]. *Institute of Competitive Intelligence, ATELIS. International Competitive Intelligence Conference* 2011 (Conference handout Day 2). Bad Nauheim, Germany: Institute of Competitive Intelligence, 2011:119-134.

Early Warning during the Industry Convergence Process: the Influence of Alliances on Acquisition Timing

Sean Tsu-Hsiang Hsu[①]   John E. Prescott[②]

Abstract

Focusing on the timing of firms' initial acquisition in an adjacent converging industry as a central aspect of the industry convergence process, we propose an early warning framework in which acquisition timing is influenced by four forms of alliances: inter-industry-horizontal, intra-industry-horizontal, intra-industry-vertical and inter-industry-vertical. As firms' alliance experience increases in the adjacent converging industry, we find that the likelihood of the timing of telecommunications equipment firms' initial acquisition in the adjacent converging computer networking industry is an inverted-U shaped form. Intra-industry-horizontal alliance experience negatively moderates the relationship. Implications for theorizing about network boundaries, rivalry, industry convergence process within an early warning context are discussed.

Keywords

Industry Convergence Process, Alliance Experience, Interfirm Relationship, Telecommunications, Early Warning, Competitive Intelligence

"… synergy is dead, and the concept of converging communications and com-

---

[①] Katz Graduate School of Business, 209 Mervis Hall, University of Pittsburgh, Pittsburgh, PA 15260, Email: thsu@katz.pitt.edu

[②] Katz Graduate School of Business, 246 Mervis Hall, University of Pittsburgh, Pittsburgh, PA 15260, Email: prescott@katz.pitt.edu

puter markets, which drove the NCR deal [AT&T's acquisition], is an illusion". (Arnst & Nathans, 1995)

"... when you look at voice networks and data networks, they're both evolving very, very rapidly. And the customers are feeling that it's very difficult to keep up. At the same time, customers want applications with much greater integration" – Interview with Lucent's Vice President, Karyn Mashima (Vizard, 1998).

"... I've long been skeptical of the convergence of telephones and computers, but my experience with these products suggests that their time has definitely come." (Wildstrom, 2004)

Researchers and practitioners treat industry convergence (IC) as an important strategic phenomenon, because it shifts industry boundaries, creates opportunities for new strategies to emerge, destroys competitive advantages while solidifying others, and establishes new institutional arrangements (Yoffie, 1997). Thus, firms need to develop early warning processes that place them in a position to act proactively rather than reactively. From a competitive intelligence (CI) perspective to understand a macro – level process such as IC one must examine the role of firms' actions during its occurrence. As the above three quotes demonstrate, the process of IC unfolds over time and is fraught with uncertainty. A growing body of evidences reveals that IC occurs not only in volatile, high – tech industries, such as telecommunications (Lee, 2007) and digital camera (Srinivasan, Haunschild, & Grewal, 2007), but also in traditionally stable industries, such as music (Burgelman & Grove, 2007), and banking (Malhotra & Gupta, 2001). Recognizing that a consensus on the definition of IC hasn't emerged, we follow the OECD's definition of IC as a process that "brings together in the same field industries formerly operating in separate markets" (OECD, 2008: 7). Because it is very likely that IC disrupts firms' strategic positions and competences through changing their landscape, scholars and practitioners alike call for theorizing and empirical analysis to better inform our understanding of the phenomenon called 'industry convergence' (Burgelman & Grove, 2007; Jacobides & Winter, 2005).

While the limited research on IC has shed light on the antecedents (e.g.

Katz, 1996) and associated outcomes of IC (e. g. Malhotra & Gupta, 2001), the process of IC receives scant attention (for an exception see Burgelman & Grove, 2007). For the definition of process, we adopt the view that IC unfolds over time as a result of events occurring in the market (Ferrier, 2001). Building on this view, we treat the process of IC as a sequence from a separate to converging to converged stage (Figure 1). In the separate stage, macro and micro drivers of IC (e. g. regulation, technology) are emerging and the industries operate relatively independently. In the converging stage, the boundaries of the industries begin to overlap (e. g. via acquisitions). At some point, the converging industry's boundaries become sufficiently blurred where the industries become de facto converged. We focus on the timing of firms' initial acquisition in an adjacent converging industry as a central aspect of the process of IC and thus a key early warning indicator. We choose this focus since acquisition activity is regarded as one indicator of IC (Chon, Choi, Barnett, Danowski, & Joo, 2003; Yoffie, 1997) but also because a firm-level investigation of IC offers a finer-grained understanding of how IC progresses over time. A key research question, then, is why and when a firm makes its initial acquisition in the adjacent industry given that IC is occurring. Our study of a firm-driven process of IC enriches theorizing of IC because it bridges and complements previous convergence-related literature which centers on its antecedents and consequences.

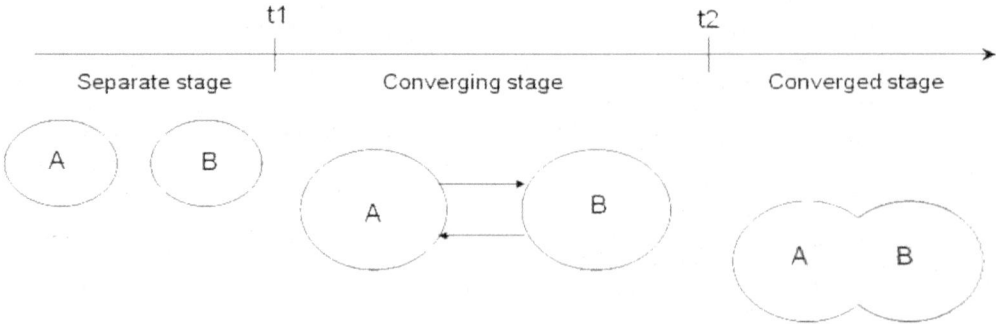

Note: The figure is under the assumption that industry convergence only occurs between two industries (A and B)

Figure 1. The Process of Industry Convergence: A Stage View

Adopting the assumption that firms are boundedly rational under uncertainty (Cyert & March, 1963), we argue that the likelihood of firms' initial acquisition in an adjacent industry will increase and then decrease as firms' alliance experience in that adjacent industry (inter – industry – horizontal alliances; e. g. , supplier – supplier) increases. Our underlying premise is that inter – firm relationships reduce institutional, industry, and firm – level uncertainties and thereby paves the path of convergence among two or more industries.

Extending from our baseline argument, we further suggest that other forms of alliances (i. e. intra – industry – horizontal and intra – industry – vertical) have a negative moderating influence on the relationship between inter – industry – horizontal alliances and initial acquisition timing. A fourth form of alliance, inter – industry – vertical is incorporated as a control, because we maintain that the influence of this form of alliance during IC hinges on the degree of vertical disintegration and/or industry – level modularity between the adjacent industry and its downstream industry (see theory section below) (Gambardella & Torrisi, 1998). The incorporation of a finer grain classification of alliances is theoretically crucial in that different types of alliances are often treated as similar in the interfirm – relationship literature (Fligstein, 2003; Lazzarini, Claro, & Mesquita, 2008; Mesquita & Lazzarini, 2008). As firms enter into vertical and horizontal alliances, they become increasingly embedded in an interconnected web (Hoffmann, 2007). Hence, it is imperative for competitive intelligence professionals to understand the consequence of the differential roles of these two types of interorganizational relationships. In this chapter, we propose and test a framework of vertical and horizontal alliances that provides a detailed examination on the effects of alliance experience on initial acquisition timing and thus an early warning process of IC.

The convergence of the telecommunications equipment and computer networking industries is our empirical context. Specifically, we examine on how "telecommunications equipment" industry firms use alliances to determine the timing of their initial acquisition in their adjacent industry – "computer networking". The context is appropriate because both practice and academia have shown that the two industries have converging industry boundaries (Lee, 2007; Shepard, 2000). During the 1990s', traditional network structure (circuit switching) in the telecommunications equipment industry was gradually challenged by Internet – protocol – based structure (packet switching). In response to threats and opportunities in the new market, telecommunications equipment firms subsequently extended their territory into the computer networking industry. The process of IC as reflected through the initiation of alliances and subsequent initial acquisition is our focus. The methodological approach used to measure the timing of firms' initial acquisition is event study analysis, since our focus centers on time – related constructs (e. g. Martin, Swaminathan, & Mitchell, 1998; Yu & Cannella, 2007). Our approach provides a template for one way that CI professionals can monitor the extent of IC and thus provide early warning assessments for their managers.

We find that as firms' alliance experience increases in the adjacent industry, the likelihood of the timing of firms' initial acquisition in the adjacent converging industry exhibits an inverted – U shaped relationship. Intra – industry – horizontal alliances negatively moderate the relationship while intra – industry – vertical alliances have no moderating effect. Our findings contribute to the nexus of IC and social network literature. Theorizing about the process of IC through an alliance and acquisition lens, our results enhance the understanding of the extent to which inter – industry – horizontal and intra – industry – vertical alliance experience influence firms' initial acquisition timing. Second, our findings serve as a strategic tool of intelligence that allows managers to monitor the timings of their competitors' acquisitions in the adjacent converging industry. Such an analytical tool of competitive intelligence is a crucial early warning indicator since the IC process often takes off when market leaders in a firm's own industry initiate acquisitions in the adjacent industry. Finally, for social network theory, our results suggest that inter – industry network ties and intra – industry network ties will dynamically co – determine the boundaries of industry networks through acquisitions and subsequently reshapes firms' network positions. This reinforces the importance of ties in overlapping industry networks and their relationship to the strategic design of interorganizational networks (Koka & Prescott, 2008).

THEORY DEVELOPMENT AND HYPOTHESES

While the concept of *industry convergence* has recently received significant attention, there are many diverging definitions that are often confused or associated with other similar concepts (Katz, 1996), such as technological convergence, service convergence and device convergence. We adopt the conceptualization of convergence developed in OECD Minister's Meeting (2007) report which states that convergence takes on several forms: network convergence, service convergence, IC, regulatory convergence, device convergence, and user – experience convergence. ① We focus on IC defined as a process that brings industries which formerly operated in separate markets together in the same industry. This definition assumes the importance of firms' action in the process of IC, which corresponds to the goal of our paper—i. e. a firm – level investigation of IC which can be part of an early warning process.

Researchers began looking at the antecedents of IC from a technological convergence perspective (Rosenberg, 1976). It is reasonable to argue that convergence between technologies that previously were rooted in different industries results in the IC. However, Katz (1996) points out that in addition to technological change, the evolution of business and regulatory thinking are drivers of IC. Maholtra and Gupta's (2001) study in the commercial and investment banking industries shows that regulation played a key role in driving their convergence. Furthermore, Broring, Cloutier, and Leker (2006) maintain that changes in the structure of consumer demand influences IC.

The associated outcomes of IC have centered on industry – wide competition and firm – level behaviors. With respect to competition, on one hand, IC creates a source of new entrants and thereby may increase the level of industry competition. On the other hand, IC may increase industry consolidation, if the convergence process moves toward an integrated service or product. Although the debate has not been resolved, the fact that cross – industry acquisitions are a part of the IC process

---

① In 2008, an OECD Minister's meeting was held in South Korea. The purpose of the meeting was to discuss communication infrastructure and the future of the internet economy. The committee agreed to declassify the paper in which the past and the future of convergence were reviewed and discussed.

is accepted (Chon and et al., 2003; Gambardella & Torrisi, 1998; Yoffie, 1997). For example, Chon and et al. (2003) use cross-industry acquisitions and social network techniques to demonstrate the existence of media convergence. In contrast to a macro-level perspective, some scholars examine firms' response to IC primarily from an organizational inertia perspective (Tripsas & Gavetti, 2000) or a vicarious-learning view (Srinivasan et al., 2007). Tripsas and Gavetti (2000) use the case of Polaroid to show that when the digital world converges with the analog world, managers who use their previous conceptual models face difficulties adapting to change no matter how much restructuring they try. Using new product introduction as an indicator of vicarious learning, Srinivasan et al. (2007) find that firms introducing new products in converging markets learn vicariously from other firms.

Arguably, phenomenon pertaining to above antecedents and associated outcomes are early warning indicators that IC is happening. Scholars identify three early warning indicators that point to the occurrence of IC: (1) the combination, integration or emergence of technologies across industry boundaries, (2) cross-industry acquisitions, and (3) the integration between services and customer markets (Wirtz, 2001; Chon et al. 2003). In other words, one can study IC by selecting appropriate contexts with some combination of these aspects (our empirical context deals with the first two).

Although the studies mentioned above establish an insightful foundation for theorizing about IC, what has been ignored is the process of IC – the study of how IC unfolds over time. This is particularly important to managers who must make resource allocation decisions that are often irreversible. One significant study that has looked at the process of IC is Burgelman and Grove's (2007) work. Using comparative case study-based findings of Apple Computer's strategic actions in different industries, Burgelman and Grove develop a concept of cross-boundary disruptor which plays a key role in accelerating the IC process. While they focus on how traditional industry boundaries are disrupted by firms in an industry where a newer and better technology originates, the influence of firms in the industry with the older technology (e.g. incumbents) is not addressed. Studies regarding firm-level processes of IC complement the antecedent and outcome streams offering a micro – foundational theory of IC. We focus on firm – level acquisition timing to investigate the IC process for several reasons. First, as mentioned above, firm acquisitions are a key indicator of outcomes of IC. Studying the timing of IC outcome will enrich our understanding as to IC process. Moreover, firm acquisition is a critical "event" that changes firm boundaries and impacts industry evolution, which is consistent with our definition of process (Haleblian & Finkelstein, 1999). Finally, firm acquisition often generates domino effect in which any acquisition may induce more acquisitions when interdependent acquirers (i. e. rivals) compete for scarce targets (Toxvaerd, 2007).

Firm acquisition timing under convergence is filled with uncertainty. When to place equity stakes in an adjacent industry is a difficult choice, even when managers know IC is happening. One important vehicle used by firms to mitigate uncertainty is strategic alliances (Hoffmann, 2007). Firms and their environment are loosely coupled through alliances, which lead to the co – evolution of firms, alliances and the environment (Koza & Lewin, 1998). The use of alliances enables firms to wade into the IC process. Previous studies have found that strategic alliances were frequently formed during periods of IC (Greenstein & Khanna, 1997; Duysters & Hagedoorn, 1998). Building on these ideas, we propose a framework of how alliances influence the timing of firms' initial acquisition in an adjacent converging industry.

A Generic Framework of Alliance Forms Operating During Industry Convergence

Our starting premise is that inter – industry horizontal alliances initiated by firms in the focal industry drive the timing of firms' initial acquisition in the adjacent converging industry. Further, other forms of alliances moderate the strength of the inter – industry horizontal alliance – initial acquisition timing relationship. To gain conceptual clarity and focus, we adopt four assumptions concerning our framework illustrated in Figure 2. First, we assume that IC occurs by the overlapping of two industries (one focal industry and one adjacent industry) and that each industry has only one downstream industry. Second, the upstream and downstream industries are assumed to have a low degree of vertical integration. This structure enables us to define four forms of alliances. *Inter – industry – horizontal alliance* is an alliance formed between a firm in the focal industry and the adjacent industry. *Intra – industry – horizontal alliance* is an alliance formed between firms within the focal industry. *Intra – industry – vertical alliance* is an alliance formed between a firm in the focal industry and the downstream industry of the focal industry. *Inter – industry – vertical alliance* is an alliance formed between a firm in the focal industry and a firm in the downstream industry of the adjacent industry. Third, we recognize that vertical alliances can involve alliances between a downstream focal firm and their upstream suppliers; nevertheless, in order to make our model concise, we choose to concentrate on upstream to downstream alliances. Finally, we adopt a focal industry perspective. We acknowledge the situation where a firm in an adjacent industry acquires a firm in the focal industry. In order to not over complicate our discussion and avoid methodological problems, we control for acquisition activity initiated from the adjacent industry into the focal industry in the empirical analysis. This treatment of a focal industry perspective has another advantage under the condition where the base of competition in the focal industry is eventually absorbed by or replaced by the adjacent industry. This is the case in our empirical setting.

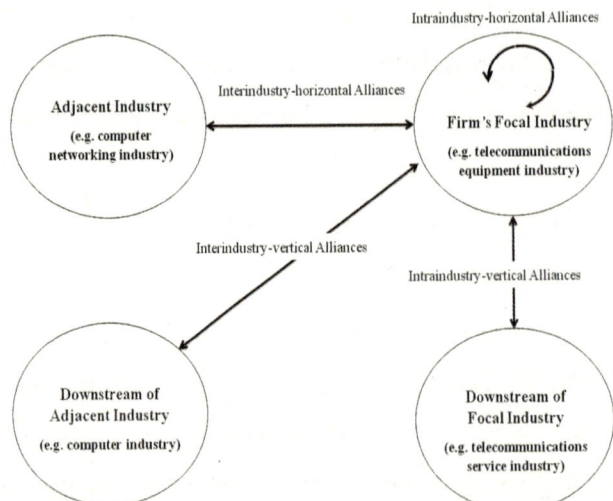

Figure 2. A Generic Framework of Alliance Forms Operating During Industry Convergence

We adopt the above approach, because we ascribe to the premise that vertical and horizontal alliances have differential influences on firm action and outcomes and that the relationship between them is interdependent (Fligstein, 2003). Vertical and horizontal alliances have been well-documented in the strategy and organizational theory literatures; however, most alliances are studied separately not as part of a portfolio (Mesquita & Lazzarini, 2008).

The role of inter-industry-vertical alliances is conditioned on the opportunity and ease of knowledge transfer between upstream and downstream stages of the adjacent industry (Gambardella & Torrisi, 1998). We maintain that two contingencies in an industry context determine whether inter-industry-vertical alliances play a moderator or control role for a particular research question. The first contingency is the degree of vertical integration between the up and downstream stages of the adjacent converging industry. Industry vertical integration between the up and downstream stages is positively associated with high capability homogeneity among firms (Jacobides & Winter, 2005). In other words, competencies in the up and downstream stages are similar. Given this condition, inter-industry-vertical alliances established in the downstream stage of the adjacent industry will moderate the timing-initial acquisition relationship in the adjacent industry because similarity of capabilities provides the opportunity to more easily transfer knowledge across down and upstream stages. On the other hand, when the adjacent industry is characterized by high vertical disintegration, the down and upstream stages co-specialize (Jacobides & Winter, 2005). Under this condition competences developed from inter-industry-vertical alliances may not transfer to the upstream stage of the adjacent industry.

A second contingency is the degree of modularity in the industry value chain. High levels of modularity in the upstream and downstream stages result in loose coupling along the production process which also produces different sets of competences in each stage (Pil & Cohen, 2006; Schilling & Steensma, 2001). Therefore, when the adjacent industry manifests a high level of vertical disintegration (and/or modularity) between its up and downstream stages, inter-industry-vertical alliances should assume the role of a control variable otherwise it should be a moderator. Our empirical context exhibits a low degree of vertical integration. Thus, we use inter-industry vertical alliances as a control variable.

Inter-industry-horizontal Alliances as a Driver of Initial Acquisition Timing

In an IC context, firms' existing capabilities in the focal industry are eroded or made obsolete. As such, the resource-based view suggests that firms embark on acquisitions in an adjacent industry to acquire or leverage resources that substitute for its existing resource base in its focal industry. Additionally, a technological innovation may manifest itself as an opportunity that two industries are likely to converge in the future. However, the timing of a firm's acquisition program is constrained, because in the adjacent industry where the resource base of firms are less understood than their own industry, firms encounter information problems regarding both locating appropriate targets and post-acquisition management issues. Respectively, these two acquisition-related problems are termed: the information asymmetry problem (e.g. Balakrishnan & Koza, 1993) and the indigestibility problem (e.g. Hennart & Reddy, 2000). The former arises from the problem that the acquiring firm finds it difficult to determine whether the information provided by the target is biased, while the latter refers to the problem that the acquiring and target firms are different in terms of resource, process and culture. Vanhaverbeke, Duysters, and Noorderhaven (2002) demonstrate that inter-industry acquisitions occur less than intra-industry acquisitions because of these problems. Therefore, both types of problems will serve as a disincentive for firm acquisition in an adjacent industry.

From the perspective of the social network and relational resource-based views, both inter-industry acquisitions problems can be mitigated under certain circumstances. The social network perspective views firm alliances as social ties that can generate social capital. Such social ties via strategic alliances allow firms to contrast the information gathered from their partners with information provided from the target (Koka & Prescott, 2002). Consistent with our logic, Beckman and Haunschild (2002) find that firm alliances enhanced the positive effect of board interlock on acquisition performance. Although the target may not be a part of a firm's alliance network, the firm's partners which are in the same industry as the target can provide information that supports the decision making process of future acquisitions.

The relational resource – based view suggests that alliances are used to access complementary resources and thereby create relational rents (Dyer & Singh, 1998). Those relations allow firms to transfer or pool such resources thus enabling firms to reduce the indigestibility problem (Gulati, Nohria, & Zaheer, 2000). Through cooperative relationships with partners that own a particular set of resources, firms can obtain those resources and recombine them with their own resources. Of course, those relationship – specific advantages do not occur in a vacuum; instead, it requires a long – time commitment and ongoing maintenance (Dyer & Singh, 1998). In the inter – industry context, prior alliances helps firms access resources specific to that industry. Alliance experience in an adjacent industry assists firms in digesting new and different resources after they acquire industry targets. Therefore, firms' alliance experience in the adjacent industry accelerates the timing of firms' initial acquisition in an adjacent industry by reducing information asymmetry and indigestibility problems. [①]

As firms' prior alliance experience increases there is a question as to if acquisition timing is a linear function of experience or a curvilinear one. We posit that the relationship is curvilinear based on two mechanisms. First, as alliance experience increases, firms become increasingly skilled at leveraging the network – form organization. The network – form organization is a governance choice that impacts firm boundaries, and therefore overtime administrative structures are designed to manage uncertainties and external dependencies. (Podolny & Page, 1998). Thus, when firms' alliance experience increases, they become increasingly embedded in an interorganizational network, learn how to leverage the network to obtain information and resources, and find that the demands of internalizing resources through acquisitions less compelling. Second, according to learning theory, after a certain point, there are diminishing returns to experience (Argote, 1999). In our case, when firms have sufficient alliance experience, additional alliances do not benefit firms in

---

① From here, we use "alliance experience in the adjacent industry" and "interindusty – horizontal alliance experience" interchangeably.

terms of accelerating the timing of making an initial acquisition in the adjacent industry. Therefore, considering the two above mechanisms, we posit that below a certain numbers of alliances, a firm's prior experience increases the likelihood of its initial acquisition. After reaching a threshold, as experience continues to grow, the likelihood decreases.

Hypothesis 1: *The likelihood of firms' initial acquisition in an adjacent converging industry will first increase and then decrease in an inverted U – shaped form as their alliance experience in the adjacent industry increase.*

Other Forms of Alliances as Moderators of Initial Acquisition Timing

Intra – industry – horizontal alliances. From a social network perspective, IC is characterized by the overlapping of two industry networks (Gulati et al., 2000). For the firm which has ties in the adjacent industry network, if it also has ties in its own industry, it is referred to as a "switcher" that occupies a position bridging two networks (Castells, 2004; White, 1995). Castells (2004) defines switcher as a controller of connecting points between various strategic networks. Burt (2007) uses the example of the development of behavioral economics to explain that people who have close contacts with psychologists and economists are able to translate tacit knowledge from both group and find commonality.

We argue that a firm that accesses information from its own and the adjacent industry will have an advantage in combining and synthesizing information from the two industries and thereby reduce or mitigates the effect of Hypothesis 1. Put differently, if a firm has alliance experience in both industries that are converging, it will have a better understanding of uncertainty and market dynamics than firms that do not have both types of ties. So the urgency of making an initial acquisition becomes less of a concern for this type of firm.

Hypothesis 2: *Firms' intra – industry – horizontal alliance experience negatively moderates the inverted U – shaped relationship between firms' alliance experience and the likelihood of their initial acquisition in the adjacent converging industry.*

Intra – industry – vertical alliances. Intra – industry vertical alliances influence firms' initial acquisition timing. Compared with horizontal alliances that mitigate information and indigestibility problems, vertical alliances influence firms through customers' power over demand. Prior literature has shown that a supplier's internal expansion will synchronize with its buyers' international expansion moves (Martin et al. 1998). Customers often use demand-based power to impact their suppliers through affecting their internal resource allocation process (Christensen & Bower, 1996). Therefore, if technology innovation drastically obsoletes customers' competences, firms that supply those customer will be negatively affected (Afuah, 2000). Although the previous evidence is built on vertical relationships characterized by monetary exchanges of supply, recent studies suggest that cooperative vertical relationships also have the power to influence firm behavior. Mesquita and Lazzarini (2008) find that vertical ties result in increased manufacturing productivity and product innovation. As vertical ties accumulate, interdependence between firms and their buyers increase as they coordinate with buyers along the supply chain (e.g. inventory control) or co-specialize with buyers.

In the IC context, ties with the focal industries' buyers inhibit or slow down firms' initial acquisition timing. When a firm which has alliance connections in the adjacent industry also has intra-industry-vertical alliances with it original industry's buyers, the likelihood that the firm makes its initial acquisition in the adjacent industry will decrease. Embedding with current industry's customers increases the firm's tendency to allocate resources in the focal industry value chain or distract the firm's attention away from the adjacent industry. Therefore, we argue that intra-industry-vertical alliances will reduce the influence of inter-industry-horizontal alliances on the likelihood of firms' initial acquisition.

Hypothesis 3: Firms' intra-industry-vertical alliance experience negatively moderates the inverted U-shaped relationship between firms' alliance experience and the likelihood of their initial acquisition in the adjacent converging industry.

RESEARCH METHOD

Empirical Context

The convergence between the telecommunications equipment (SIC: 3661, 3663, and 3669) and computer networking (SIC: 3576) industries serves as our empirical context for four reasons. First, their blurred industry boundaries have been recognized as one salient case of IC (Lee, 2007; Shepard, 2002). In the 1980s, these industries belonged to the telecommunications and the computer sectors respectively. Firms in the telecommunications equipment industry (e. g. Nortel and Alcatel) relied on circuit switching technology, while firms (e. g. Cisco and 3Com) in the computing networking industry adopted packet switching technology. Circuit switching was designed for voice traffic of telecommunications network service. When someone dials a voice call, the network saves a network path for the entire duration of the call but can't share it with others. In contrast, the packet switching is designed for data traffic of Internet Protocol (IP) in which data are broken into small segments called packets. IP does not need to save a path for the entire duration of the call. Although circuit switching has the advantage of quality for voice calls, it is inefficient for data transmission. As the usage of the Internet grew in the 1990s, telecommunications equipment firms found that traditional circuit switching technology made network capacity insufficient and that they couldn't fulfill the demand for data traffic (e. g. surfing over the Internet). Increased price competition in the voice traffic market created incentives for telecommunications equipment vendors' to develop internet telephony by switching to packet – switching technology, since its cost per minute was lower (Dodd, 2002). Like other firms, telecommunications firms have three choices to pursue growth: internal development, cooperative alliance, and acquisition. However, resource commitments in the new IP market were a risky pursuit because equipment costs are higher in computer networking and because packet – switch technology was still new. Thus, firms formed alliances to mitigate these uncertainties.

Second, many telecommunications equipment makers whose previous expertise was in circuit switching technology begun to beef up their packet switching capability by way of acquisition in the computing networking industry. Because the new technology (packet switching) originating in computer networking was subsuming the old technology (circuit switching), most of acquisitions across the two industries were initiated by telecommunications equipment firms (our focal industry). These deals provide us with a rich context to examine determinants of the timing of firms' initial acquisitions. Third, both the telecommunications equipment and computer networking industries have only one major downstream industry: the telecommunications service industry (e. g. MCI Worldcom and British Telecom) and the computer industry (e. g. Compaq and Hewlett – Packard) respectively, which allows us to clearly identify intra – industry – vertical and inter – industry – vertical alliances. Finally, financial data for key foreign telecommunications equipment firms are in COMPUSTAT allowing us to include influential worldwide players (e. g. Alcatel and Ericsson) in the telecommunications equipment industry.

Data

COMPUSTAT was used to identify firms in four industries consistent with our framework shown in figure 2. Specifically, we used: the telecommunications equipment industry (SIC: 3661, 3663, and 3669) as the focal industry, computer networking industry (SIC: 3576) as the adjacent industry, telecommunications service industry (SIC: 4812 and 4813) as the downstream of the focal industry, and computer industry (SIC: 3571, and 3572) as the downstream of the adjacent industry. All alliances formed between 1989 and 2004 in the Thompson Financial SDC database were identified. The SDC database has been recognized as the most comprehensive sources of information on alliance deals, so using it to assemble our dataset is sensible choice particularly when research context is characterized by technology – intensive operation (Anand & Khanna, 2000; Schilling, 2009). The earliest packet – switching communication equipment product was introduced in 1989, so our data collection started from the year 1989. With the four – industry set of firms, we were able to identify alliances formed (1) between telecommunications equipment and computer networking industry (inter – industry – horizontal alliances), (2) within the telecommunications equipment industry (intra – industry – horizontal alliances), (3) between telecommunications equipment and telecommunications service industry (intra – industry – vertical alliances), and (4) between telecommunications equipment and computer industry (inter – industry – vertical alliances). The total number of alliances belonging to the four sets is 484. Of theses, 172 are intra –

industry – horzonzontal alliances, 211 are intra – industry – vertical alliances, 46 are inter – industry – vertical alliances, and 55 are inter – industry – horizontal alliances. The number of telecommunications equipment firms that had at least one alliance during the period 1989 – 2004 is 64 and are classified as the sample set of focal firms. ①

The SDC database was used to retrieve acquisition deals that telecommunications equipment firms completed with computer networking firms. The total number of initial acquisition deal initiated during the 1989 – 2004 period is 26. These deals were verified with the news database, Lexis – Nexis.

Measurement

Dependent variables. The dependent variable, *acquisition timing*, is the amount of time elapsed between the emergence of IC and a telecommunications equipment firm's initial acquisition event in the adjacent industry (computer networking). The acquisition event is the initial acquisition assessed from the SDC and COMPUSTAT database.

Independent variables. For the independent variable *alliance experience in the adjacent industry*, following previous work (Anand & Khanna, 2000), we measure the cumulative number of prior alliances that a telecommunications equipment firm had in the computer networking industry by taking count of all alliances formed from 1989 for each year through 2004. Since we are testing an inverted – U relationship, a square of this variable, *alliance experience in the adjacent industry – square*, is used. For the variable of *intra – industry – horizontal alliance experience*, we measure the cumulative number of prior alliances that a telecommunications equipment firm

---

① In order to confirm the representativeness of these 64 equipment firms, we divide the total sales revenue of the sample firms in 1999 by the total sales revenues of the overall telecommunication equipment market size in 1999 estimated from STANDARD & POOR'S INDUSTRY SURVEY. The result (76%) shows that the samples represent a major portion of the industry's sales revenue. Recognizing that the categories of SIC 3661/3663/3669 also contain firms which don't have any alliances under our framework, we reviewed all of these non – alliance firms (24% of sales). None of them are powerful firms (global top 10 players). The telecommunications equipment industry was historically dominated by a few of giant firms which had significant influence on industry evolution.

had in its industry by taking count of all its alliances formed from 1989 for each year. For the variable of *intra – industry – vertical alliance experience*, we measure the cumulative number of prior alliances that a telecommunications equipment firm had in the telecommunications service industry by taking count of all its alliances formed from 1989 for each year through 2004. In order to create the other two interaction variables, these two measures are multiplied by the variable alliance experience in the adjacent industry. All of these above variables are one – year – lagged, since we assume that alliance effects on the occurrence of an acquisition event are not immediate.

Control variables. We control for variables that have an influence on the timing of the initial acquisition: inter – industry – vertical alliance experience, firm size, firm age, consolidation, alliance portfolio diversity, dissolution by acquisition, prior acquisition experience, and prior firm performance.

According to our theory, we treat inter – industry – vertical alliance experiences as a control variable since in our sample setting, high vertical disintegration exist between the upstream computer networking and downstream computer industry. Throughout the time period of our study, the up and downstream stages of the two industries increasingly became more disintegrated. The battle between Cisco and IBM exemplifies this case (Christensen, Anthony, & Roth, 2004). Local area network (LAN) was dominated by computer firms in the 1980s under IBM's proprietary structure, called system network architecture (SNA). However, Cisco's design of the router increased the efficiency of LAN management and reduced equipment cost simultaneously. Most computer firms, such as IBM and Digital Equipment, retreated from the LAN market and sold their business units to router firms. The variable of *inter – industry – vertical alliance experience* is measured as the cumulative number of prior alliances that a telecommunications equipment firm had in the computer industry by taking count of all its alliances formed from 1989 for each year through 2004.

Firm size is controlled by using the natural logarithm of net sales, because large firms usually have more resources to complete acquisitions than small firms. In addition, *firm age* may result in inertia for pursuing acquisitions, so it is controlled by measuring the nature logarithm of the difference between the firm's founding year and the year in which it first entered our observation period. Previous literature suggests consolidation may correlate with across – industry acquisition under IC (Katz, 1996; Maholtra & Gupta, 2001). Thus, the number of annual intra – industry acquisitions that occurred in the telecommunications equipment and computer networking industry is calculated for the variables of *telecommunications consolidation* and *computer networking consolidation*.① Note that only buyers that are public firms are included. Public firms reflect the significance of intra – industry acquisitions deals, since firms may not know all of the acquisitions in their population, but are more easily able to pay attention to public firms.

Prior studies show that heterogeneity in a firm's alliance portfolio influences firm entry into new markets (Lee, 2007); therefore, a firm's partner heterogeneity across the four forms of alliances is assessed by Blau's heterogeneity index (Blau, 1977)② for the variable of *alliance portfolio diversity*. The variable of *dissolution by acquisition* is controlled by measuring whether the firm was acquired by its competitors in the telecommunications equipment industry. If it is acquired, the variable is coded as 1, otherwise 0. This variable helps us reduce estimation bias for the case in which a firm that has already engaged in several alliances in the adjacent industry and thus has a higher likelihood of making its initial acquisition later in the study time period, but was acquired by its competitor. In addition, according to previous studies (Haleblian & Finkelstein, 1999), acquisition experience may shorten the

---

① . One control variable that may influence firm acquisition timing is the opportunity set of acquisitions in the adjacent industry. The decreasing number of available targets in the computer networking industry may increase the bidding competition on targets. Anticipating that more premiums would need to be paid, firm may postpone acquisition timing. This variable highly correlates with another control variable (computer networking consolidation), since in our context, many targets had been acquired by top 4 computer networking firms (STANDARD & POOR'S INDUSTRY SURVEY, 1999). Thus, we did not incorporate it into the model.

② Blau's heterogeneity index: $\eta = 1 - \sum_{i=1}^{n} P_i^2$, where Pi is the percentage of the group in the ith category. Since we have four forms of alliances, the number of categories (n) in this index is four. The more heterogeneous composition of four forms, the higher the Blau's heterogeneity index becomes. Its value is 0 when the firm only has a completely homogeneous form of alliance. If a firm has no alliances, the index will be 1. Thus, we recode the case into 0.

decision – making time of firm acquisitions, so a measure of the cumulative number of acquisition deals that the firm previously had is included for the variable of *prior acquisition experience*. Finally, inter – industry acquisitions are more risky than intra – industry acquisitions. Firms who have low prior performance may be more willing to take such risky strategic actions (Cyert & March, 1963). So, we control for *firm prior performance* by measuring one – year – lagged return on asset (ROA).

Analytical Model

Since our data contain right – censored data, which means that some firms may initiate acquisitions beyond the observation period, ordinary least regression analysis is not appropriate. In addition, our purposes is to examine the determinants of firms' initial acquisition timing, thus, event history analysis that enables us to model the hazard rate: the likelihood that an acquisition will be observed at time t, given that no acquisition occurred prior to time t, is appropriate. With a hazard rate function, one can estimate acquisition timing. Researchers have used event history analysis to measure timing – related constructs, such as response speed in competitive dynamics (Yu & Cannella, 2007), the timing of international expansion (Martin et al. 1998) and the timing of alliances and acquisitions (Shi & Prescott, 2009).

A piecewise exponential model is used because no assumptions are made regarding the duration (period) dependence which would require a specific parametric distribution (Blossfel & Rohwer, 1995). This approach is appropriate for our framework where IC consisted of three periods of transition as we mentioned in the outset of the paper. We interviewed an academic professor who was also a former practitioner who has specialized in the telecommunications field for over twenty years to assess our approach and pinpoint markers that divide the three periods. From 1989 to 1993, it was a period of the emergence of packet switching technology applied in telecommunications products, whereas from 1994 to 2001, it was in the converging period in which two industries increasingly converged. [①] After that, from 2002 to 2004,

---

[①] The Clinton administration convened a "National Infrastructure Initiative" (NII) in 1994 and 1995. NII has been regarded as a key mark where the "convergence era" age started (Sterling, Brent, & Weiss, 2006).

the convergence slowed down in anticipation of deregulation and new technology—the industry started to migrate toward a new generation network structure (OECD, 2008: 15). The flexibility of the piecewise exponential model allows us to model the differentiation across these periods. ①

Given the time periods, the transition rate from a given origin state to destination state k is defined as follows in which the rate stays constant within each period I_l to I_{l+1}

$$\gamma_k(t) = \exp\left\{\bar{\alpha}_l^{(k)} + A^{(k)}\alpha^{(k)}\right\} \text{ if } t \in I_l$$

For each transition to destination state k, $\bar{\alpha}^k$ is a constant coefficient associated with the l th time period. A^k is a row vector of covariates, and $\alpha^{(k)}$ is an associated vector of coefficients assumed not to vary across time periods (Blossfeld, Golsch, & Rohwer, 2007).

RESULTS

Table 1, reports means, standard deviations and pair-wise correlations. The table shows high correlations among intra-industry-horizontal and intra-industry-vertical alliances. The high correlation between vertical and horizontal alliances is consistent with the empirical results of previous studies that the formation of vertical and horizontal relationships is interdependent (Lazzarini et al., 2008). Also, the interaction and quadratic variables would inevitably increase the correlation level. To avoid problems of multicollinearity, the following steps were taken. First, two partial models were run to test H2 and H3, rather than in one model specification. This helped us to distinguish the effect of the two moderators. Second, for testing interaction effects, variables were centered by subtracting the sample mean from the individual values and then creating the interaction variables (Aiken & West, 1991). Such a method can significantly reduce the values of variance inflation factors (VIF) and thereby avoid multicollinearity problems.

---

① We conducted a sensitivity analysis to assess if changes in the dates of the time periods influenced our statistic outcomes. The results show that coefficients were similar; thus, we retained the usage of these periods in the model.

Table 1. Descriptive Statistics and Correlation Matrix

		Mean	S.D.	1	2	3	4	5	6	7	8	9	10	11	12	13
1	Alliance experience in the adjacent industry	0.58	1.49													
2	Intra-industry-horizontal alliance experience	2.01	4.28	.67**												
3	Intra-industry-vertical alliance experience	2.11	5.64	.67**	.88**											
4	Alliance experience in the adjacent industry x Intra-industry-horizontal alliance experience	5.42	20.18	.81**	.90**	.88**										
5	Alliance experience in the adjacent industry x Intra-industry-vertical alliance experience	6.82	28.11	.78**	.81**	.93**	.94**									
6	Inter-industry-vertical alliance experience	0.68	2.63	.56**	.93**	.87**	.85**	.77**								
7	Firm size	5.37	2.41	.61**	.59**	.50**	.51**	.46**	.50**							
8	Firm age	2.19	1.40	.41**	.33**	.23**	.32**	.28**	.26**	.44**						
9	Telecommunications consolidation	2.15	2.58	.15**	.14**	.09**	.12**	.09*	.07+	.13**	-.03					
10	Computer networking consolidation	1.24	1.29	-.01	.01	-.06	-.04	-.08*	-.01	-.00	-.07+	.16**				
11	Alliance portfolio diversity	0.20	0.27	.60**	.59**	.50**	.48**	.42**	.45**	.61**	.32**	.13**	.05			
12	Dissolution by acquisition	0.32	0.47	-.21**	-.23**	-.16**	-.18**	-.16**	-.16**	-.22**	-.22**	-.19**	.10**	-.27**		
13	Prior acquisition experience	3.79	8.82	.80**	.82**	.78**	.89**	.83**	.73**	.59**	.44**	.15**	-.07+	.52**	-.22**	
14	Firm performance	-0.09	.81	.02	.03	.01	.01	.00	.02	.20**	.06	-.10	.09*	.04	.09*	.00

+p<0.10; *p<0.05; **p<0.01

Table 2 illustrates the result of each variable on the timing of firms' initial acquisition in the adjacent industry from the hazard rate function. All coefficients in Table 2 are not estimated hazard rates. To derive hazard rates, one needs to obtain the exponential values of the coefficients. Model 1 includes only the control variables and then we test the hypotheses in Model 2 – 4. The outcome of control variables shows that firm size has significantly positive effects on the likelihood of initial acquisition in the adjacent industry (Model 1, 2, 3, and 4: $p < 0.1$), while firm age has a weak negative influence (Model 3: $p < 0.1$). The latter corresponds to the predication of ecology theory where firms experience inertia as they age leading to resistance to changing. The positive effect of firms' prior acquisition experience on the likelihood of firm acquisition is significantly supported in Model 1 ($p < 0.05$), but it becomes insignificant after including the independent variables. Similarly, the control variable of inter – industry – vertical alliance experience is significant in Model 1 ($p < 0.01$), but not in Model 2, 3, and 4.

Table 2. Results from Hazard Rate Analysis of Initial Acquisition in An Adjacent Converging Industry

		Model 1	Model 2	Model 3	Model 4
	Time period 1989-1993	-6.131***	-5.015***	-4.473**	-5.569**
	Time period 1994-2001	-5.394***	-4.326**	-3.816**	-4.686**
	Time period 2002-2004	-5.343***	-4.026**	-3.512**	-4.322**
	Firm size	0.314†	0.304†	0.330†	0.320†
	Firm age	-0.282	-0.386	-0.489†	-0.437
	Telecommunications consolidation	0.005	0.006	0.012	0.014
	Computer networking consolidation	-0.027	-0.066	-0.081	-0.064
	Alliance portfolio diversity	0.303	-1.113	-2.386	-0.966
	Dissolution by acquisition	0.381	0.479	0.579	0.681
	Prior acquisition experience	0.215*	0.130	0.140	0.127
	Inter-industry-vertical alliance experience	-0.181†	-0.154	-0.001	0.124
	Firm performance	-0.190	-0.187	-0.222	-0.213
H1	Alliance experience in the adjacent industry		1.240†	1.964**	1.722*
H1	Alliance experience in the adjacent industry square		-0.160†	-0.310*	-0.296*
	Intra-industry-horizontal alliance experience			0.040	
H2	Alliance experience in the adjacent industry x Intra-industry-horizontal alliance experience			-0.159*	
H2	Alliance experience in the adjacent industry square x Intra-industry-horizontal alliance experience			0.032†	
	Intra-industry-vertical alliance experience				-0.297
H3	Alliance experience in the adjacent industry x Intra-industry-vertical alliance experience				0.002
H3	Alliance experience in the adjacent industry square x Intra-industry-vertical alliance experience				0.015
	Log-likelihood	-24.71***	-22.64***	-20.79***	-20.62***
	Wald chi-squared	147.28	141.74	130.81	132.28

The analysis is based on 549 firm-year observations covering 64 firms and 17 events of firms' initial acquisitions.
†$p<0.10$; *$p<0.05$; **$p<0.01$; ***$p<0.001$.

Model 2 reveals that the estimation coefficient of alliance experience in the adjacent industry is positive and significant ($p < 0.05$) and that the coefficient of the square term of this variable is negative and significant ($p < 0.1$) supporting hypothesis 1. The result is quite robust, since Model 2, 3, and 4 all show significance for these variables. To examine the result more closely, we transform coefficients in Model 3 into hazard rates to interpret how alliances influence acquisition timing. In Model 3, the exponential coefficient of alliance experience in the adjacent industry and its square term is 7.128 ($e^{1.964} = 7.128$). In hazard rate analysis, this means that a one unit increase in the variable of alliance experience in the adjacent industry results in the hazard rate of the initial acquisition to increase by 713 percents. For the square term, the exponential coefficient is 0.734 ($e^{-0.310} = 0.734$). This suggests that for a one unit increase in the squared amount of alliance experience in the adjacent industry, the hazard rate of acquisition will decrease by 26.6 percent. The combination of results from these two variables further confirms Hypothesis 1 that as firms' alliance experience in the adjacent industry increase, the likelihood of firms' initial acquisition will first increase and then decrease.

The moderator effect of intra-industry-horizontal alliance experience is included in Model 3. The interaction variable of interaction of alliance experience in the adjacent industry and intra-industry-horizontal alliance experience has a significant negative effect on acquisition likelihood ($p < 0.05$), and the hazard coefficient is 0.853 ($e^{-0.159} = 0.853$), meaning that an increase of one unit in the interaction effect will reduce the hazard rate of acquisition by 14.7 percent. On the other hand, the interaction variable of square of alliances in the adjacent industry and intra-industry-horizontal alliances has a significant positive effect on the likelihood of acquisition ($p < 0.1$), and the hazard coefficient is 1.032 ($e^{-0.032} = 1.032$), though the effect is very small (3.2%). Therefore, as firms' alliance experience in the adjacent industry and in the focal industry both increase, firms' initial acquisition likelihood will be lower than the case in which firms only have alliances in the adjacent industry but no intra-industry-horizontal alliances. This supports Hypotheses 2. In Model 4, the hypothesis that intra-industry-vertical alliance experience negatively affects the timing of telecommunications equipment firm acquisition in the converging adjacent industry is not supported.

DISCUSSION AND CONCLUSION

We have two goals for this chapter. Our first goal is to explain how alliances influence the timing of firms' initial acquisition in an adjacent converging industry, one central aspect of the process of IC. We hypothesize that an increase in alliance experience in the adjacent industry will first increase and then decrease the likelihood of firms' initial acquisition in the adjacent industry in an inverted – U shaped relationship, while two other forms of alliances: intra – industry – horizontal and intra – industry – vertical alliance experience negatively moderate the inverted – U shaped relationship. The empirical findings support the inverted – U shaped relationship and that intra – industry – horizontal alliances negatively moderate the inverted – U shaped relationship, but the findings do not confirm the moderating effect of intra – industry – vertical alliances.

Our second goal is to propose that our approach can be adapted by CI professionals to develop an early warning process. While we focused on an empirical model using sophisticated analytics, the approach can be modified to track firm alliance and acquisition initiations that can be used to predict not only industry convergence but which firms are likely to be first movers in the IC process. The rationales of early warning systems are to avoid surprise and provide managers with sufficient time to undertake action that protects a firm's market position. During IC, this is indeed an important task for CI professionals.

Our findings contribute in several ways. First, our approach provides a close look at the extent to which alliance experience in an adjacent industry and intra – industry – horizontal alliance experience simultaneously influence the timing of firms' initial acquisitions in the adjacent industry. We use Figure 3 generated from Model 3 to demonstrate this point. As Figure 3 illustrates, in the case of telecommunications equipment firms, when a firm does not have any intra – industry alliance experience, the inverted – U shaped curve is greatly amplified. On the other hand, if the firm has four alliances, the likelihood of the curve is suppressed.① This figure also reveals several characteristics of the inverted – U shaped curve. The peak of the curve shows that four alliances in the adjacent industry is the threshold after which the likelihood of an initial acquisition becomes a decreasing function. This suggests that for telecommunications equipment firms, the sufficient cumulative number of alliances in the adjacent converging industry to maximize the likelihood of an initial acquisition is between two to four alliances. Further, the argument that the extent to which intra – industry – horizontal alliance experience provides switcher benefits and thus slows initial acquisition timing is not supported. The results show that the interaction effect on the likelihood of initial acquisition given high levels of intra – industry – horizontal alliance experience is larger than one, which means that firms still have a positive likelihood of an initial acquisition. This implies that benefit of switcher that straddle in two industry networks from alliances within the telecommunications equipment industry is not strong enough to suppress the likelihood of initial acquisition. Regarding the question as to when a firm accumulates sufficient experience to significantly lower the likelihood of an initial acquisition in the adjacent industry, this figure tells us the number is seven. Care must be taken in these interpretations since we are dealing with the likelihood of a sample and not specific firm decisions.

Second, the findings inform managers regarding competitive intelligence processes and rivalry capabilities. Understanding the structure of other firm's inter – industry and intra – industry alliances provides valuable intelligence. If the alliance structure of a competitor in the focal industry is sparse, one may foresee that a couple of inter – industry horizontal alliances will greatly increase the likelihood of an initial acquisition in the adjacent industry, since the constraining force from intra – industry alliances is attenuated. If market leaders in a firm's industry have shifted their focus from intra – industry alliances to alliances in the adjacent converging in-

---

① We did not use the mean of intra – industry – horizontal alliance experience plus or minus one standard deviation to represent the low level and the high level of alliance experience because it generate negative values (see Table 1). This characteristic is not surprising since prior study has found the distribution of alliances in the telecommunication industry is skewed (Rosenkopf & Schilling, 2007).

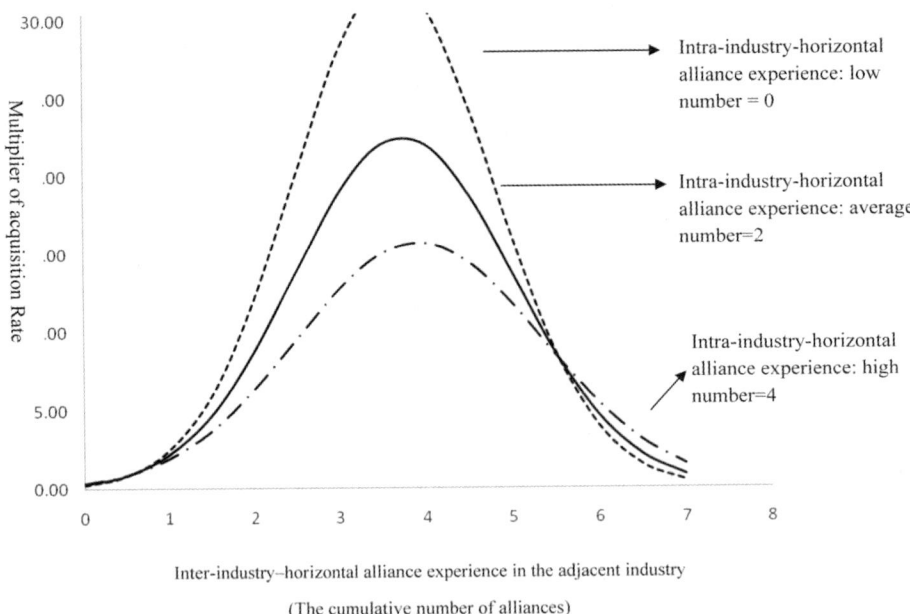

Figure 3. Effects of Intra-industry-horizontal and Inter-industry-horizontal Alliances on Initial Acquisition Timing

dustry, they will very likely initiate their initial acquisition which may greatly impact the competitive landscape. This type of strategic initiative can be interpreted as an early warning signal that IC is beginning to take off. To illustrate our conjecture, we created a map in which one axis is firm alliance experience in the adjacent industry and the other axis is intra – industry – horizontal alliance experience. Then, we placed all of the firms in the focal industry on the map based on their alliance activities (see Figure 4). This map creates a picture of the forest regarding the likelihood of competitors' initial acquisitions. This tool can provide significant informational advantage to firms during IC.

Finally, our study suggests how IC impacts outcomes associated with a firm's position in their alliance network. Our observation consistent with Powell, White, Koput, and Owen – Smith's emphasis (2005: 1134) is that an understanding of the emergence of a new field requires "the analysis of interactions of overlapping networks". Traditionally, scholars adopt industry membership as a criterion to determine the boundary of a network and then generate each firm's network position (Koka & Prescott, 2008). However, during IC, intra – industry and inter – industry

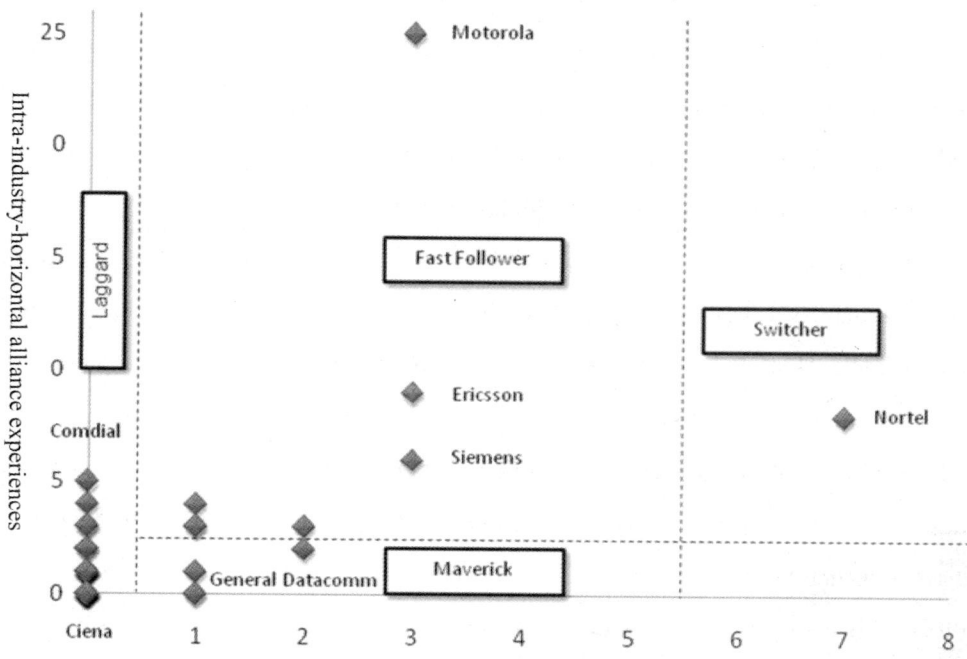

Inter-industry-horizontal alliance experiences in the adjacent industry
(The cumulative number of alliances)

Note: The four labels (maverick, fast follower, switcher, and laggard) inside the figure identify the likelihood of initial acquisition that range from high to low level respectively. The dividing lines that distinguish four types of acquisition timing are drawed according to different levels of inter-industry-horizontal and intra-industry-horizontal alliance experience from our dataset in year 1996. The locations of dividing lines inside the map are the authors' estimates based on Figure 3. Thus, the purpose of this map is to not suggest that the typology of initial acquisition timing presented for this sample is generalizable, but to highlight the potential value of the application of our results for managers. The firms noted in the figure are examples drawn from our sample.

Figure 4. Types of Acquisition Timing of Firms in Year 1996

ties co – determine the timing of firms' initial acquisitions in the adjacent industry network, thereby introducing new members in the industry and changing the network boundaries. For firms which do not have inter – industry ties, a change in the network boundary will likely weaken their centrality and possibly brokerage network positions. When the relative number of inter – industry ties is increasing and intra – industry ties is shrinking (industry – level changes), firms who based their network positions on intra – industry ties will likely be disrupted as the two industries converge.

Before moving to limitations and future research, we discuss why intra – industry – vertical alliance experience does not moderate firm initial acquisition timing. We speculate that the pull force of intra – industry – vertical alliances is countervailed by the push force of inter – industry – horizontal alliances. In Model 4, despite the non – significance of intra – industry vertical alliance experience, its direction is negative (coefficient = -0.297, p = 0.3). Thus, intra – industry vertical alliances may still impose a negative influence on firms' initial acquisition timing to some extent. However, the countervailing force of inter – industry – horizontal alliances is strong (Model 4: $e^{1.715}$ = 5.56), such that the interaction effect of intra – industry – vertical alliances is not significant. It is likely that the relative strength of these pull and push forces vary across sample settings. For example, in the context of convergence between the music and internet industry, the music industry had tight relationships with its downstream (e.g. retailers). This force explains why music firms have not acquired online firms in an aggressive manner (Rivkin & Meier, 2000). In contrast, unlike music firms, telecommunication equipment firms have been situated in a dynamic within – industry change of technology and regulation which has weakened inertia resulting from customer connections. Therefore, we believe that Hypothesis 3 warrants empirical examination in different IC contexts.

Our results should be viewed in light of several limitations. First, the evidence supporting the intra – industry – vertical alliances hypothesis is not supported. However, rather than abandoning this hypothesis, we call for further studies which explore how the net effect of intra – industry – vertical and inter – industry – horizontal alliances differs across industry contexts and their reasons. Second, we recognize that generalizing our framework to other industries is important to the accumulating knowledge of the convergence process. Industries which are undergoing the emergence of IC, such as the food and pharmaceutical industry (Broring et al., 2006) and the convergence of semiconductor and biotech industries (Avenel, Favier, Ma, Mangematin, & Rieu, 2007) would be ideal for studying the generalizability of our findings. Third, our emphasis is the process of IC, not its antecedents or outcomes. Thus, our findings should be generalized to industries where the triggers of IC have been observed or given. Future research could integrate convergence triggers and our process framework to study other interesting questions. For example, why do some industries not converge even though there are strong exogenous forces pushing towards convergence?

Fourth, our framing centered on the permeation of the telecommunications equipment firms into the computer networking industry through initial acquisitions. We focused on how firms from an industry with the older and would – be – replaced technology rely on alliances to help drive the IC process. One future research direction could be to include initial acquisitions in the other direction: acquisitions by computer networking firms into the telecommunications equipment industry. The computer networking firms have newer and substituting technology. Although reviewing historical data tells us that the telecommunication equipment firms' market which used to have good relationships with telecommunication service firms were not replaced by computer network firms; the sustainable growth of Cisco is a noteworthy case. A reasonable speculation would be that Cisco aggressively bought intra – industry valuable firms to prevent cross – industry acquisitions from telecommunication equipment makers. So, a comparative study of a two – way IC process can inform us as to why they acquire at different rates, how competitive dynamics occur between these two industries, and so forth. Fifth, this chapter focuses on one aspect of the IC process—i. e. initial acquisition. Future research can extend our approach in other respects and mechanisms. For example, the process of convergence between telecommunications service and cable industries mostly occurs through the aspect of integration of product services (the bundle of triple services), but not through acquisitions. Also, there could be other mechanisms that firm can rely on (e. g. open innovation environment or TMT diversity) rather than alliances to make progress along the path of convergence. These directions will more fully complete our theorizing of the IC process and their mechanisms. Finally, our analysis does not cover the relationship among alliance experience, initial acquisition timing, firm performance, sustainability or survival. In the face of convergence and change, some firms failed, while other firms survived. Under what conditions can alliances and initial acquisition timing assist firms confronted with the disruption of their competences? How the interaction of alliances and acquisitions create new business models is another intriguing question.

As Hamel and Prahalad (1996: 240) suggest, our industrialized society has shifted toward a new economy in which many industries are in "a state of flux". Nevertheless, the theorizing regarding IC has been under – developed for over a decade. Our framework uses prior alliance experience and subsequent initial acquisition timing to examine the process of IC. A firm – level focus enabled us to provide several fine – grain implications and several interesting future research questions. Our framework serves as one stepping stone to an enhanced understanding of the ambiguous process through which one industry converges with another industry.

ACKNOWLEDGMENTS

We would like to thank Professor Weiss for his constructive inputs. Additionally, the Strategy Research Group Brown Bag series at the University of Pittsburgh provided a rich context for us to share and improve our ideas.

REFERENCES

[1] Afuah, A. 2000. How much do your co – opetitors' capabilities matter in the face of technological change? *Strategic Management Journal*, 21(3): 387 – 404.

[2] Aiken, L. S. & West, S. G. 1991. *Multiple regression: Testing and interpreting interactions.* CA: Sage.

[3] Anand, B. N. & Khanna, T. 2000. Do firms learn to create value: The case of alliances. *Strategic Management Journal.*, 21(3): 295 – 315.

[4] Argote, L. 1999. *Organizational learning: Creating, retaining and transferring knowledge.* Norwell, MA: Kluwer.

[5] Arnst, C. & Nathans, L. S. 1995. Divide or conquer? *BusinessWeek.* October 2: 56 – 57.

[6] Avenel, E., Favier, A., Ma, S., Mangematin, V., & Rieu, C. 2007. Diversification and hybridization in firm knowledge bases in nanotechnologies. *Research Policy*, 36(6): 864 – 870.

[7] Balakrishaman, S. & Koza, M. P. 1993. Information asymmetry, adverse selection and joint – ventures: theory and evidence. *Journal of Economic Behavior and Organization*, 20: 99 – 117.

[8] Beckman, C. M. & Haunschild, P. R. 2002. Network learning: The effects of partners' heterogeneity of experience on corporate acquisitions. *Administrative Science Quarterly*, 47(1): 92 – 124.

[9] Blau, P. 1977. *Inequality and heterogeneity: A primitive theory of social structure*. New York: Free Press.

[10] Blossfeld, H. &Rohwer, G. 1995. *Techniques of event history modeling*. Mahwah, NJ: Lawrence Erlbaum Associates.

[11] Blossfeld, H. , Golsch, K. & Rohwer, G. 2007. *Event history analysis with stata*. Mahwah, NJ: Lawrence Erlbaum Associates.

[12] Broring, S. , Cloutier, L. M. , Leker, J. 2006. The front end of innovation in an era of industry convergence: Evidence from nutraceuticals and functional Foods. *R&D Management*, 36(5): 487 – 498.

[13] Burgelman, R. A. & Grove, A. S. 2007. Cross – boundary disruptors: Powerful inter – industry entrepreneurial change agents. *Strategic Entrepreneurship Journal*. 1: 315 – 327.

[14] Burt, R. S. 2007. Secondhand brokerage: Evidence on the importance of local structure for managers, bankers, and analysts. *Academy of Management Journal*, 50(1): 119 – 148.

[15] Castells, M. 2004. *The Network Society: A Cross – cultural Perspective*, Cheltenham, UK; Northampton, MA: Edward Elgar Pub.

[16] Chon, B. S. , Choi, J. H. , Barnett, G. A. , Danowski, J. A. , & Joo, S. – H. 2003. A structural analysis of media convergence: Cross – industry mergers and acquisitions in the information industries. *Journal of Media Economics*, 16(3): 141 – 157.

[17] Christensen, C. M. , Anthony, S. D. , & Roth, E. A. 2004. *Seeing what's next: Using the theories of innovation to predict industry change*. Cambridge, MA: Harvard Business School.

[18] Christensen, C. M. & Bower, J. L. 1996. Customer power, strategic investment, and the failure of leading firms. *Strategic Management Journal*,17(3): 197 – 218.

[19] Cyert, R. M. & J. G. March. 1963. *A Behavioral Theory of the Firm*, NJ: Prentice Hall, Inc.

[20] Dodd, A. Z. 2000. The Essential Guide to Telecommunications. (2nd Eds.) Prentice Hall, Upper Saddle River, NJ.

[21] Duysters, G. & Hagedoorn, J. 1998. Technological convergence in the IT industry: The role of strategic technology alliances and technological competencies. *International Journal of the Economics of Business*, 5(3): 355 – 368.

[22] Dyer, J. H. & Singh, H. 1998. The relational view: Cooperative strategy and sources of interorganizational competitive advantage. *Academy of Management Review*, 23(4): 660 – 679.

[23] Ferrier, W. 2001. Navigating the competitive landscape: The drivers and consequences of competitive aggressiveness, *Academy of Management Journal*, 44 (4): 858 – 877.

[24] Fligstein, N. 2003 Agreements, disagreements, and opportunities in the "new sociology of

markets". In Guillen, M. F. (Eds.). *The New Economic Sociology: Developments in an Emerging Field*. New York: Russell Sage Foundation.

[25] Gambardella, A. & Torrisi, S. 1998. Does technological convergence imply convergence in markets? Evidence from the electronics industry. *Research Policy*, 27(5): 445 – 463.

[26] Greenstein, S. & Khanna, T. 1997. What does industry convergence mean? In Yoffie, D. B. (Eds.), *Competing in the age of digital convergence*:201 – 223. Cambridge, MA: Harvard business school press.

[27] Gulati, R., Nohria, N., & Zaheer, A. 2000. Strategic networks. *Strategic Management Journal*, 21(3): 203 – 215.

[28] Haleblian, J. & Finkelstein, S. 1999. The influence of organizational acquisition experience on acquisition performance: A behavioral learning perspective. *Administrative Science Quarterly*, 44(1): 29 – 56.

[29] Hamel, G. & Prahalad, C. K. 1996. Competing in the new economy: Managing out of bounds. *Strategic Management Journal*, 17(3): 237 – 242.

[30] Hennart, J. & Reddy, S. B. 2000. Digestibility and asymmetric information in the choice between acquisitions and joint ventures. *Strategic Management Journal*, 21(2): 191 – 193.

[31] Hoffmann, W. H. 2007. Strategies for managing a portfolio of alliances. *Strategic Management Journal*, 28(8): 827 – 856.

[32] Jacobides, M. G. & Winter, S. G. 2005. The co – evolution of capabilities and transaction costs: Explaining the institutional structure of production. *Strategic Management Journal*, 26(5): 395 – 413.

[33] Katz, M. L. 1996. Remarks on the economic implications of convergence. *Industrial & Corporate Change*, 5(4): 1079 – 1095.

[34] Koka, B. R. & Prescott, J. E. 2002. Strategic alliances as social capital: A multidimensional view. *Strategic Management Journal*, 23(9): 795 – 816.

[35] Koka, B. & Prescott, J. E. 2008. Designing alliance networks: The influence of network position, environmental change, and strategy on firm performance. *Strategic Management Journal*, 29(6): 639 – 661.

[36] Koza, M. P. & Lewin, A. Y. 1998. The co – evolution of strategic alliances. *Organization Science*, 9(3): 255 – 264.

[37] Lazzarini, S. G., Claro, D. P., & Mesquita, L. F. 2008. Buyer – supplier and supplier – supplier alliances: Do they reinforce or undermine one another? *Journal of Management Studies*, 45(3): 561 – 584.

[38] Lee, G. K. 2007. The significance of network resources in the race to enter emerging prod-

uct markets: The convergence of telephony communications and computer networking 1989 – 2001. *Strategic Management Journal*, 28(1): 17 – 37.

[39] Malhotra, A. & Gupta, A. K. 2001. *An investigation of firms' strategic responses to industry convergence*. Paper presented at the Academy of Management Proceedings.

[40] Martin, X., Swaminathan, A., & Mitchell, W. 1998. Organizational evolution in the interorganizational environment: Incentives and constraints on international expansion strategy. *Administrative Science Quarterly*, 43(3): 566 – 601.

[41] Mesquita, L. F. & Lazzarini, S. G. 2008. Horizontal and vertical relationships in developing economies: Implications for smes' access to global markets, *Academy of Management Journal*, 51(2): 359 – 380.

[42] Organization for Economic Co – operation and Development (OECD). 2008. *Convergence and next generation netwroks*, Seoul, Korea: OECD.

[43] Pil, F. K. & Cohen, S. K. 2006. Modularity: Implications for imitation, innovation, and sustained advantage. *Academy of Management Journal*, 31(4): 995 – 1011.

[44] Podolny, J. M. & Page, K. L. 1998. Network forms of organizations. *Annual Review of Sociology*, 24(1): 57 – 76.

[45] Powell, W. W., White, D. R., Koput, K. W., & Owen – Smith, J. 2005. Network dynamics and field evolution: The growth of interorganizational collaboration in the life sciences. *American Journal of Sociology*, 110(4): 1132 – 1205.

[46] Rivkin, J. W. and Meier, G. 2000. *BMG Entertainment*. Harvard Business School, Case Teaching Note 5 – 701 – 049.

[47] Rosenberg, N. 1976. *Perspectives on Technology*. Cambridge Univ. Press, Cambridge, UK

[48] Rosenkopf, L. & Schilling, M. A. 2007. Comparing alliance network structure across industries: Observation and explanations. *Strategic Entrepreneurship Journal*, 1: 191 – 209.

[49] Schilling, M. A. 2009. Understanding the alliance data. *Strategic Management Journal*, 30(3): 233 – 260.

[50] Schilling, M. A. & Steensma, H. K. 2001. The use of modular organizatinal forms: An Industry – Level Analysis. *Academy of Management Journal*, 44(6): 1149 – 1168

[51] Shepard, S. 2002. *Telecommunications Convergence*. (2nd Ed.). New York: McGraw – Hill.

[52] Shi, W. & Prescott, J. E. 2009. A temporal perspective of corporate M&A and alliance portfolios. In Finkelstein, S. & Cooper, C. (Eds.) *Advances in Mergers and Acquisitions*, Elsevier Publishers.

[53] Srinivasan, R., Haunschild, P., & Grewal, R. 2007. Vicarious learning in new product

introductions in the early converging market. *Management Science*,53(1): 16 – 28.

[54] Standard & Poor's. 1999. *Industry surveys: Communications equipment.* NY: Standard & Poor's.

[55] Sterling, C. H. , Bernt, P. W. , & Weiss, M. B. H. 2006. *Shaping American telecommunications: A history of technology, policy, and economics*, Mahwah, NJ: Lawrence Erlbaum.

[56] Tripsas, M. & Gavetti, G. 2000. Capabilities, cognition, and inertia: Evidence from digital imaging. *Strategic Management Journal*, 21(10/11): 1147.

[57] Toxvaerd, F. 2007. Strategic merger waves: A theory of musical chairs. *Journal of Economic Theory*, 1 – 26.

[58] Vizard, M. 1998. Lucent vice president on her company's future in data. *InfoWorld*, Feb 23: 53.

[59] White, H. C. 1995. Network switchings and bayesian forks: Reconstructing the social and behavioral sciences. *Social Research*, 62(4): 1035 – 1063.

[60] Wildstrom, S. H. 2004. Net phoning is starting to make sense. *BusinessWeek*, May 24: 28 – 28.

[61] Wirtz, B. W. 2001. Reconfiguration of value chains in converging media and communications markets. *Long Range Planning*,34(4): 489 – 506.

[62] Yoffie, D. B. 1997. *Competing in the age of digital convergence*, Cambridge, MA: Harvard business school press.

[63] Yu, T. & Canella, A. A. Jr. 2007. Rivalry between multinational enterprises: An event history approach, *Academy of Management of Journal*, 50 (3): 665 – 686.

近 25 年我国竞争情报研究进展

查先进① 刘莉②

[摘要] 本文以中国知网(CNKI)数字出版平台所收录的文献为数据源,采用文献计量方法,对 1987—2011 年 10 月我国有关竞争情报的 2683 篇论文进行统计,分别从文献外部特征(发表年代分布、期刊分布、核心著者及著者单位分布)、文献内容特征(关键词分布、研究热点)和文献所使用的研究方法等方面进行分析和探讨,旨在对近 25 年来我国竞争情报研究的发展状况进行概要性总结,并在此基础上对我国竞争情报研究未来发展趋势进行展望。

[关键词] 竞争情报 研究现状 研究趋势 文献计量分析

Progress in Competitive Intelligence Research in China over the Past 25 Years

[**Abstract**] We analyze 2683 research papers relating to competitive intelligence published in China from 1987 to October, 2011 based on CNKI, using bibliometric methods. We explore the external characteristic of literature such as the distribution of time, journals, core authors and their affiliation, as well as the content characteristic of literature such as the distribution of the keyword and hot topics. Meanwhile, we discuss the research method used in the literature. In this case, we frame the status quo of competitive intelligence research in China over the past 25 years and thus look into the research trend in the field of competitive intelligence.

[**Keywords**] Competitive Intelligence, Research Status Quo, Research Trend, Bibliometric Analysis

---

① 查先进,教授,博士生导师,武汉大学信息资源研究中心,xianjinzha@163.com
② 刘莉,硕士研究生,武汉大学信息管理学院,liu32330017@163.com

1 引 言

作为一种竞争理念,竞争情报兴起于 20 世纪 80 年代以后,起源于军事情报和政治情报领域,并率先和重点推广应用于企业界,形成企业竞争情报。在美国竞争情报专业人员协会(Society of Competitive Intelligence Professionals,简称 SCIP)官方网站上,对于"什么是竞争情报",其所做的最新解释是:"竞争情报是一个过程,它侧重于监控竞争环境、分析内部问题,以便支持企业的决策。竞争情报使得各类企业中的高层管理者能够制定从市场、研究与开发、投资策略到长期商业战略的更优决策。高效的竞争情报活动是一个连续的过程,包括合法的信息搜集、导致各种结论的信息分析、向决策者有效发布可实施的情报等。"[1]从实践上看,竞争情报研究很早就在我国出现,例如,早在科技情报系统建立之初,我国就已经在外国封锁的特定条件下独立自主地发展了一系列与现代竞争情报方法(如技术跟踪、反求工程、定标比超等)完全一致或十分相似的方法,其实质是科技领域的竞争情报研究,只是在当时没有运用"竞争情报"这个名称而已。[2]在竞争情报概念进入我国之后,为顺应改革开放需要,上海科学技术情报研究所率先从环境扫描与分析、高技术情报预警系统研究等角度对竞争情报功能进行了实证研究,此后又进行了"上海轿车工业竞争环境监视系统"的实践探索,从而拉开了我国竞争情报研究的序幕,基于企业性质的竞争情报研究活动开始此起彼伏。为了更好地引进竞争情报的理论和技能,1994 年 1 月中国科学技术情报学会在北京成立了情报研究暨竞争情报专业委员会,北京科学技术情报学会和中国兵工学会情报分会也相应建立了北京竞争情报研究会和兵工竞争情报研究会。1994 年 9 月,又由中国科学技术情报学会、北京科学技术情报学会、上海科学技术情报学会和中国兵工学会情报分会联合召开了"全国竞争情报与企业发展研讨会"。这表明我国竞争情报研究工作开始走上了有组织和相对正规化的道路。1995 年 4 月,经中国科协批准、民政部登记,中国科学技术情报学会情报研究暨竞争情报专业委员会改组为中国科学技术情报学会竞争情报分会(Society of Competitive Intelligence of China,简称 SCIC)。SCIC 的主要任务是竞争情报理论和实践的学术研究和交流活动、普及竞争情报知识、传播竞争情报技能、开展竞争情报咨询服务、帮助企业获得竞争优势、发展国际竞争情报的合作与交流、维护竞争情报从业者的合法权益、奖励优秀论文和优秀人才、编辑出版竞争情报学术书刊和科普读物,为提高我国企业竞争力,加速发展信息咨询业做出贡献。

值得注意的是,越来越多的研究者开始认为,竞争情报并不仅仅局限于企业,其他组织也可能会引入竞争情报思想,从而形成诸如"政府竞争情报"、"国家竞争情报"、"图书馆竞争情报"等竞争情报活动空间。近25年来,我国竞争情报研究工作发展迅速。本文拟对这一时期我国关于"竞争情报"的研究论文进行统计分析,以期从不同角度回答"我国竞争情报领域文献数量的增长趋势"、"该领域文献的期刊分布状况"、"该领域文献的发文机构分布状况"、"该领域的关键词分布"、"研究热点有哪些"、"该领域的研究方法有哪些"等问题。

2 数据搜集和研究方法

2.1 数据搜集

本文以中国知网(CNKI)为数据来源,以"竞争情报"为检索词、"题名"为检索项、"1987—2011年"为时间范围(检索截止时间为2011年10月),采用精确检索,对CNKI中的"中国期刊全文数据库"、"中国重要会议论文全文数据库"进行跨库检索,共检索出2960条记录,其中来自"中国期刊全文数据库"的有2903条记录,来自"中国重要会议论文全文数据库"的有57条记录。在文献阅读的基础上,剔除涉及秘密、文献损坏以及内容相关度不大的文章,最后选取2683篇相关文献作为统计分析的原始数据。

2.2 研究方法

本文的研究采用文献计量学方法。文献计量学方法是一种建立在文献基础上的基于数学和统计学的定量分析方法,其主要研究对象是文献的特征。本文针对所选取的"竞争情报"相关文献,重点从三个方面展开研究,即:基于文献外部特征(文献年代、来源期刊、论文作者等)的分析;基于文献内容特征的分析;基于文献研究方法的分析。

(1) 基于文献外部特征的分析

文献外部特征主要包括文献的篇名(题目)、作者、出版物、出版年代、作者单位以及某种特殊文献自身的特征标识,如标准文献的标准号等。本文通过对文献出版年代、来源期刊和论文作者三方面文献外部特征的量化分析来描述和揭示竞争情报领域的研究现状和变化规律。其中文献的年代分布情况可以从时间维度上系统地反映该学科领域产生、发展与成熟的过程,有助于了解、把握该领域研究的发展历程,揭示其发展趋势。[3] 而对发表竞争情报相关论文的期刊的载文量、载文比例以及期刊数量和发文篇数的对应关系予以统计分析,有助于确定研究竞争情报的核心期刊、所属学科以及学科融合状况。此外,从文献计量的角度,探讨论文作者的著述规律及其与相关文献之间的数量关系,包括统计作者的出现频次、发文所占比例、合著率、作者单位等,可以此来确定竞争情报研究领域的核心作者、核心研究机构,了解该学科研究的发展规模。

(2) 基于文献内容特征的分析

文献内容特征主要是指文献所论述的主题、观点、见解和结论,关键词是具有情报特性的词汇,常常能反映文献的主题。由于学术论文中的关键词不重复出现,因此一个关键词出现的频次等于附有该关键词的论文篇数,研究关键词的出现频次可以有效地判断该研究领域研究内容的集中与分散规律,此外关键词可以揭示研究成果的总体内容特征、研究内容之间的内在联系、学术研究的发展脉络与发展方向。[4] 本文在关键词频次统计分析的基础上,结合论文的内容以及该领域的相关著作,确定竞争情报领域的研究热点。

(3) 基于文献研究方法的分析

当代学科发展的一个重要特点是不同学科之间的联系越来越紧密,这个特点在研究方法上体现为应用一门或几门学科的研究方法去研究另一门学科的研究对象,这种研究方法的移植、渗透和融合,极大地推动了学科的发展与进步,推动了不同学科研究对象的有机结合。对一个学科的研究方法进行分析,可以了解一个学科的发展脉络与发展阶段,与其他学科的融合状况,以及其研究对象的特征与变化趋势。

3 基于文献外部特征的分析

3.1 论文发表年代分布

论文发表的年代数量分布可以系统地反应该学科在一定时间段内的发展历程和研究水平,揭示其发展趋势。图 1 显示了 1987—2011 年 10 月我国竞争情报领域论文发表文献数量年代分布及累计百分比年代分布。从图中我们可以看出,我国对竞争情报的研究起始于 20 世纪 80 年代,CNKI 收录的我国与竞争情报研究相关的论文基本成增长态势,从 1987 年的 1 篇增长到 2010 年的 331 篇,其中 1994 年竞争情报论文数量陡然增加,本文认为这主要是由于 1994 年 1 月我国成立了中国科学技术情报学会情报研究暨竞争情报专业委员会,促进了我国的竞争情报研究走向职业化、系统化。

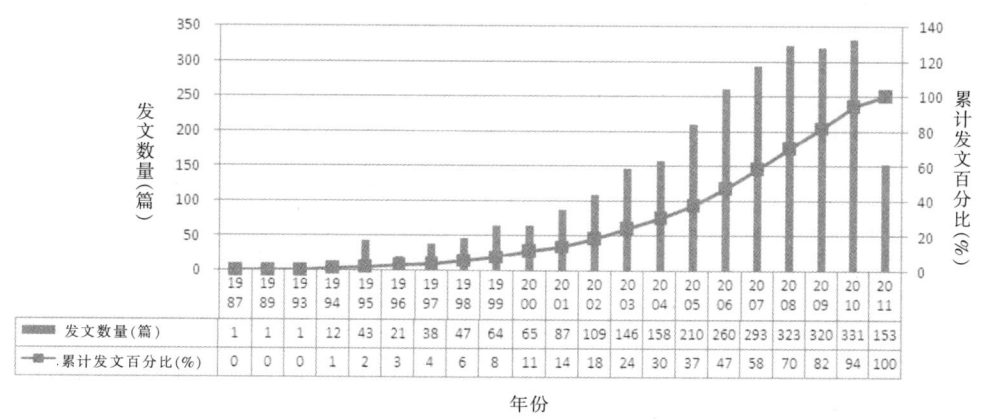

图 1 论文发表年代分布情况

根据图 1 的论文数量分布情况,我们可以将竞争情报的研究大致分为四个阶段:1987—2000 年为我国竞争情报研究的起步阶段,论文数量占全部论文的 11%,数量相对较少,学界对于竞争情报的关注度不高,对竞争情报的研究还处于散乱零星的状态;2001—2004 年为平稳发展期,论文量占全部论文的 19%,在这个阶段竞争情报的研究越来越受到业界关注,逐渐形成了竞争情报领域的专业研究队伍;2005—2008 年为我国竞争情报研究的快速发展阶段,该阶段的文献发表量明显大于前两个阶段,文献数量占论文总量的 40%;2009—2010 年为成熟稳定期,这个阶段的论文数量基本持平或略有下降,这是一个学科趋于成熟和稳定的标志。文献量的持平或者下降并不意味着一个学科的发展已然停滞,更可能是这个学科将进入新的发展阶段,此时虽然文献量未有增加,但会涌现出新的研究热点。

3.2 论文期刊分布

(1)研究领域分析

CNKI 将收录的论文分为基础科学、工程科技Ⅰ辑、工程科技Ⅱ辑、农业科学、医药卫生科学、哲学与人文科学、社会科学Ⅰ辑、社会科学Ⅱ辑、信息科学、经济与管理科学十个学科领域。对竞争情报相关论文的文献来源按学科领域进行统计分析(见表1),发现我国有关竞争情报的论文主要刊载在信息科学类(32.39%)、经济与管理科学类(58.20%)期刊上。此外,CNKI 所划分的十个学科领域内均有论述竞争情报的相关论文,说明竞争情报作为一门交叉学科,开始被更多的学科所接受,其研究呈现出多学科的态势,涉及各个学科的渗透与融合。

表1　　　　　　　　　学科领域论文分布情况

学科类别	载文量(篇)	载文比例(%)
基础科学	11	0.33
工程科技Ⅰ辑	132	4.01
工程科技Ⅱ辑	21	0.64
农业科学	2	0.06
医药卫生科学	16	0.49
哲学与人文科学	25	0.76
社会科学Ⅰ辑	25	0.76
社会科学Ⅱ辑	78	2.37
信息科学	1067	32.39
经济与管理科学	1917	58.20

(2)核心期刊分析

对论文的期刊来源进行统计发现,竞争情报相关的论文分布在554种不同的期刊上,这些期刊属于不同的学科,包括情报学、经济学、医学、信息技术等。表2列出了其中载文量在15篇及15篇以上的期刊。其中,《情报杂志》、《现代情报》、《情报理论与实践》、《图书情报工作》、《情报科学》5种期刊包含了全部论文的34.40%,载文量均在150篇以上。同时,全部论文的57.81%仅分布在19种期刊上,有367种期刊发文量仅为1篇,这符合文献的布拉德福定律,即相关论文高度集中于核心区的少数几种期刊,其余数量的论文高度分散于其他各区。此外,表2所列举的前10种期刊均为情报学的专业期刊,可见对竞争情报的研究仍主要集中于情报学领域,其他学科领域对其略有关注,但关注度不够高。然而,竞争情报的实践应用主要是在企业,应该注重推动竞争情报与企业实际经营工作的结合。

表2　　　　　　　　　　期刊论文分布情况

期刊名称	载文量(篇)	载文比例(%)
情报杂志	213	7.94
现代情报	206	7.68
情报理论与实践	173	6.45
图书情报工作	173	6.45
情报科学	158	5.89
科技情报开发与经济	129	4.81
情报探索	120	4.47
情报学报	93	3.47
情报资料工作	42	1.57
农业图书情报学刊	41	1.53
中国信息导报	33	1.23
商场现代化	31	1.16
图书馆学研究	31	1.16
内蒙古科技与经济	20	0.75
图书与情报	20	0.75
科技信息	19	0.71
图书馆理论与实践	17	0.63
图书情报知识	17	0.63
图书馆学刊	15	0.56
累计	1511	57.81

3.3 论文作者分布

(1) 核心作者分析

在此次统计过程中,参与发表论文的作者共有 2646 个(不计重复出现,包括第二作者、第三作者等)。对这 2683 篇论文的 2646 个作者进行统计分析,发现发文最多的是彭靖里(64 篇)、王知津(42 篇)、陈峰(39 篇)、吴晓伟(37 篇)。此外,发表文献数量在 10 篇以上的作者共有 30 人,他们可以被看做是竞争情报领域的核心作者。仅发表过一篇文章的共有 2029 人,占总作者人数的 76.7%。

若只统计第一作者,共有 1769 个作者,将其依据论文发表数量的多少按递减规律排序,统计其发表文献的数量占全部文献数量的百分比及累计百分比,绘制成图 2。从图 2 中可以看出,我国竞争情报研究领域已经形成了相应的核心作者群,他们的研究促进了我国竞争情报的发展。

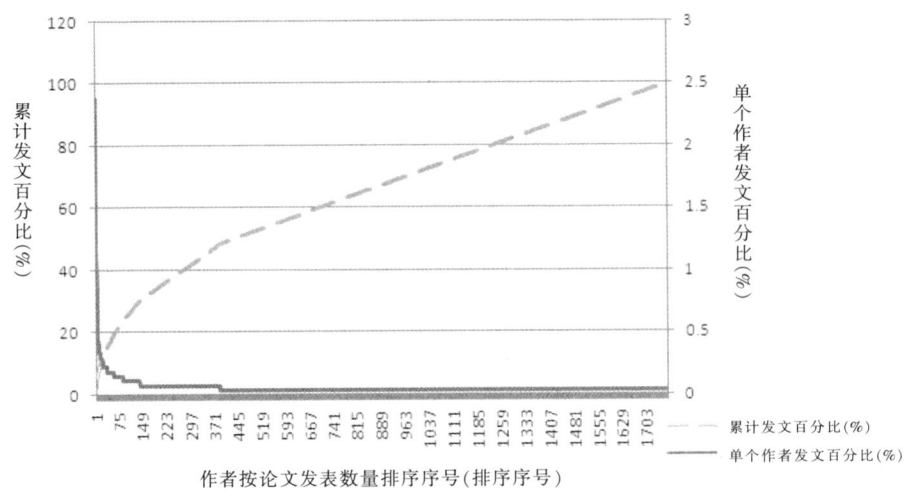

图 2 作者排序与文献百分比对应关系

(2) 著者合作度分析

统计论文的合著情况可以分析出竞争情报研究中的合作状况,在测量竞争情报研究中的合著状况时本文以论文作者人数为测量标准,将论文作者分为 1 人、2 人、3 人及以上三种情况。经过统计,竞争情报研究领域论文合著情况如表 3 所示。从表 3 中可以看出,竞争情报领域论文合著比例基本呈逐年上升趋势,其中 2011 年(截至 10 月份)论文著者合作度高达 56.2%,3 人及以上合著论文有35篇,2人合作论文数有51篇。这说明随着信息技术的革新,企业经营管理的复杂化,学科之间的交叉融合,竞争情报研究的难度日益加大,单一的学科知识已经无法应对复杂的竞争情报研究问题,必须寻求合作研究。这种跨学科背景、跨机构甚至跨国籍的学术交流与合作有助于形成各种研究社群,解决各种理论和实践上的问题,推动竞争情报研究在纵向上和横向上得到更深更广的发展。

表3 著者合著度分析

年份(年)	1987–1994	1995–1996	1997–1998	1999–2000	2001–2002	2003–2004	2005–2006	2007–2008	2009–2010	2011
1人(篇)	12	50	66	97	124	189	284	373	357	67
2人(篇)	1	11	13	26	47	75	116	163	162	51
3人及以上(篇)	1	3	6	6	25	40	70	80	142	35
总计(篇)	14	64	85	129	196	304	470	616	651	153
合著比例(%)	14.3	21.9	22.4	24.8	36.7	37.8	39.6	39.4	46.7	56.2

(3)作者单位分析

若只考虑第一作者的来源单位,不排除重复出现的情况(如武汉大学信息管理学院、武汉大学信息资源研究中心、武汉大学图书情报学院),共有1233个来源单位,其主要为大学或者学院,其余的为各类研究机构、企业、公共图书馆、政府机构,可见在竞争情报研究领域,依然是以"学院派"为主,但另一方面竞争情报的研究已经受到社会各界的关注与重视。在全部发文机构中,发文量为1篇的有871个单位,占总发文单位的70.6%,发文量少于或等于3篇的有1117个单位,其发文量占总发文量的90.2%。可见,竞争情报领域的研究机构范围广泛,相对分散。

对发文数量排名靠前的机构进行统计(见表4),可以发现,在竞争情报领域已经出现了一批核心研究机构。其中,南京大学信息管理系发文90篇,占总数的3.35%;武汉大学信息管理学院发文78篇,占总数的2.91%;中国科学技术信息研究所发文47篇,占总数的1.75%;北京大学信息管理系、南开大学商学院信息资源管理系各发文41篇,共占总数的3.06%;云南省科学技术情报研究所发文32篇,占总数的1.19%。这些单位地域分布广泛,其中湖北、北京等地发文量遥遥领先,可见我国竞争情报研究呈现出地区发展不均衡的态势。

表4　　　　　　　　　　　核心发文机构分布

发文数量排名	机构名称	发文数量(篇)
1	南京大学信息管理系	90
2	武汉大学信息管理学院(含武汉大学信息资源中心,武汉大学图书情报学院)	78
3	中国科学技术信息研究所	47
4	北京大学信息管理系	41
5	南开大学商学院信息资源管理系	41
6	云南省科学技术情报研究所	32
7	云南省科技情报研究所	25
8	中山大学资讯管理系	24
9	南开大学商学院	23
10	华中师范大学信息管理系	20
11	西南大学计算机与信息科学学院	18
12	吉林大学管理学院	17
13	福州大学图书馆	17

4　基于文献内容特征的分析

4.1　关键词频度分析

统计1987—2011年竞争情报领域2683篇文献的关键词出现频次,基于本文是以"竞争情报"为检索词,"题名"为检索项进行的数据收集,故去除"竞争情报"、"竞争情报研究"等关键词,将关键词按其出现频次降序排列,得到表5统计结果。从表5中可以看出,"企业"(239次)、"竞争情报系统"(209次)、"知识管理"(97次)、"企业竞争情报"(96次)、"反竞争情报"(63次)排名前五位,是竞争情报领域研究的热点。其中,"企业"、"企业竞争情报"体现了竞争情报活动与企业的经营活动密切相关,企业既是竞争情报活动的主要行为主体,又是竞争情报的主要应用者,所以竞争情报研究更多地与企业密切相关。此外,知识管理和竞争情报系统推动了竞争情报工作的开展,反竞争情报与竞争情报则是"一枚硬币的两面"。"高校图书馆"(59次)排名第六,"图书馆"(40次)排名第九则从一个侧面说明了对竞争情报的研究依然是以高校为中心,研究人员也主要集中于图书情报学领域,且随着图书馆经营环境的变化,竞争情报也被引入到图书馆的经营管理中。而"专利分析"、"统计分析"、"案例"等词则表明在竞争情报研究中,实证研究开始受到研究者的关注。

表5　　　　　　　　　　　　关键词频次分布

中文关键词	频次(次)	中文关键词	频次(次)	中文关键词	频次(次)
企业	239	竞争对手	23	情报搜集	15
竞争情报系统	209	信息	23	信息系统	15
知识管理	97	商业秘密	22	产业竞争情报	15
企业竞争情报	96	发展	22	中国	15
反竞争情报	63	高校	22	服务	14
高校图书馆	59	企业发展	21	竞争环境	14
企业竞争情报系统	45	竞争情报工作	21	网络环境	14
数据挖掘	41	现状	20	网络组织	13
图书馆	40	市场竞争	20	专利	13
信息服务	36	核心竞争力	20	国家竞争情报	13
技术竞争情报	35	企业竞争力	20	竞争策略	13
中小企业	35	作用	19	人才培养	13
战略管理	32	竞争战略	18	专利分析	13
情报研究	32	网络	18	情报分析	13
企业竞争	32	应用	18	信息源	13
竞争情报服务	30	对策	18	统计分析	13
情报	29	电子商务	18	情报收集	13
情报服务	29	构建	18	教育	13
企业管理	28	知识经济	17	情报工作	13
人际网络	28	技术创新	17	信息管理	13
竞争	27	情报学	17	案例	13
竞争情报教育	27	企业信息	17	方法	12
竞争优势	23	比较研究	16	运行机制	12

从时间这个轴线来分析(见图3),我们可以发现有些关键词突显,并在短

时间内出现频次急剧增长,快速成为竞争情报研究的热点,如"高校"、"产业竞争情报"。同时,一些关键词出现频次急剧增长后又明显下降,逐渐成为往年研究的热点,比如"技术竞争情报"、"人际网络"等,这类关键词可以审视其获得的成果,从中总结其研究方法与思路,为相似问题的研究提供参考。还有类关键词(如企业),它们一直呈现着波动增长的态势,这些关键词可以继续挖掘其内在价值,创造新的研究点。

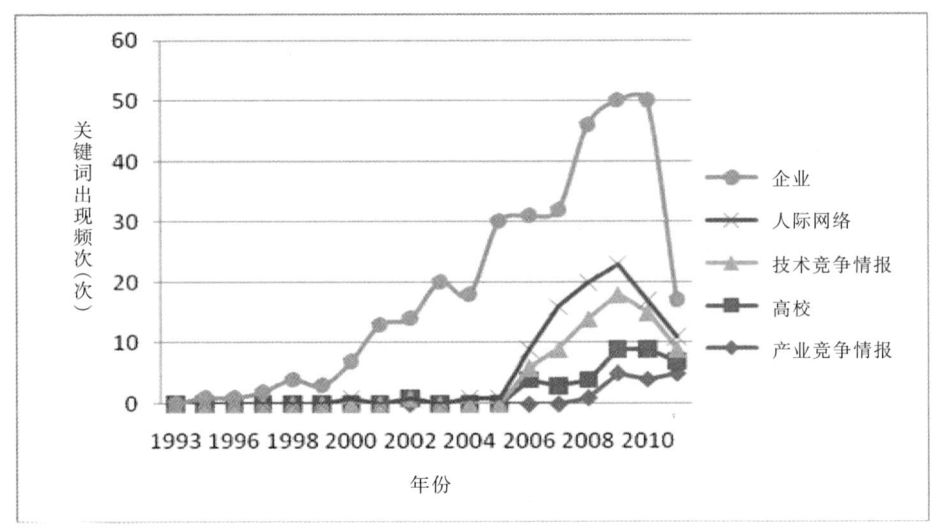

图3 关键词变化趋势

4.2 研究热点分析

根据中国科学技术情报学会竞争情报分会策划的《竞争情报丛书》,在分析中,本文将竞争情报论文所论述的问题分为:竞争情报理论研究、竞争情报系统、商业企业竞争情报、商业秘密、竞争情报服务、竞争情报教育与人才、行业竞争情报、竞争情报技术等问题。[5]统计相关关键词出现频次,结合论文的内容以及该领域的相关著作,本文综合归纳出我国竞争情报研究的热点问题主要集中在以下几个方面:

(1)商业企业竞争情报

在此次统计分析中,"企业"、"企业竞争情报"、"中小企业"、"企业竞争"、"企业管理"、"企业发展"、"市场竞争"、"核心竞争力"、"企业竞争力"等关键词出现频次均大于18次,总共出现556次。可见,在市场竞争日益加剧的今天,竞争情报如何为企业战略决策提供服务,如何为企业获得持续竞争优势,如何应用于企业危机管理,是企业竞争情报工作者和企业高层管理者关注的焦点。

在危机管理方面(关键词"危机管理"出现7次,"危机预警"出现9次),国内最早由任皓和邓三鸿发表了"竞争情报与企业风险管理"一文,阐述了竞争情报在企业风险管理中的重要作用。[6]张左之则在2003年11月中国竞争情报第九届年会上提出竞争情报应从危机管理走向危机预警。[7]随后的研究就主要集中在危机预警的探讨上,如彭靖里等重点研究了竞争情报危机预警体系的功能结构设计、工作目标和建设步骤等问题,并进行了案例分析[8];史尚元、糜凯探讨了竞争情报与危机预警的契合之处,从竞争情报在企业危机预警中的作用、企业危机预警中竞争情报战略价值、企业危机预警中竞争情报工作原则和企业危机预警中竞争情报工作应关注的问题四个方面对竞争情报在企业危机预警中的应用进行了分析。[9]

企业多样化战略(关键词"战略管理"出现32次,"发展战略"出现10次)有两种基本方式,即内部发展和外部扩张,主要通过企业战略联盟与企业并购完成。战略联盟背景下竞争情报工作具有重大的意义[10]:如可以帮助企业进行基于战略联盟获取互补性资源和能力的前期分析[11];帮助企业应对激烈的市场竞争[12];帮助企业发展规模经济[13];规避竞争中的风险[14]等。在企业并购方面,SCIP主席Paul Dishmanren认为企业并购就是一项竞争情报活动[15];李国秋则指出企业并购战略制定的核心问题之一是目标行业及目标企业的选择,而竞争情报对于正确选择目标行业和目标企业具有极其重要的保障作用。[16]基于此,他提出了一个基于竞争情报的并购目标选择和评估模型,并运用实证数据验证了并购案例失败的原因。[17]

此外,还有学者对竞争情报在企业市场营销活动、产品创新、技术改造等多个方面的应用进行了探讨。如刘冰认为市场营销活动中的竞争情报工作重点是企业营销战略,应从竞争对手监测与环境情报搜集两方面着手[18];彭靖里等从研究产品创新及类型与技术竞争情报的关系入手,运用历史追溯描述性案例分析方法对云南锡业集团公司在无铅焊料新产品研发决策中的技术竞争情报应用案例进行了实证分析。[19]

(2)竞争情报系统

我国对竞争情报系统的研究起步较晚,但经过几年的迅猛发展,它已迅速成为竞争情报研究的重要内容之一。在此次统计分析中,"竞争情报系统"、"企业竞争情报系统"、"构建"等关键词均为高频词汇,同时还存在着许多诸如"智能采集"、"文本挖掘"、"系统设计"、"云计算"等具有一定出现次数且与竞争情报系统密切相关的关键词。通过对以竞争情报系统为主旨的论文进行分析,发现对竞争情报系统的研究主要集中在竞争情报系统的构建模式、相关理论在竞争情报系统中的应用及竞争情报系统的评价三个方面。

在竞争情报系统的构建模式上,我国学者主要对基于某项信息技术平台的竞争情报系统架构展开研究,如刘玉照等以 C/S 与 B/S 的集成模式作为技术平台,按照信息系统的设计思想与生命周期,从系统分析、系统设计等方面,对企业竞争情报系统的构建进行了初步的探讨[20];朱永武在数据挖掘的概念和数据挖掘的一般过程的基础上提出了一个基于数据挖掘的企业竞争情报系统模型,并介绍了相应的构建过程[21];李钧民通过分析内容管理系统的结构功能,结合竞争情报系统的业务流程,依据内容管理技术构建竞争情报系统模型,实现竞争情报系统中内容与形式的分离。[22]

相关理论在竞争情报系统中的应用方面,杨勇通过研究知识管理与竞争情报两者的关系,发现知识管理作为新时代条件下一种先进的企业管理思想,在企业构建竞争情报系统的过程中有着重要的启发作用,并对于切实提高企业竞争力具有非常重要的意义。[23]

对竞争情报系统的评价也是国内学者的研究重点,目前的研究内容主要集中在评价指标体系的确定上。例如,李纪等认为可以从组织结构资本、人力资本、技术资本、竞争情报产品服务和竞争情报被关注程度五个方面考核企业竞争情报系统的绩效[24];邱均平等则提出了包括系统质量、系统技术水平、系统运行质量、系统成本、用户需求、系统效益、对企业文化的影响、知识管理能力、外界环境管理水平九个方面的企业竞争情报系统效益评价指标体系。[25]

(3)竞争情报服务

竞争情报服务是上个世纪末兴起的一项新型的企业咨询服务(同时也面向政府机构、社会公益机构),其一经出现就快速地在发达国家传开。在本次统计分析中,"信息服务"、"竞争情报服务"、"情报服务"等关键词频繁出现,可见,我国竞争情报服务研究发展迅速。本文通过对题目中含有"竞争情报服务"的论文进行分析,发现我国对于竞争情报服务的研究主要集中在图书馆竞争情报服务上,且主要论述图书馆与企业竞争情报的关系,图书馆开展竞争情报活动的方法与途径,图书馆开展竞争情报服务的优势与不足等基本问题。

在图书馆与企业竞争情报的关系上,我国学者基本上持一致的观点:图书馆和企业可以优势互补,共同创造经济效益。如范艳芬讨论了社会主义市场经济体制中图书馆的竞争性和图书馆在市场竞争中开展竞争情报服务的优势及策略,提出开展竞争情报咨询服务是图书馆增强竞争能力的有效途径[26];周秀卿认为图书馆信息咨询人员在为企业提供竞争情报的同时,一方面可以拓展图书馆的服务领域,另一方面,在把竞争情报产品有偿提供给企业的同时,自己也得到了丰厚的经济回报。[27]

在图书馆开展竞争情报活动的方法与途径方面,魏丽敏认为主要有七种途径:做高校决策层竞争情报参谋;做高校生源、毕业生就业竞争的宣传窗口;做高校教学科研人员参与竞争的情报顾问;做高校科研成果商业转化的桥梁;做企业的竞争情报知识技能和相关法律法规的培训站;高校图书馆应建立完善的竞争情报系统;为企业竞争情报系统的建立提供支持。[28]此外,许真玉等也给出了相关建议:主动走向市场,为企业服务;定题情报服务;开发深层次情报资源;网上情报服务方式等。[29]

此外,很多学者探讨了图书馆开展竞争情报服务的优势与不足,例如,范艳芬认为图书馆开展竞争情报工作具有信息资源优势、技术优势、人才优势、信息用户优势[30];贺志刚等则认为图书馆开展竞争情报工作存在着对竞争情报认识不足、信息咨询人员的信息综合和分析能力较低、信息咨询人员缺乏沟通能力、缺乏协调管理、信息资源建设偏重科学研究等问题。[31]

自包昌火(1998)将竞争情报的研究内容归纳为竞争环境、竞争对手、竞争策略三大方面[32]以来,我国大多数学者将竞争情报概括为是关于竞争对手、竞争环境和竞争战略的研究。基于此,本文从这三方面考察近25年来我国竞争情报研究热点,根据样本的关键词内容含义将关键词进行统计整理,其中"竞争战略"相关关键词出现56次,"竞争环境"相关关键词出现49次,"竞争对手"相关关键词出现38次。

(1)竞争战略研究热点

在对竞争战略的研究过程中,我国学者往往将其与具体的行业、具体的企业相结合。如刘文云等在对我国C2C电子商务网站各个内外部影响因素进行

SWOT定性分析的基础上,运用层次分析方法分析影响我国C2C网站发展的关键性因素,然后构建SWOT四边形进行战略分析,最终提出提高C2C网站竞争力的发展策略和建议[33];傅家荣认为虚拟教育正是在信息通讯技术运用于教育领域的背景下,教育机构为适应日益激烈的全球化竞争而产生的竞争战略。[34]

(2) 竞争环境研究热点

随着Internet的快速发展,网络逐渐改变了我们的生活方式以及交流方式,基于"网络环境"(关键词出现14次)、"动态环境"(关键词出现6次)的竞争环境研究逐渐成为我国学者研究的热点。如路永和等介绍了网络信息环境下我国购物网站的发展现状,从宏观的角度对网络环境下购物网站的竞争环境、竞争对手进行讨论,并提出相应的竞争策略[35];张收棉等则探索了在竞争态势复杂多变、信息价值加速提升、反应速度面临挑战的动态竞争环境下的企业竞争情报问题解决方案。[36]

(3) 竞争对手研究热点

在有关竞争对手的研究中,我国学者主要对各种理论方法在竞争对手识别以及分析中的运用进行研究。如我国某机构曾应用专利分析法研究了世界各国微波炉的专利申请情况,发现世界各国微波炉的专利技术主要集中在日本,其中松下、东芝、日立、夏普和三洋的实力较为雄厚,是最为强劲的竞争对手[37];查先进等研究了竞争对手实力分析和评估、竞争对手动向预测的方法[38];彭靖里等则应用模糊数学中的Blin方法原理,提出了一种企业竞争对手的模糊判别模型,将竞争情报分析中多因素且不同权重的对手判别问题简化为单指标的比较问题,并给出了实际应用的案例。[39]此外,还有学者对财务报表分析[40]、Porter模型[41]、价值链分析[42]、社会网络分析[43]等方法在竞争对手识别与分析中的应用进行了研究。

5 基于文献研究方法的分析

在进行竞争情报领域研究方法的分析时,本文依据席西民等在《我国管理科学发展纲要研究报告》中的归纳,将研究方法分为规范研究和实证研究两大类。[44](1)规范研究:以方法导向为特征,从假设出发,以现有的理论为基础,遵循严密的逻辑推理体系,目的是为了得出新的知识。(2)实证研究:是指通过归纳的思维方式,以观察事实和归纳逻辑为基础,透过对现象的描述和解释概括出理论命题,最后再通过实际案例进行验证。实证研究以问题导向为特征,包括案例分析、实验、实地考察等。

对竞争情报领域论文中所使用的研究方法进行统计分析后的结果见表6。由表6可以看出,在竞争情报研究领域,规范研究仍然占据着主要阵地,所占比例高达82.7%。但从总的趋势来看,实证研究的比例在逐年升高,越来越受到人们的关注。

表6 论文研究方法使用分布

年份(年)	实证研究		规范研究		总计(篇)
	论文数(篇)	构成比(%)	论文数(篇)	构成比(%)	
1987	0	0	1	100	1
1989	0	0	1	100	1
1993	0	0	1	100	1
1994	0	0	12	100	12
1995	3	6.98	40	93.02	43
1996	1	4.76	20	95.24	21
1997	1	2.63	37	97.37	38
1998	2	4.26	45	95.74	47
1999	4	6.45	58	93.55	62
2000	6	9.23	59	90.77	65
2001	10	11.49	77	88.51	87
2002	14	12.84	95	87.16	109
2003	19	13.01	127	86.99	146
2004	21	13.38	136	86.62	157
2005	30	14.29	180	85.71	210
2006	40	15.38	220	84.62	260
2007	46	15.86	244	84.14	290
2008	63	19.50	260	80.50	323
2009	68	21.66	246	78.34	314
2010	85	25.68	246	74.32	331
2011	49	32.03	104	67.97	153
总计	462	17.30	2209	82.70	2671

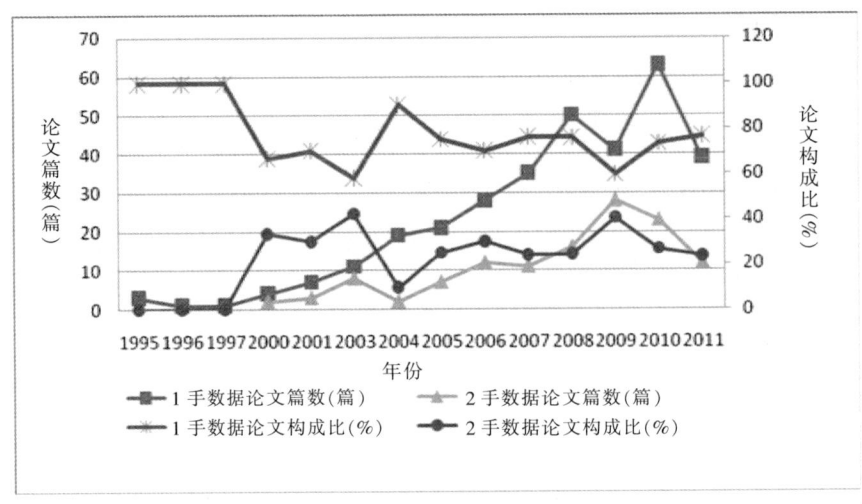

图 4 实证研究构成分析

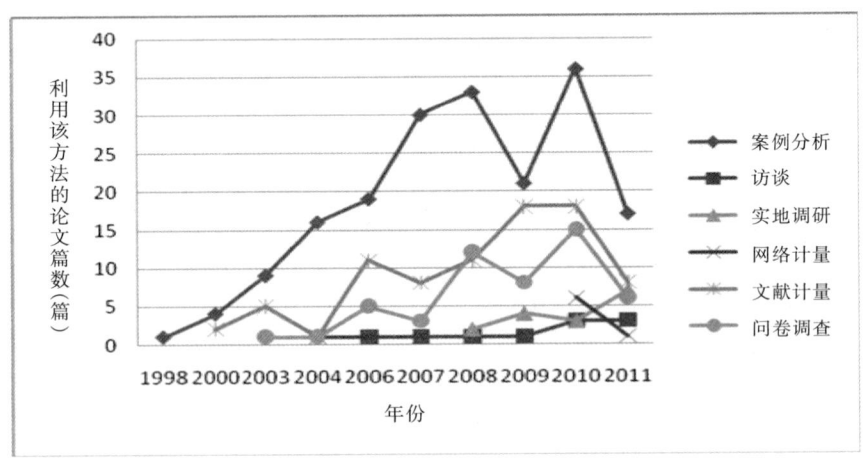

图 5 实证研究方法分布

对实证研究进一步探索,将其分为基于一手数据的实证研究(包括案例分析、问卷调查、实地考察、访谈等)和基于二手数据的实证研究(主要为文献计量与网络计量),统计结果见图4和图5。从图4中我们可以看出,竞争情报领域的实证研究主要是基于一手数据的实证研究,然而自1998年文献计量的研究方法引入竞争情报领域以来,这种基于二手数据的实证研究方法也得到了稳定的发展。从图5中可以看出,在各种方法的使用中,案例分析在实证研究中所占的比例最大(53.6%),成为主流的研究方法,这主要归因于竞争情报与企业密切相关,竞争情报的研究人员有一部分来自于企业,对具体企业实际经营活动的分析是竞争情报研究的一个重要组成部分。同时,文献计量的研究方法也占据了很大的比例(22.58%),这从另一个侧面说明了竞争情报的研究人员很多来自于情报学领域。此外,实地调研最近几年也逐渐运用到竞争情报领域,并越来越受到重视,体现出我国对于竞争情报的研究越来越注重于实际。多种研究方法的并用既体现了竞争情报研究方法的灵活性、多样性,又反映了其研究对象的复杂性和研究难度的增大,仅靠一种研究方法无法解决问题,必须融合多种研究方法。

6 我国竞争情报研究发展趋势

在对 CNKI 中题目中出现"竞争情报"的论文进行统计分析、科学总结的基础上,结合近年来竞争情报领域发展的总体形势和基本情况,我们可以对我国竞争情报研究发展趋势做一些总体上的判断和展望。

(1)竞争情报研究环境的变迁

第一,我国竞争情报研究越来越具有自主性。从竞争情报领域论文发表数量来看,这两年已趋于稳定;从作者分布、期刊分布及发文机构分布来看,竞争情报领域已经形成了其核心作者群、核心期刊群及核心研究机构。可见,竞争情报作为一个较为年轻的研究领域,从诞生之日起就不断地从别的学科汲取养分,经过数十年的发展,逐渐成为独立的具有自主性的研究领域。

第二,我国竞争情报研究呈现出以情报学为主,多学科融合的趋势。纵观国内的竞争情报研究,从相关论文的核心研究机构分布、核心期刊分布、核心作者分布不难看出图书情报学依旧是其主要的学科背景。但另一方面,其在研究领域、研究机构、研究人员上的多元化分布则体现了其与其他学科融合的趋势。

第三,合作研究呈现出增多趋势。竞争情报领域的分散研究、个体研究正在向合作研究和团队研究方向转变。在 CNKI 的 2683 篇论文中,平均著者合作度为 40%,并且在 2000 年以后呈现出加速增长的趋势,其中,2011 年(截至 10 月份)合著比例高达 56.2%。可见,合作研究不仅成为了竞争情报研究领域的普遍现象,也是一种重要的发展趋势。

(2)竞争情报研究内容的变化

第一,我国竞争情报研究将会越来越关注于企业经营现实。竞争情报最早产生于企业中,企业是竞争情报活动的行为主体也是竞争情报的利用者,在市场竞争环境下如何提高企业竞争力,形成企业竞争优势,促进企业发展将持续成为竞争情报研究的一个热点主题,并将越来越受到研究人员的重视。

第二,竞争情报的研究将更加注重实际应用。从研究方法上来看,案例分析、实地调研、访谈等占据了一个很大的比例,这说明竞争情报这一领域的研究,已不仅局限于规范研究,而是更多地注重于应用实践。从关键词来看,关键词"信息服务"出现36次,"竞争情报服务"出现30次,甚至关键词中直接出现"作用"(19次)、"应用"(18次)、"对策"(18次)等词,可见,越来越多的竞争情报研究人员关注于竞争情报的实际应用。

第三,竞争情报的思想将应用于更多的组织。越来越多的研究者开始认为,竞争情报并不应该仅仅局限于企业,其他组织诸如图书馆、政府机构、高校等也需要引入竞争情报思想,从而形成许多诸如"政府竞争情报"(关键词出现6次)、"国家竞争情报"(关键词出现13次)、"图书馆竞争情报"(关键词"高校图书馆"出现59次,"图书馆"出现40次)等竞争情报研究领域。

(3)竞争情报研究方法的变革

第一,我国竞争情报研究方法日益多元化。从总体趋势来看,规范研究仍将是研究的主体,但网络计量、文献计量、案例分析、问卷调查等研究方法越来越受到研究人员的重视;此外,社会网络分析、专家评价法、德尔菲法、层次分析法、模糊综合评价法、灰色综合评价法、数据包络分析法等方法也逐渐运用于竞争情报领域。可见,竞争情报领域正不断从经济学、管理学、社会学、情报学等学科领域吸收研究方法,以解决日益复杂的研究问题。

第二,我国竞争情报研究将越来越重视一手数据的采集与运用。竞争情报的研究需要与整个竞争环境、竞争对手、竞争战略保持一致、积极互动、有机协调,需要同变化了的现实紧密联系在一起,这种研究对象的依赖性、研究环境的动态性要求竞争情报的研究不能脱离现实,不能脱离具体的研究对象,而一手数据是最具有现实敏感性的,基于一手数据的研究将成为竞争情报研究的一个重要趋势。

致 谢

特别感谢饶怡情、娄海凤、郭玥、周芬、李改霞等人在数据搜集过程中给予的支持和帮助。

参考文献

[1] 美国竞争情报从业者协会.竞争情报的定义[EB/OL].http://www.scip.org/content.cfm?itemnumber=2214&navItemNumber=492.[2008-07-03].

[2] 查先进.竞争情报与企业危机管理[M].武汉:武汉大学出版社,2010:15.

[3] 查先进,曹晨.近20年我国信息资源配置研究文献计量分析[J].图书情报工作,2010,54(20):6-10.

[4] 李文兰,杨祖国.中国情报学期刊论文关键词词频分析[J].情报科学,2005,23(1):68-70.

[5] 蒋一平,邵利勤,杨惠明,万跃华.我国竞争情报研究的文献计量学分析[J].新世纪图书馆,2011(6):12-16.

[6] 任皓,邓三鸿.竞争情报与企业风险管理[J].图书情报工作,2001(11):16-18.

[7] 张左之.竞争情报:从危机管理到危机预警[C].中国竞争情报第9届年会论文集,2003:63-68.

[8] 彭靖里,周勇胜,邓艺.基于竞争情报的危机预警体系构建及其应用研究[J].情报理论与实践,2009(6):46-50.

[9] 史尚元,糜凯.竞争情报在企业危机预警中的应用[J].情报科学,2008(2):192-196.

[10] 李家清.合作竞争时代的竞争情报战略[J].情报科学,2008(2):183-187.

[11] 王玉.企业战略联盟的竞争情报研究[J].情报理论与实践,2005(3):300-302.

[12] 孔德超.企业战略联盟的情报活动运行探析[J].现代情报,2008(12):170-172.

[13] 胡琳.企业战略联盟的竞争情报支持研究[J].科技情报开发与经济,2009(7):75-76.

[14] 夏咏梅.试用博弈论分析竞争情报与企业合作[J].科技情报开发与经济,2007(17):86-88.

[15] 陈峰,梁战平.竞争情报与战略管理[M].北京:科学技术文献出版社,2004:152.

[16] 李国秋.企业并购战略制定的竞争情报保障研究[J].图书情报知识,2004(5):73-75.

[17] 李国秋.企业并购目标选择的竞争情报评估模型—兼论中信证券并购广发证券失败的竞争情报缺失[J].情报理论与实践,2008(1):55-59.

[18] 刘冰.企业竞争情报基础[M].北京:首都经济贸易大学出版社,2010:354.

[19] 彭靖里,张勇,可星.论技术竞争情报在新产品开发中应用的实证研究[J].现代情

报,2010(6):16-19.

[20] 刘玉照,刘建准,范志雯. 基于 C/S 与 B/S 集成模式的企业竞争情报系统构建研究[J]. 情报科学,2005(3):411-412.

[21] 朱永武. 基于数据挖掘的企业竞争情报系统[J]. 现代情报,2005(6):168-172.

[22] 李钧民. 基于内容管理技术的竞争情报系统构建[J]. 情报资料工作,2010(4):41-43.

[23] 杨勇. 试论知识管理思想在企业竞争情报系统中的应用[J]. 现代情报,2006(1):188-189.

[24] 李纪,孙颖. 企业竞争情报系统绩效评价指标体系研究[J]. 商业研究,2006(16):68-71.

[25] 邱均平,张蕊. 企业竞争情报系统效益评价分析[J]. 情报科学,2005,22(6):649-652.

[26] 范艳芬. 论图书馆的竞争性与竞争情报服务[J]. 现代情报,2004(11):2-3.

[27] 周秀卿. 图书馆为经济建设服务的新领域—竞争情报服务[J]. 图书馆工作与研究,2004(1):56-57.

[28] 魏丽敏. 竞争情报崛起对高校图书馆服务的影响[J]. 情报杂志,2005(6):131-133.

[29] 许真玉,王文佳,杨晓玉. 企业竞争情报研究与图书馆情报服务[J]. 现代情报,2006(11):185-190.

[30] 范艳芬. 论图书馆的竞争性与竞争情报服务[J]. 现代情报,2004(11):2-3.

[31] 贺志刚,隋银昌. 竞争情报服务—高校图书馆信息咨询服务的新课题[J]. 图书馆论坛,2002(6):66-68.

[32] 包昌火. 加强竞争情报工作,提高我国企业竞争能力[J]. 中国信息导报,1998(11):33-36.

[33] 刘文云,韩晓红. 我国C2C电子商务网站竞争战略研究[J]. 图书情报工作,2010,54(22):126-130.

[34] 傅家荣. 虚拟教育—高等教育面向全球化的竞争战略[J]. 湖北社会科学,2004(10):145-147.

[35] 路永和,张晓琴. 网络信息环境下我国购物网站的竞争情报分析[J]. 现代情报,2007(11):2-5.

[36] 张收棉,刘建准. 基于动态竞争环境的企业竞争情报问题诊断与分析[J]. 情报资料工作,2009(1):106-108.

[37] 陆海红. 基于专利文献信息中竞争情报价值的分析[J]. 江苏科技信息,2010(1):27-28.

[38] 查先进,严亚兰. 论企业竞争对手[J]. 情报科学,2000,18(2):123-125.

[39] 彭靖里,赵光洲,宋林清,马敏象.论企业竞争对手的模糊判别模型及其应用[J].情报理论与实践,2004(2):160-161.

[40] 殷春连,曹霜.论财务报表中的企业竞争情报[J].情报探索,2007(4):79-81.

[41] 包昌火,谢新洲.竞争对手跟踪分析[J].情报学报,2003(2):194-205.

[42] 包昌火,谢新洲.竞争对手跟踪分析[J].情报学报,2003(2):194-205.

[43] 吴晓伟,徐福缘,宋文官.社会关系态势图在竞争对手分析中的应用[J].情报学报,2007(1):100-105.

[44] 席酉民,梁磊,郭菊娥.我国管理科学发展纲要研究报告[R].西安:西安交通大学,2001(1).

Waste Management Data Collection during Disaster Recovery

– A Case Study of the Great East Japan Earthquake –

Yoshinari Noboru[1]　Ohuchi Azuma[2]　Sugasawa Yoshio[3]

Abstract

In the event of great disasters such as earthquakes, tsunami and floods, disaster waste, including trash and debris are generated in enormous quantities. Disaster waste is normally disposed of by municipalities (by departments in special instances) as general waste. However, when its quantity becomes excessive it cannot be dealt by municipalities alone, and the association with private disposal services such as local industrial waste disposers becomes a requirement. After the Great East Japan Earthquake, one of the local corporations of the affected area, Sendai Kankyo Kaihatsu Co., Ltd., took various measures as part of its corporate defenses. In this paper, we shall analyze and put in order our company's activities during the three months from the Great Earthquake, following the disaster from the initial measures of disaster waste treatment and emergency recovery, to the recovery phase. We shall then discuss the correct uses and applicability of intelligence necessary for industrial waste disposal contractors located in devastated areas, and efficient techniques, as well as the characteristics of the intelligence cycle during the recovery phase.

Competitive Intelligence (CI) is believed to create excellent information in order to make decisions for performing specific measures to counter the strategies of rivals and

---

[1] Sendai Waste Management Ltd., Sendai, Japan
[2] Gracudate School of Hokkai School of Commerce, Sapporo, Japan, ohuchi@hokkai.ac.jp
[3] College of Economics, Japan University of Economics, Tokyo, Japan, sugasawa@tk.jue.ac.jp

competitors, by gathering, analyzing, and evaluating information. Since competitors still exist, even during disasters corporations need to enact both defensive and aggressive intelligence activities as part of their risk management.

Keywords

The Great East Japan Earthquake, Disater recovery, Intelligence cycle, Scenario analysis, Internet community

INTRODUCTION

In the event of great disasters such as earthquakes, tsunami and floods, disaster waste including trash and debris are generated in enormous quantities. The measures of disaster waste disposal during the recovery and restoration period starts with the initial disaster measures, then proceeds to the emergency recovery, recovery and restoration phases.[1] The type (category), quantity, and manner of treatment of the waste differ according to each phase.

Disaster waste is normally treated by municipalities (by departments in special instances) as general waste. However, when its quantity becomes excessive, it cannot be disposed of by municipalities alone, and an association with private disposal services such as local industrial waste disposers becomes a requirement. At this point, it is assumed that the disposers themselves have also been exposed to the disaster.

In fact, after the Great East Japan Earthquake (hereinafter referred to as the "great earthquake"), Sendai Kankyo Kaihatsu Co., Ltd. (hereinafter referred to as "our company")[2] was forced to take various unprecedented measures, as one of the industrial waste disposal contractors (hereinafter referred to as "waste disposal contractors") located on the area stricken by the earthquake. In the immediate aftermath, due to the effect of the earthquake and tsunami, gathering information necessary to business activities was extremely difficult, and various uncertain information had spread. The measures countering harmful rumors and cooperation with the authorities that we conducted under these circumstances can all be attributed to managerial decisions. These decisions were made based on the experience and instinct of the management, and were not a result of intelligence analysis made consciously at that point. However, looking back, after a few months, we realize that these are examples of intelligence activities.

In this paper, we shall analyze and put in order our company's activities during the three months from the great earthquake, from the initial measures of disaster waste treatment, emergency recovery, to the recovery phase. We shall then discuss the correct uses and applicability of intelligence necessary to the industrial waste disposal contractors located on the disaster sites, the efficient techniques, as well as the characteristics of the intelligence cycle during the recovery phase.

"Intelligence", in this paper, refers to exact and actionable information useful for decision making, gathered at the time of disaster. "Intelligence activities" refer to the enactment of the gathering, analysis, and evaluation of information that a corporation must carry out in times of disaster as part of an entire intelligence cycle.[3-5]

In recent years, disaster intelligence activities are attracting rising attention along with intelligence activities against terrorism[7]. However, as far as the author has observed, there are no proposals of taking the disaster recovery in hand, coming from industrial waste disposal contractors. Disaster waste disposal is an indispensable activity in disaster recovery. It is rare to give an intelligence research opportunity during the course of a disaster recovery phase. Therefore, we report the knowledge acquired through this experience, hoping that it will encourage intelligence research in future disaster recovery phases.

We shall not discuss the matter of the Fukushima Nuclear Plant accident here, though its aftermath is equivalent to the great earthquake.

1 GENERAL DESCRIPTION AND TERMINOLOGY OF WASTE DISPOSAL BUSINESS AND OUR COMPANY

We shall outline the basic points of the waste disposal business in order to help understand this dissertation, and the terminology used here.

1.1 Laws Related to Waste and Definitions

Among the Japanese laws related to waste disposal, we shall outline the "Law Regarding Waste Disposal and Cleaning (abbreviated as Waste Disposal Law)".

1.1.1 *Waste Disposal Law (Law Regarding Waste Disposal and Cleaning)*

It is the most important law related to waste disposal. It defines the different types of waste, such as general waste, industrial waste, etc., stipulates the disposal responsibility of municipalities and generators, and sets up the rules of the waste disposal business and facilities, as well as the various measures of environmental conservation.

1.1.2 *Waste*

Article 2 of the Waste Disposal Law defines waste as "garbage, bulk garbage, combustion residue, sludge, excreta, waste oil, waste acid, waste alkali, animal carcass, and other litter or unwanted solid or liquid objects (radioactive matters and contaminated matters are excluded)". Radioactive matters are not industrial waste as defined by this law.

1.1.3 *Industrial Waste and General Waste*

Waste is broadly divided into industrial waste and general waste.

Industrial waste refers to the twenty – one (21) types of waste defined by the Waste Disposal Law, and is generally regarded as waste generated through business activities of companies and factories.

General waste is any waste that is not industrial. General waste is disposed of by municipalities, and industrial waste by waste disposal contractors.

1.1.4 *Disaster Waste*

Disaster waste is any waste generated as a result of natural disasters such as earthquakes, tsunami and floods. It includes debris (pieces of concrete, waste wood, etc., generated when removing damaged buildings), domestic garbage (domestic and bulk garbage that is temporarily generated in big quantities due to an earthquake), raw sewage (raw sewage scooped up from portable toilets), and waste with risks of environmental pollution (asbestos, PCB, etc.). Since it is difficult to separate general waste from industrial waste, in cases of disaster the municipalities (departments in special cases) shall dispose of them as general waste.

In the great earthquake, a lot of waste (mainly debris) was generated. The Ministry of the Environment estimates its total quantity to be 24.9 million tons over the three prefectures Tohoku, Miyagi, Iwate and Fukushima. This volume is 1.7 times bigger than that of the Great Hanshin Earthquake. The volume broken down per prefecture is as follows: 16 million tones in Miyagi, 6 million in Iwate, and 2.9 million in Fukushima. Assuming that these 24.9 million tons are all general waste, it would be the equivalent of the quantity generated by 10 million people over six years.

1.2 Industrial Waste Disposal System

Industrial waste disposal is conducted through the following processes: collection and transportation, intermediate processing, recycling, final disposal, water treatment (Figure 1).

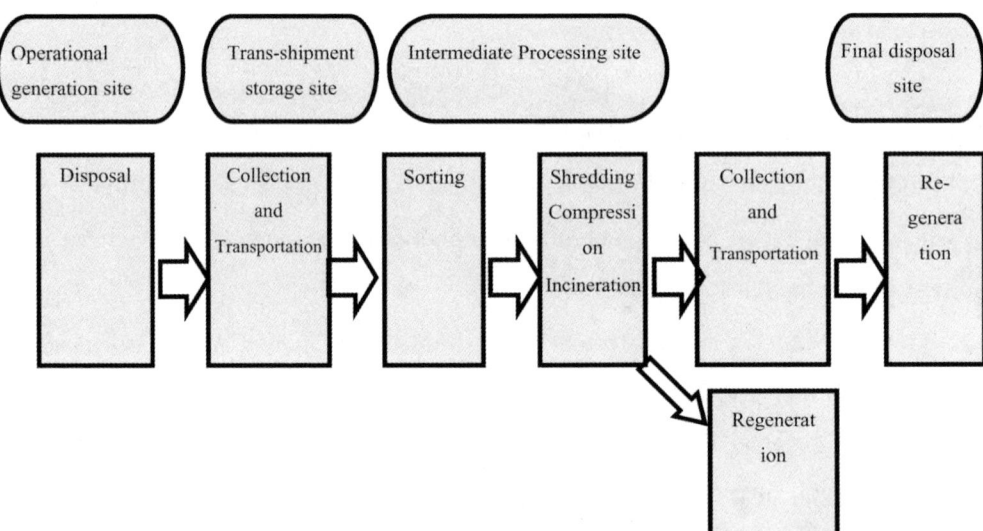

Figure 1. Waste disposal process

1.2.1 Collection and Transportation

The industrial waste generated is taken to intermediate or final disposal facilities using the company's or a contractor's transportation facilities. The means of transportation must be chosen according to the characteristics of the waste, in order to prevent dispersion, draining, leakage of bad smells, etc. Vehicles specialized in waste transportation include dump trucks, container cars, high-power suction cars, powder and granular material transporter vehicles, etc.

1.2.2 *Intermediate Processing*

Intermediate processing is conducted for the purpose of volume reduction, outage, detoxification, stabilization, recycling, etc. of the waste, through appropriate processing such as sorting and screening for recycling and final disposal, shredding, mutilation, compression, incineration, fusion and dehydration.

1.2.3 *Recycling*

Waste is recycled through reclaim, heat recovery, etc.

1.2.4 *Final Disposal*

Residue from the intermediate processing that cannot be recycled is collected and transported to final processing facilities. The final disposal facilities are roughly classified as "inert", "controlled", and "strictly-controlled" landfill sites.

At inert landfill sites, inert industrial waste, such as plastic, scrap rubber, scrap metal, scrap glass, scrap concrete, debris, etc. are dumped. Incineration residue or sludge needing leachate treatment are disposed of at controlled landfill sites, where seepage control work and leachate treatment facilities are required. Toxic industrial waste is placed in strictly-controlled landfill sites.

1.3 Industrial Waste Disposal Business

Industrial waste disposal businesses deal with part of or the entirety of industrial waste disposal. In order to become an industrial waste disposal contractor, the acquisition of authorization of industrial waste collection and transportation, industrial waste disposal, etc. is required for each treated item.

1.4 Guidelines of the Ministry of the Environment Concerning Disaster Waste Measures

Under supposition of a large production of waste due to earthquakes and flood disasters, the Japanese Ministry of the Environment issued the "Guideline of Earthquake Waste Management"[10] in 1998, and the "Guideline of Flood Disaster Waste Management"[11] in 2005. The contents are as follows.

- Development of disaster damage prevention system including waste disposal
- Emergency measures at the occurrence of disasters
- Recovery and restoration measures from disasters

In regards to the planning of disaster waste disposal, which is the subject of this paper, we detail the necessity of the following.

- Collection and transportation plans of disaster waste
- Estimation of the quantity of debris, etc.
- Plans for the securing and arrangement of temporary debris storage
- Drawing – up of a debris disposal plan

The measures taken by Sendai City in the event of the great earthquake in regards to debris disposal were more or less based on these guidelines.

2　OUR COMPANY'S RESPONSE FROM THE OCCURRENCE OF THE EARTHQUAKE

The actions taken by our Company after the great earthquake are the following:
(1) grasping the damage details of our own company
(2) cooperation with the government
(3) countermeasures against damage caused by misinformation

In (1), we grasped the degree of damage of our Company, and the operation status of our resources. (2) is a corporate defense against damage caused by misinformation which occur after disaster. On the other hand, cooperation with Sendai City is considered a social mission of industrial waste contractors dealing with disaster waste in the aftermath of disaster, as well as a corporate activity on the offensive by an enterprise focusing on future business development. The details are outlined below.

2.1　Outline of our Company

Our Company is a private corporation specializing in industrial waste disposal including the collection, transportation, intermediate processing, recycling, and controlled final disposal. We have our headquarters in Sendai, a business office in Tokyo, a research centre on the Aobayama campus of Tohoku University, an intermediate processing facility, and a controlled landfill in the Aonogi district of Sendai City.

Our Company's organization is structured so that the headquarters, operational headquarters, managerial strategy office, and the technical research institute may each fulfill their responsibilities and roles, under the command of the company proprietor. The managerial side is headed by the proprietor, and the operational section by the president. Information/intelligence is run by the managerial strategy office and the technical research institute.

2.2 Verification of the Degree of Damage on the Occurrence of the Earthquake

When the great earthquake took place on March 11, the executive staffs, including the proprietor and the president, were all gathered in Tokyo for a meeting. The site supervisor and other executives were immediately en route for Sendai. However, the Tohoku Expressway was shutdown, and they were forced to take local roads. By the time they arrived in Sendai, 14 hours later, it was 6 a.m., March 12. They started gathering information on human and facility damage, etc., upon arrival. The result of this investigation revealed that apart from some office equipment that had fallen at the headquarters and at the Technical Research Institute, there was no damage to human resources (staff members and their families) or any facility in the disposal sites. Having confirmed this, preparation for restarting corporate activities were made in the afternoon. As part of crisis management preparations, we had been preparing an emergency contact network, and a crisis management manual against natural disasters. We believe that the existence of these measures resulted in the grasping of the damage situation in such short notice.

2.3 Damages Caused by Misinformation and Their Prevention Measures

The first concern around the great earthquake was damage caused by misinformation. We had to swiftly inform our customers and partners that we had, by miracle, no reported damage. Misinformation might have caused damage based on the following two premises.

1. Although we had no damage, people might have believed that we would not be able to deal with industrial waste because we are a Sendai – based enterprise and the waste disposal sites would be seriously damaged by the earthquake and tsunami.

2. People might have believed that we would not take in regular industrial waste, giving priority to disaster waste disposal.

In fact, there have been misunderstandings on the part of some of our customers who saw news footage immediately after the earthquake, thinking that Sendai City was also affected by the tsunami. Later, as information became more accurate, there were clients who got worried about premise 2.

We started taking measures against damage caused by March 12.

We telephoned, faxed, and e – mailed our clients from the Tokyo office and the headquarters, explaining that we had no reported damage and will accept their refuse as usual. Thanks to these efforts, we were able to prevent our customers from going to our competitors, and managed to continue our contracts. We understood that in order to prevent damage caused by misinformation, it is important to swiftly spread accurate information and prevent misunderstandings.

2.4 Participation to Recovery Works

On March 12, the day after the earthquake, after confirming that our Company suffered no damage, we visited the city of Sendai and informed them that our situation allowed us to cooperate in the disaster waste disposal. Learning our situation, Sendai City requested our help in various matters related to the restoration of the city. Among the projects we put in place upon this request, where we were able to make our knowledge and expertise useful as professionals, was the installation, management, and supervision of temporary depositories of household and disaster waste generated in enormous quantities by the tsunami.

Immediately after the earthquake, Sendai City installed two types of temporary waste depositories in order to dispose of the waste generated by the tsunami. One was a depository of waste generated in each household, such as broken dishes and furniture. The other was the depository for disaster waste generated in great quantities by the earthquake.

2.4.1 *Household Waste Temporary Depository*

Since Sendai City stopped collecting household waste the day after the earthquake, a temporary depository was in need as a collection site of daily garbage and for the disposal of broken furniture. Sendai City installed five temporary depositories, March 14, the third day after the earthquake. These were installed in parks of 5000 to 10000 m^2 around the city, situated in residential areas.

Having to handle matters upon very short notice, we first provided transportation vehicles (with drivers), heavy machinery (with operators), iron plates, workmen for the sorting of waste and guidance of vehicles, etc. Since there was no data available for estimation of the needed number of machinery, we had to rely completely on our past experience. When looking back at the results, our estimation seems to have been correct, and we were able to efficiently manage and supervise the temporary depositories.

2.4.2 *Disaster Waste Depository*

It is needless to say that the greatest cause of devastation from the earthquake was the tsunami. As the area affected by the tsunami in Sendai City was mainly residential, agricultural and a shelterbelt, after the disaster, it was a mess of various objects used in people's lives and the fallen windbreaks.

The schemes planned by Sendai City in order to remove the debris were as follows

• First, Self – Defense Forces would secure the roads and start searching for survivors

• Construction companies and demolition contractors would start removing tsunami waste

• Install three temporary disaster waste depositories on the coastline to shore tsunami disaster debris.

Among these, our Company was in charge of the 40ha disaster waste depository in the Inoue district. We started by installing the temporary waste depository according to Sendai City's plan. While doing that, we relied on our past experience to devise more efficient ways for management and disposal.

3 INTELLIGENCE ACTIVITIES DURING THE RECOVERY PHASES

Based on the analysis and evaluation of the practices executed after the great earthquake, we shall examine the intelligence activities leading to the resumption of corporate activities during the recovery phases following the chaotic situation of the aftermath, as a reference for future earthquakes.

We will first verify the three phases of disaster recovery, then the intelligence cycle. Thereupon, we shall examine the characteristics of each step of the intelligence cycle at the time of recovery from natural disasters. These steps are: intelligence requirement, information collection, information analysis, and publication of intelligence.

3.1 The Three Phases of Post – Disaster Recovery

First, we would like to stress that when carrying on an intelligence activity soon after a natural disaster, three recovery phases need to be carefully verified.

These three phases that will be carried out according to the time axis are the following.[6]

Phase 1: Lifesaving/rescue

A phase during which rescue operations supersede all other matters. It is usually said that the time limit for saving life is 72 hours. However, there are cases where there are still survivors after the 72 hours have elapsed, so the decision to close this phase is a difficult one to make.

Phase 2: Restoration of social infrastructure

A phase for the restoration of social infrastructure essential to everyday life, including electricity, gas, water, transportation (road, railway, air, etc.), communication (telephone, internet), etc.

Phase 3: Recovery from economic damage

A phase of financial support to the people affected by the disaster, and for the resumption of corporate activities. The time needed for recovery will vary greatly according to the type of business.

Intelligence activities are said to be best acknowledged socially when the collection of information starts during the above phase 2, and the management activities along with the economic recovery of phase 3.

3.2 Intelligence Cycle

We shall examine the intelligence cycle of the recovery phases, based on the analysis and evaluation of the practices following the g earthquake.

According to Kitaoka[3], intelligence is defined as "knowledge necessary for judgment and action". The intelligence cycle[3, 8] processes for the production of intelligence triggered by the intelligence requirement from the decision makers who require the acquisition of intelligence. These processes are: collection of information done by the information side, information analysis (integration, analysis, evaluation, and interpretation of information), and publication of intelligence (Figure 2).

Compared to a regular intelligence cycle, the intelligence cycle during recovery is unique the following four points:

First - the time period of the intelligence cycle is extremely short

Second - it is an intelligence requirement unique to the recovery phase

Third - the information collection step is unique

Fourth - the analysis/evaluation step is unique

We shall explain these particularities below.

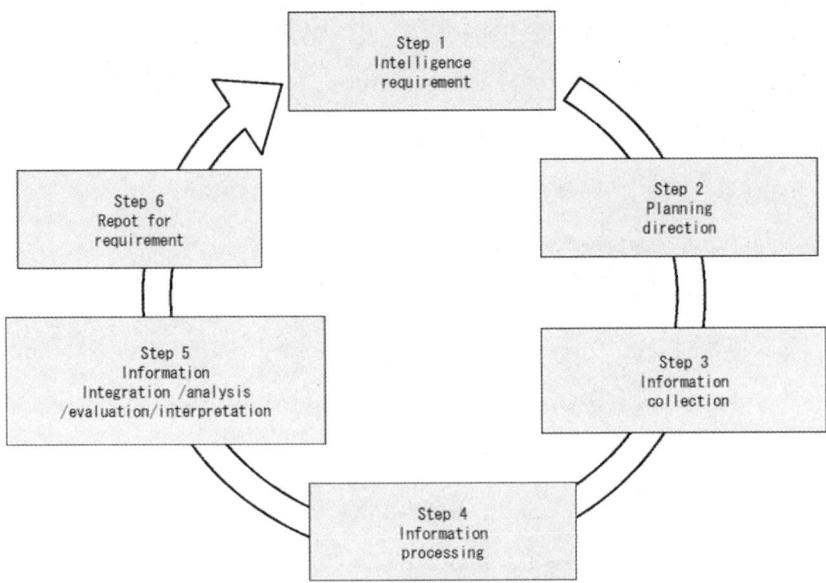

Figure 2. Intelligence cycle

3.3 Intelligence Cycle Time Period

The biggest difference between the intelligence cycles of normal times and of a recovery phase is its time period. More specifically, the length of time tolerated until the information side reports the intelligence results to the decision makers, from the moment the intelligence requirement is made. Under normal circumstances, the time period would vary from a few months to a year, or a few years. However, the intelligence cycle time period allowed during recovery is very short. In the case of the great earthquake, the scale of time restriction varied from 3 – 4 hours to 24 hours. In most cases, it should be a matter of days.

3.4 Intelligence Requirement Step

The measures to be taken and intelligence requirement to be made by enterprises located in areas affected by natural disasters in order to resume business activities during the recovery phase are the following (Table 1).

Table 1. Requirements in terms of intelligence during the recovery phase (intelligence requirement)

Management side		Information side		
Requirement	Detail	Information collection	Analysis methods	Report
Damage situation of earthquake/tsunami Amount of disaster debris Living environment Local infrastructure	Company (human resource, transportation vehicles, intermediate processing facilities, final processing facilities, headquarters, R&D center), related companies, clients, competitors, municipalities, department, broad area, country, electricity, gas, water, communication, transport, daily commodities (clothing, food, shelter), oil	Company's contact network Fixed phone Satellite phone Fax Media coverage Website of related authorities Satellite photograph map of the devastated area Grey-zone information	Macro-environment analysis Issue analysis Scenario analysis Image analysis Competition analysis matrix Client value matrix	Devastated area's map Competition analysis result Client analysis result
Recovery of local infrastructure Living environment Government's recovery plan	Electricity, gas, water, communication Railways (conventional lines, Shinkansen) Road (general road, highway), airways, seaways, daily commodities (clothing, food, shelter), oil Debris disposal	Media coverage Website of related authorities Website of enterprises Blogs Twitter SNS Satellite photograph map of the devastated area	Macro-environment analysis Issue analysis Scenario analysis Image analysis	Recovery scenario
Company's business activity resumption plan	Full operation of disposal system Cooperation with related enterprises Waste collection/transport & logistics Resumption of business operations	Report from division managers Situation of related enterprises	Issue analysis Scenario analysis	Resumption scenario Plan document of recovery from disaster

3.4.1 *Requirement to comprehend the damage situation of the enterprise*

Comprehend the damages affecting the corporate activities, such as human and facility damages of companies, clients, competitors and the industry segment.

3.4.2 *Requirement to comprehend the damage situation of the region*

Comprehend the damage situation of the municipalities, the departments, a broader area, and the country. In the case of the great earthquake, aside from the destruction of housings by the earthquake itself, damage caused by the tsunami was great. The quantity and quality estimation of the disaster debris generated by the tsunami is important, since it would be one of the bases for the planning of recovery.

3.4.3 Requirement to comprehend the damage on the lifelines and recovery status

The comprehension of damage and recovery status of the infrastructure essential to the citizens' lives, such as electricity, gas, water, transportation (railways: conventional lines, high speed rail such as Shinkansen, roads (local road), and highway), airway, seaway, etc., is an important step for the resumption of corporate activities. In our case, being a contractor in charge of disaster waste disposal, this information is especially vital.

3.4.4 Requirement of the company's corporate activity resumption plan

A requirement designed to plan the resumption of businesses by restoring the production lines through the procurement of damaged parts, the securing of sources, and logistics of raw materials, etc.

The management shall make a required report of the above items for information centralization. Normally, a company should have in-house manuals regarding this requirement, as part of their own emergency risk management.

3.5 Information Collection Step

The first step taken by the information side for any intelligence requirement is the collection of information. However, the following difficulties exist as a characteristic of a recovery phase.

- Information on the damage and prevalence (existence, location) is unknown
- Information reliability is low
- The information changes rapidly in a short period of time
- Means of access to information cannot be secured

We shall discuss the policies of information collection under such difficult circumstances. It should be conducted in a target-oriented manner, as indicated below.

1. List necessary information drawn from the ultimate strategy (action, necessary item).

2. Collect information with consideration to the time and cost allowance of the investigation and analysis, and pre-determined method of analysis.

3. Verify the existence of good-quality data sorted into "indispensable information", "useful information", "known information", and specified priority order.

4. Acquire data necessary to the analysis through indirect investigation.

5. Acquire data necessary to the analysis through direct investigation.

6. Present the analysis result to management or superiors, and a brain storm weakness.

7. Collect data once again, and conduct analysis repeatedly (combine the different analysis methods).

That is to say, instead of coming up with the analysis method after the collection of information, the analysis method should be postulated in order to get the intended result. Necessary information should be collected in accordance with it. It is difficult to obtain the intended results if you start by tentatively collecting information and thinking about the analysis method later.

3.6 Information Analysis/Evaluation Step

We believe that the analysis/evaluation intelligence activity is a process of creating intelligence (information contributing to decision making) by joining the pieces of information (raw information and/or data) together.

For an enterprise aware of its competitors, competitive analysis is a means to build up a competitive advantage and continually improve a performance superior to them, by making necessary decisions, developing strategies and better understanding the business sector and the competitors.

The analysis result must be viable. They should be future-oriented, helping the decision makers to develop more competitive strategies, better understood than the competitors' strategies, and identifying the current and future competitors plans and strategies. The ultimate goal of an analysis is to create better business results.

Environmental analysis is believed valid for an intelligence analysis at the time of recovery from disasters. We shall discuss the issue analysis and scenario analysis which are especially effective when information is scarce, in chapters 5 and 6.

3.7 Publication of Intelligence

Intelligence activities become diverse during a recovery phase, depending on the information requirement. Depending on the situation, one may or may not obtain a lot of knowledge from public information in the information collection step. An adequate analysis method well suited for the requirement must also be adopted in the analysis step. Since the publications may also include qualitative or quantitative reports, the publication of the various reports obtained by the intelligence activity must also be adequately adapted to the information requirement[8].

3.8 Heuristics within the Intelligence Activity

In an urgent situation following a great earthquake, there is no time for a detailed intelligence analysis. The management has to react based on results derived from experience and intuition. In the intelligence world, the heuristics that would drive intuition is also called a "mindset". There are merits and demerits to heuristics. The demerits are the following.

- Intuition in an analysis may lead to a belief that "analysis is an art".
- CIA analyst Morgan Jones[7] points out that heuristics is the cause of all biases formed during analysis.

On the other hand, it can be considered as a merit in the following ways.

- The heuristics that have been developed little – by – little through numerous past mistakes, allow an experienced old hand to make a quick and accurate analysis.
- Heuristics are "a shortcut in the mind, leading to judgment and evaluation". At times, we have to judge or evaluate something by carefully thinking, step by step. This process leading to judgment and evaluation is called an algorithm. However, we rarely reach judgment or evaluation through a step – by – step algo-

rithm. We judge and evaluate by subconsciously shortcutting in our minds, i. e. through heuristics. (David Welch, researcher of people's decision making mechanism)

Heuristics are said to be a cause of biases, as stated above, but also lead to accurate judgment. Especially in times of disaster, such as this paper focuses, we are forced to rely on heuristics created by experience and intuition, as decision making is constrained any by time limits before making a decision.

4 ISSUE ANALYSIS DURING A RECOVERY PHASE

Issue analysis[5] is an analysis enabling an organization to predict changes of the external environment, and aspires to becoming a more proactive player in the shaping of the external environment while exerting influence on the expansion of public policies. When analyzing our company's corporate activity in the aftermath of the great earthquake, from an issue analysis perspective, we feel that an issue analysis based on intelligence is on – the – point, and will affect the enterprise's future intelligence activities. In this paper, we shall execute an issue analysis based on document[5] (pages 274 – 291), and show that issue analysis is an effective means of analysis in times of natural disaster.

4.1 Issue Analysis

Issue analysis enables accurate analysis by collecting information of matters influencing an enterprise, such as social issues surrounding the company, trends and events within the political environment, etc., through intelligence activity. In Western societies, it is widely used, especially by large organizations such as enterprises and associations. It holds good for organizations dealing with external politics such as community relations, government issues, or public affairs.

It is said that an issue analysis happens when trends and events get intense. Here, a trend refers to the trajectory of an issue. It evokes a lot of discussion, and social/political dynamics will influence the issue.

The intensity of trends and events will become apparent through either of the following methods.

4.1.1 The current policy opposes an interest

A group would evoke an issue in order to chance a policy opposing them. The fact that a group thinking that the Great Earthquake would change their business policy according to the stakes is a good example.

4.1.2 Unpredictable events

People tend to get interested in unpredictable accidents. Some believe that the leakage of oil from the tanks after this earthquake would lead to stricter regulations from the government.

4.1.3 Public interest

Some groups and individuals wish to advertise their own concerns, when they believe the public would generally be interested. The great Earthquake was the best opportunity as a public interest. In terms of damage, it was a worldwide concern involving housings' collapse, damage done by the tsunami triggered by the earthquake, and the accident of the Fukushima Daiichi Nuclear Power Plant.

4.1.4 Overseas development

Since the issue is a big problem in other countries, it also becomes a subject of debate in our own country. The Fukushima Nuclear Plant accident impacted nuclear plants in countries all over the world, including most adversely Germany.

4.1.5 Mindset as a political entrepreneur

Politicians and political parties present issues as public agendas in order to attract attention or gather votes for elections. We hope this great earthquake will not become an example of such behavior.

4.2 Issues' Order of Priority, Issues' Life Cycle

For any enterprise, a lot of issues exist in its environment. Criteria are needed in order to decide what problems a company must choose and act on, or whether it should outsource the operating resources. The operating resources are limited for each corporation, and it is difficult to judge where the ceiling of their activities lies.

Needless to say, corporate activities require an especially difficult judgment in great earthquakes such as this one.

When such difficult judgment is required, accurate answers to the following important problems are in need.

- In which development phase does the issue lie?
- How probable is it that governmental organizations would pick up the issue and enshrine it into law, and that it would develop to a level giving tangible impact to enterprises?
- What is the extent of impact that the new prospective public policy would give to the final profit and loss of corporations?
- Do the corporations possess the ability to affect the process of issue development, or to the dimension and/or the nature of the probable governmental reaction?

When considering the reaction of the enterprises after the great earthquake as necessary elements for an issue analysis, many of the suggestions are accurate, and we believe corporate efforts are needed.

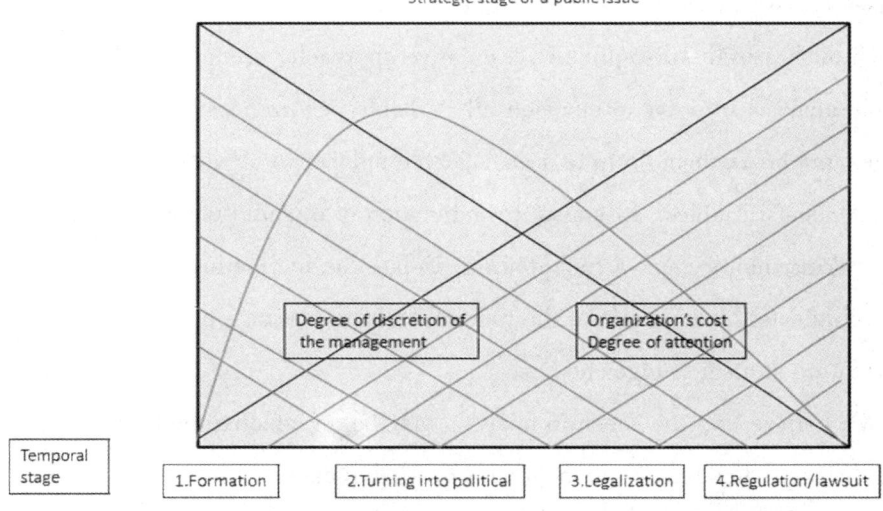

Figure 3. Life cycle of an issue, strategic stage of a public issue
(reprint form [3] with authorization)

Figure 3 is a visual indication of the issue's life cycle, and it shows how the four stages develop. The parabola represents the degree of attention from society. The triangle on the left represents the degree of discretion of the business manager, and the triangle on the right the costs the enterprise has to pay.

The period of three months after the occurrence of the Great Earthquake was a shifting phase of the formation in Stage 1 turning into a political problem in Stage 2. The degree of attention from the society was extremely high, and the practical handling within the cooperation with the authorities was mostly left to our Company's free hand.

As a result, we believe that issue analysis is an effective method in defining the way corporations should make decisions in times of earthquakes.

5 SCENARIO ANALYSIS DURING A RECOVERY PHASE

The creation of scenario and analysis[5,7] are known to be systematical approaches for the formulation of several scenarios for the purposes of correcting overestimation or underestimation of changes, and showing the right direction. The overall objective of an analysis framing a scenario as a plan is to formulate a base line for enterprises and organizations to share strategic mindsets.

Through a well-disciplined yet creative approach, scenario analysis comprises sensible analysis in order to envision all probable occurrences due to environmental changes and break them down to a manageable number to identify the relationships of the dependent variables. It is also a combination of quantitative and qualitative analyses, taking into account a framework to isolate the inclinations and patterns in order to eliminate the loopholes at the time of decision making, and to realize the ideas in the future strategic judgments.

We believe that the scenario analysis may be an effective tool on how to understand the unpredictable situation in case of earthquakes.

The analysis method to use in combination with the scenario analysis is the growth vector analysis[5]. In order to apply the growth vector analysis, supposing that the enterprise will grow, one needs to conduct a thorough analysis of the sales amount and the sales growth rate, evaluate the choices and estimate the return from the current services. However, judging that these would be impossible in this case, we only conducted the scenario analysis independently, without combining it with the growth vector analysis.

Ultimately, the "extracted scenario" would be an extremely precise strategy. In order to construct a strategy demanding expediency for the handling of unexpected events, it is important to act whilst being strongly conscious that it is an intelligence activity that creates intelligence by collecting accurate and prominent information in the shortest time possible.

In this paper, we shall indicate the analysis results of the three steps (scope definition of Figure 4, basic trend of Figure 5, space analysis of Figure 6) required for the analysis obtained by the scenario analysis conducted according to document[5] (pages 310 – 325), and the extracted scenario of Figure 7. In particular, the four scenarios of Figure 7 extracted from Figure 6 can all be adopted as an actual scenario.

It is certain that the extreme validity of the construction of scenarios as a strategy demanding expediency in times such as natural disasters has been confirmed. However, it was also a chance to re-acknowledge the importance of the collection of information using a scenario analysis, as an intelligence activity at normal times.

Definition of Scope	* Time frame : months after the earthquake
	· Product(service) : disposal of disaster waste generated by the earthquake
	· Market : municipalities of Miyagi prefecture surrounding Sendai city
	· Customer group: Sendai city
	· Technology: intermediate processing, recycling, management of a controlled landfill site in the industrial waste disposal business
	· Regional: Sendai city and Miyagi prefecture
Main stakeholder	· Ministry of land, infrastructure, transport and tourism, Ministry of Internal affairs and communications, Sendai city, etc.
	· Provider of service(Sendai Kankyo Kaisha Co,. Ltd.)
	· Disaster waste disposal contractors
	· Proprietor/manager of housings, factories, etc. of the devastated area, local governments

Figure 4. Scenario analysis(process of framing a scenario)

Social	• Disaster waste disposal is the key to recovery from disaster(positive fir the society) • Vast amounts of industrial waste will have to be disposed (Positive for the entire company) • It is becoming difficult to newly establish businesses emitting industrial waste(Positive for the entire company)
Technological	• New disposal technologies for the treatment of tsunami waste in needed(positive for the entre company) • Only one company is able to dispose of waste after the earthquake(positive for the entire company) • Total treatment including collection and transport, intermediate processing and final processing is possible(positive for the entire company)
Economic	• Disaster waste disposal is the top priority for the recovery from disaster(positive foe the entire company) • Price competition will become intense due to the participation of other industrial waste disposal contractors(negative for the entire company)
Ecological	Stricter attention to the environment will be required in the field of waste disposal(negative for the entire company) Management of harmful objects among the tsunami debris
Political	Special provision regarding the handling of general waste (positive for Sendai Kankyo Kiisha Co,. Ltd.)

Figure 5. Scenario analysis(process of framing a scenario)

	Name of scenario	Possi-bility	Exclusive Appointment form public agencies		Disposal Under special provisions in times of earthquake		Entirely free entry	
			Possible	Impossible	Possible	Impossible	Possible	Impossible
1	Monopoly by Sendai Kankyo Kaisha Co,. Ltd.	Y		●	●			●
2	Fierce competition due to the participation of several contractors	Y	●		●		●	
3	Oligopoly by specific enterprises	Y		●	●			●
4	A new ara of disposal	Y	●			●		●

Figure 6. Scenario analysis (space analysis)

Scenario 1 Monopoly by Sendai Kankyo Kaisha Co., Ltd.	The company will continue to undertake the business under special provision, with the cooperation of Sendai city.
Scenario 2 Several contractors	Intensification of price lowing competition of disposal fees.
Scenario 3 Oligopoly by specific enterprises	Concentration to contractors with strong collaborative relations with Miyagi prefecture and Sendai city.
Scenario 4 New disposal technology	No new technology will arise for the time being, since the competitors are also absorbed in the disposal after the great earthquake.

Figure 7. Extracted Scenario

6 DEFENSIVE AND AGGRESSIVE INTELLIGENCE ACTIVITIES DURING A RECOVERY PHASE

Intelligence activities can generally be categorized into defensive and aggressive intelligence activities.[8] The following details are known to be their characteristics.

The purpose of the defensive intelligence activity is to find the answer to the set-up theme from the flow of data. Defensive intelligence is valid in the following situations.

• In terms of existing competition, changes in the current situation may be detected by following up changes through the flow of data.

• For example, when changes in the product mix and price strategy, or dangers jeopardizing the position of the company are found, management will immediately be placed on alert.

• The fact that it allows a company to become a market leader putting greater effort in strategies to maintain market share, rather than revolutionary actions, is a good example.

Aggressive intelligence activities aim at nailing down the coming opportunities. Aggressive intelligence activities are effective in the following situations.

• Changes in data collection means, according to environmental changes and management policy, changes are needed.

• A broad range follow-up is needed, and an elaborate information collection means is required.

• For example, to urge the management's swift caution based on the fact that prominent competitors have fired certain experts from Research and Development sections, due to the recent decline of the economy. As a result, the management can consider this situation a favorable opportunity.

Detecting, collecting and analyzing hidden information and indications regarding competitors is important in a CI. We confirmed that upon occurrence of the great earthquake, other industrial disposal contractors located in the affected area, who are our competitors, were harmed by the disaster and our company was the only enterprise able to proactively operate the following day of the earthquake.

The observation obtained through experience from the defensive and aggressive intelligence activities in response to the earthquake are the following.

• Aside from grasping the company's damage situation and working on the recovery from the damage, get across defensive intelligence activities such as measures against damage caused by misinformation, in the immediate aftermath of the earthquake.

• Swiftly identify the movements of competitors and start aggressive intelligence activities, at the point where the prospect of intelligence needed for defense is secured.

6.1 Damage Caused by Misinformation and Its Mechanism

Damage caused to many businesses by misinformation became a topic of talk after the great earthquake. In this clause, we shall discuss the prevention of such damage as a defensive intelligence activity.

"Damage caused by misinformation" became an issue in relation with the problem of compensation to the economic damage that the safe food and products would actually bare because of the nuclear plant accident, etc.[9] However, the phrase is now used not only about the nuclear plant accident, but in a broader sense referring to "economic damage caused by the fear of diminished quality of products and services of businesses and contractors unharmed by or unrelated to direct damages caused by natural disaster, accidents, and inadequate or false press report".

In terms of academic research of the damage caused by misinformation, there are only a few reports of its history and cases, mechanism of its generation, questionnaire surveys in the areas of its occurrence, etc. There are few studies on the damages caused by misinformation related to the great earthquake, and their effective means of prevention.

Nagao[6] and his group have made a detailed report on the damage caused to the tourism industry by misinformation related to earthquakes such as the Niigataken Chuetsu – oki earthquake. The generation mechanism of damage caused by misinformation is as follows.

- Misidentify untruths for truth
- Exaggerated degree by the media
- Geographical errors

In addition, they state the following after effects are the characteristics of damage caused by misinformation to tourism.

- Uneasiness, voluntary restraint mood, deterioration of transport access, devastated mood, government dependent mood

In addition, according to the results of the research on the amount of media coverage and its contents regarding the Niigataken Chuetsu – oki earthquake and the Noto – oki earthquake, the countermeasures against damage caused by misinformation is most effective at the time of the economic restoration of the third disaster recovery phase previously mentioned. When executed earlier, it would be criticized for not valuing human life, and would only make matters worse. The Third Phase is the period where economic restoration is publicly acknowledged. They mentioned that in the case of the studied earthquake's scale, the practice of countermeasures against damage caused by misinformation is effective after one – and – a – half to two months after the disaster.

6.2 Defensive Intelligence Activity – Countermeasures against Damage Caused by Rumors in the Industrial Waste Disposal Business

The nature of damage caused by rumors in the industrial waste disposal business differs from that of tourism.

• Tourism is not indispensable to everyday life, but industrial waste disposal is.

• While the countermeasures against damage caused to tourism by misinformation is effective during the Third Phase's economic restoration, waste disposal has to start immediately in the First Phase. That is to say, countermeasures against damage caused by misinformation in the waste disposal industry would be more effective when implemented as early as possible.

The countermeasures we took as a company are as mentioned in 3.2, and we were able to prevent damage caused by misinformation. The greatest countermeasure against damage caused by misinformation is to be conscious of defensive intelligence activities, swiftly communicate accurate factual situations to relative parties on our own, and prevent misunderstandings.

6.3 Aggressive Intelligence Activity – Proactive Participation to Disaster Recovery Projects

Recovery from disasters need cooperation between government, industry and academia, i.e. the collaboration of the government's planning ability with the intellect of the academia, and the faculty of the industry. The disposal of disaster waste especially directly affects the recovery activities that would start later. It is not too much to say that recovery from disaster starts here. The waste disposal contractors should participate proactively to restoration activities, though they will have to be prepared for a considerable burden.

As mentioned in 3.4, the fact that our Company promptly offered our services to Sendai City for the recovery from disaster and was practically in charge of waste disposal for the city, is expected to relate to an aggressive strategy in future corporate activities, and can be positioned as an aggressive intelligence activity.

7 CHARACTERISTICS OF THE INFORMATION COLLECTION STEP IN THE RECOVERY PHASE OF AN INFORMATION – DRIVEN SOCIETY

The modality of the information collection step in the recovery phase has been mentioned in 4.5. Here, we shall discuss the characteristics of the information collection step in the recovery phase of an information – driven society.

7.1 Location and Collection Method of Information

Needless to say, it is the data collection on site that is considered valid in order to create intelligence in an intelligence collection step. However, information collection was extremely difficult in situations where transportation and communication means were divided. The most important intelligence collection step possible at this point was to identify the location of the intelligence, and collect the information with the highest degree of accuracy possible.

The most efficient means of information collection under the circumstances was the use of the internet. While mobile phones were ineffective due to a limitation of incoming calls by the provider, data communication was.

It is characteristic of the media to deliver daily information through the internet, weekly information in newspapers, and monthly information in magazines information collection on the internet required a repetition of the following operations.

- Search and access websites containing necessary information, and read their contents.
- If several websites deliver the same information, make a comparison of their contents and arrange them as more accurate information.
- Search for newly created websites providing related information.
- Collect, arrange and put the information together.

Damage information delivered on the internet by the Geographical Information Authority of Japan (Note 2) and the e – Community Map created base on this (Note 3) were very useful sources.

On the other hand, information delivery sites on the internet evolve in the following ways.

- First, individual sites provide information on their own.
- Next, articles introducing them are delivered.
- Lastly, curator sites putting the information together and diffusing them are created (Note 1 and Figure 8). For example, the e – Communication Map is a sort of curator site based on geographical information.

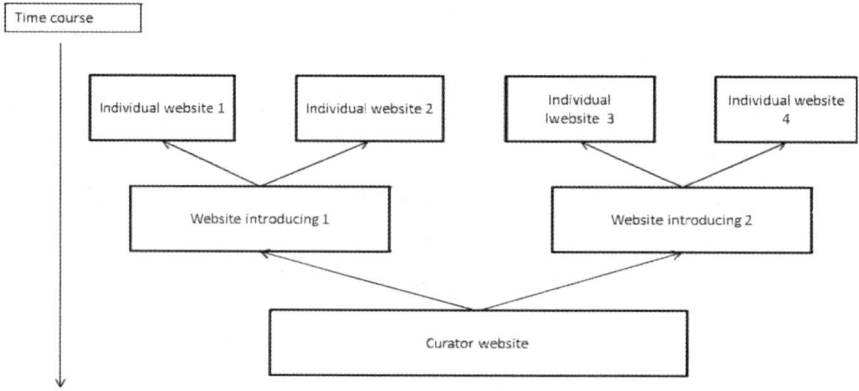

Figure 8. Formulation of curator website

It seems that, in the occurrence of the great earthquake, the act that these information bases were strongly present in our country took its effect. We believe that it is an unprecedented experience worldwide. As an experimental rule of experts actually conducting intelligence research, it is said that "80% of intelligence is obtained through publicly delivered information" (for example, the Intelligence Forum documents of the Japan Productivity Center, June 14, 2011). However, if you limit the topic to this Great Earthquake, the information sources during the three months were 100% published information on the network.

7.2 Hardiness of the Distribute System

As seen in the limitation of cellular communication in times of natural disaster, public communication systems failed and the top – down (formal, centralized) communication route collapsed. On the other hand, the bottom – up (private, decentralized) communication routes where information exchange would be done on the internet through data communication systems of mobile devices such as individually owned mobile phones, survived.

It has been said in system theory, that a centralized system is efficient but vulnerable to crisis, and divided systems are ineffective but robust in crisis. It seems that this theory has unexpectedly been proven to be true in the communication system by the great earthquake. As part of the intelligence activity in times of disaster, it is important to secure a communication route that connects the divided sources, in order to collect information.

7.3 Building of an Internet Community

People of the area affected by the disaster know best the information regarding their surroundings. In the past, there was no means to deliver such information owned by individuals. However, at the time of this great earthquake, as mentioned in 8.2, bottom-up communication routes survived, and the means to deliver individually owned information was ready in several forms. As communities mediated by the internet were built, individually owned information was effectively utilized though means such as the sharing of information through the World Wide Web on the internet, communication between individuals by e-mail, blogs, Twitter, SNS using websites provided by volunteers. We imagine that, along with the development and growth of the intelligence infrastructure, this trend will speed up. In the field of intelligence activity, this kind of relationship with the communities should be a topic to study.

8 CONCLUSION

Through this paper, we have analyzed and sorted out our Company's business activities during the recovery phase in the three months following the great earthquake from an intelligence perspective, and made suggestions as to how intelligence should be utilized by industrial waste disposal contractors located in the area affected by the disaster, and what techniques are effective, along with the characteristics of the intelligence cycle during a recovery phase.

The novelty of this paper as a research outcome can be roughly summed up in the following two points.

- We identified the fact that in a situation like the recovery phase from a disaster, where the amount of information to be collected is considerably limited, and uncertainty increases compared to normal competitive intelligence, the complementary use of the heuristics method, that was said to be unwise to rely on in conventional competitive intelligence theories, is an effective tool to accelerate the speed of decision making.

- In the intelligence of disaster times, there coexist two domains that appear during a normal competitive intelligence, which are the intelligence domain related to social economic environment, such as damage caused by misinformation, and the information analysis for corporate competition. We clearly distinguished the intelligence methods applied to each domain as "aggressive intelligence" and "defensive intelligence", and identified that it holds good to apply them at the same time, while differentiating the application methods.

More precisely,

- We identified the characteristics of each step of the intelligence cycle, i.e. intelligence requirement, information collection, information analysis during the recovery phase.

- Issue analysis and scenario analysis are believed to be valid as CI methods for the building of strategies. The fact that the management's intuition deriving from heuristics cultivated through daily experience is also an important element, and plays an important role in an intelligence activity.

- As a defensive intelligence activity, it is important to conduct risk management by making facility investments on a regular basis as a precaution against earthquakes, or creating an in-house system preparing against accidents. In addition, we identified detailed responses in regards to damage caused by misinformation that would affect all enterprises located in the area touched by the disaster.

- It has been identified that an aggressive intelligence activity, where the company would swiftly participate to recovery projects of the government side once it has secured the soundness of its own, and relate this move to the aggressive strategy of future corporate activities is effective. As a management activity, it is effective to use both the defensive and aggressive intelligence consciously.

- We put together the characteristics of the information collection during a recovery phase in a society highly information - oriented, along with the influence of SNSs. We have also proposed some hints as to the information collection in times of expected future earthquakes.

Our task is to continue studying the shape of the intelligence activities, the required information and sources, as preparation for future occurrences of world - scale earthquakes.

There is a grave problem we did not touch in relation to the great Earthquake, namely the Fukushima Nuclear Plant accident. This accident greatly affected the energy policies, not only of Japan but of the entire world. In addition, the damage caused by radioactivity has not only affected people's lives including food and housing, but is causing various difficult problems in terms of radioactive waste disposal. We would like to report our intelligence activities in regards to this problem on a different occasion.

NOTES

1) Curator

It derives from the English "Curator", referring to a staff of a museum in charge of planning exhibitions, collecting exhibits according to the theme of the plan, and arranging these exhibits through the exhibition area in order to let a lot of people see them. On the internet, a curator would collect and select information according to a set theme, from the flood of information available. He/she would then add comments, etc. to these selected information to give them a meaning, and provide them to various people by means of services such as blogs, Twitter, SNS, etc.

2) Overall chart of the range flooded by the tsunami

Geospatial Information Authority of Japan (GSI), Ministry of Land, Infrastructure, Transport and Tourism

A chart depicting the deciphered range flooded by the tsunami. Website of GSI

http://danso. env. nagoya - u. ac. jp/20110311/

(Accessed on July 20, 2011)

3) e - Communication Map

http://danso. env. nagoya - u. ac. jp/20110311/ecom. html

(Accessed on July 20, 2011)

REFERENCES

[1] Japan Society of Material Cycles and Waste Management (JSMCWM), "Disaster Waste Disposal Measures/Recovery Task Team". *Strategic Manual for the Separation and Disposal of Disaster Waste - On the Event of the Great East Japan Earthquake -*.

http://eprc. kyoto - u. ac. jp/saigai/. [2011 - 7 - 20].

[2] Website of Sendai Kankyo Kaihatsu Co., Ltd

http://www. sendaikankyo. co. jp/. [2011 - 7 - 20].

[3] Kitaoka Hajime. 2006. *Intelligence History*. Keio University Press.

[4] Ishikawa Akira, Nakagawa Juro. 2009. *From business Intelligence to Knowledge Management Science*. Zeimu Keiri Kyokai.

[5] Fleisher Craig, Bensoussan Babette. 2005. Japanese translation by Sugasawa Yoshio, Others. *Strategic and Competitive Analysis*. Corona Publishing Co., Ltd.

[6] Nagao Mitsuyoshi, Others. 2006. Echigo - Yuzawa's Approach to Damage Caused by Rumors in the Niigataken Chuetsu - oki Earthquake. *Society for Tourist Informatics Magazine* 2, 1, 30 - 40.

[7] Kitaoka Hajime. 2009. *Business Intelligence - Scenario Analysis Technique Predicting the Future -*. Toyo Keizai Inc.

[8] Sugawasa Yoshio, Other. 2010. *Technology Marketing and Intelligence*. Corona Publishing Co., Ltd.

[9] Sekiya Naoya. 2009. *Psychology of Damages Caused by Rumors*, *Psychology of Disaster Prevention*, 101 - 134. Toshindo Publishing Co., Ltd.

[10] Guideline of Earthquake Waste Management. Environment Section, Water Supply Division, Health Service Bureau, Ministry of Health, Labor and Welfare, Japan. 1998.

[11] Guideline of Flood Disaster Waste Management. Office of Waste Disposal Management, Industrial Waste Management Division, Waste Management and Recycling Department, Minister's Secretariat, Ministry of Health, Labor and Welfare, Japan. 2005.

人际情报网络研究进展

李纲[①]　王忠义[②]

[摘要]　人际情报网络是应情报活动的需要而构建的一种人际网络,是情报从业者获取、分析和传播非公开信息和隐性知识的重要平台,对于企业来说具有重要的意义和价值。本文在对人际情报网络的基本理论进行分析的基础上,论述了人际网络、人际情报网络的国内外研究进展,并通过比较分析,对人际情报网络的研究进行了展望。希望能够有助于加深人们对人际情报网络的认识,以促进人际情报网络研究的进一步深化。

[关键词]　人际网络　人际情报网络　研究进展　发展趋势

Research Progress in Human Intelligence Network

[Abstract] Human intelligence network is a kind of human network which is constructed to meet the needs of intelligence activities. Human intelligence network can be used to obtain, analyze and disseminate tacit information and knowledge, so it has an important significance for enterprises. This paper, based on the analyses of the theory of human intelligence network, discussed the research progress of human network and human intelligence network. Based on comparison, this paper prospected the development trends of human intelligence network. Through such studies, this paper wants to deepen people's understanding of human intelligence network and promote the research on human intelligence network.

---

① 李纲,博士生导师,武汉大学信息管理学院副院长,武汉大学信息资源研究中心研究员
② 王忠义,情报学博士研究生,武汉大学信息管理学院

[**Keywords**] Human Network, Human Intelligence Network Research Progress, Development Trends

在经济全球化的大趋势下,世界经济日益成为一个紧密联系的整体,贸易自由化、生产国际化、金融和科技的全球化等趋势越来越明显。企业之间的竞争也越来越激烈,呈现白热化的发展趋势。为了能在激烈的市场竞争中占据一席之地,企业需要拥有自己的核心竞争能力,以保持自己的竞争优势。企业的核心竞争能力是企业所独有的,难以转移,难以为其他组织所模仿,支撑企业不断发展和保持竞争优势的核心知识和技能。在当今知识经济时代里,人们越来越强烈地意识到知识尤其是隐性知识已经成为企业核心竞争能力的一个主要来源。在这种背景下,如何及时准确地采集、分析企业内外的知识或情报并将它们及时提供给需求者,以促进企业自身的创新,成为企业成功的关键。当前,企业获取这些竞争情报或知识的主要途径有两个:信息网络和人际情报网络。随着信息技术的发展,信息网络不再为少数企业所特有,而且信息网络在获取竞争情报或知识尤其是隐性知识方面具有一定的局限性,这些因素导致企业在开展竞争情报活动时,也不再完全崇尚技术,而是越来越注重于人的活动和交际能力。在这种情况下,企业员工的人际网络成为企业获取情报和知识的重要情报源,关系着企业竞争情报或知识的搜集、分析和使用。由此可见,人际情报网络作为企业竞争情报工作和知识管理的重要平台对于企业来说具有重要的意义和价值。为此,国内外相关领域的学者对人际情报网络的相关理论、分析方法及其实践应用进行了广泛而深入的研究,并取得了大量的研究成果。

1 人际情报网络

人际情报网络(Human Intelligence Network)是应情报活动的需要而构建的一种人际网络,是情报从业者获取、分析和传播非公开信息和隐性知识的重要平台。[①] 从本质上来说,人际情报网络其实就是一个"谁认识谁"和"谁知道什么"的人际资源地图,借助于该地图,不仅能够有目的拓展自己的人脉,而且能

---

① 包昌火等. 人际情报网络[J]. 情报理论与实践,2006,29(2):129–141.

够借助于这些关联获取各种稀缺的隐性知识资源。人际情报网络是应情报工作的需要而构建的一种特殊的人际网络，与一般的人际网络相比，其具有不同于人际网络的自身所特有的属性。这些属性表现在以下几个方面。

(1) 人际情报网络是一种基于业缘关系的特殊的人际网络

在企业中，无论是高层管理者还是一般员工，由于个人能力的局限性，都不可能拥有企业所需要的全部知识，因此，在日常工作中，他们经常会产生对各种类型的知识或情报的需求，这些需求促使他们去与拥有他们所需知识或情报的人建立联系，进而通过这些联系达到最终获取自己所需要的知识或情报的目的。而这些节点和联系也就共同构成了企业的人际情报网络。由此可见，人际情报网络不是基于血缘、地缘等关系的一般的人际情报网络，而是一种基于业缘关系的一种特殊的咨询网络。该咨询网络是以提高企业的竞争能力为导向，以收集、分析和利用人际网络中的各种情报或知识为目的的一种特殊人际网络。在该人际网络中节点之间交流的是知识和情报，节点之间建立联系的目的是获取其他节点所拥有的知识和情报，节点之间建立联系的动机是对知识和情报的需求。

(2) 人际情报网络是一个具有自适应复杂演化特性的动力系统

企业构建人际情报网络的目的是获取企业所需要的各类隐性知识或情报，以保持企业的竞争优势，谋取企业的发展。为达到这一目的，人际情报网络作为一个开放的系统，需要不断地吸纳新的节点。而新节点的进入，又会给原人际网络造成各方面的影响：一方面，新节点的进入可能会取代原网络中某节点，或削弱某节点在人际情报网络中影响力；另一方面，新节点进入人际情报网络之后会与网络中的其他节点建立新的联系，这些新的联系同时也会对人际网络中的其他联系造成影响，从而使得人际情报网络表现出复杂动态变化的特征。此外，人际情报网络中已有节点自身的属性和关系也处于不断变化的过程之中，如节点通过不断的学习，使得自己的能力不断地提升，进而引起其在人际情报网络中的地位和关系发生变化，这也使得人际情报网络处于不断的变化之中。需要说明的是，人际情报网络的这一动态变化的过程是自适应演化的结果，是人际情报网络为完成自己的使命而不断优化自身节点和联系的过程。正如吴晓伟和李丹所说：人际情报网络是一个不断吸收中心节点而生长的自适应复杂动力系统。①

(3) 人际情报网络具有内紧外松的小核心、大范围的网络特征特点

尽管不同的企业构建的人际情报网络在节点属性、关系类型、网络规模等方面各不相同,但这些人际情报网络在总体结构上都不约而同地表现出内紧外松的结构特性。人际情报网络的内紧表现在组织内部的人际情报网络的闭合性和强联系;人际情报网络的外松表现在组织外部人际情报网络的非闭合性(存在结构洞)和弱联系。在这种小核心、大范围的人际情报网络结构中,核心中运行的是紧密型网络,大范围运行的是松散型网络,也即核心以外的各种联系,如企业与政府、客户、供应商的联系等。小核心、大范围的人际情报网络结构,一方面可以保证人际情报网络的正常运行,另一方面可以保证搜集到各种类型的异质知识或情报,以满足企业对各类知识或情报的需求。

(4) 人际情报网络是一种具有知识特性的人际网络

人际情报网络是应情报工作的需要而构建的一种人际网络。从人际情报网络的目的来看,企业之所以要构建人际情报网络是为了收集、分析和利用人际网络中的各种隐性知识或情报;从人际情报网络的功能来看,其主要体现在将隐性知识或情报及时传递给所需的人之上;从人际情报网络形成的动机来看,在人际情报网络中,节点之间建立关系的动机是对知识的需求;而从人际情报网络中建立节点之间关系的依据来看,在人际情报网络中,节点之间建立关系的依据从本质上来看是知识之间的相关关系。通过上述分析不难发现,无论是从人际情报网络的目的、功能来看,还是从人际情报网络形成的动机和建立节点之间关系的依据来看,人际情报网络都具有知识的特性。在人际情报网络中,节点所拥有的隐性知识或情报通过人际情报网络不断地从知识势能高的节点流向知识势能低的节点,最终达到这些隐性知识的使用和共享。

2 人际情报网络的类型

依据构成人际情报网络的节点不同,人际情报网络可以分为企业内部人际情报网络和企业外部人际情报网络两种类型。

---

① 吴晓伟,李丹.企业人际竞争情报网络复杂性研究[J].图书情报工作,2007,51(9):75-78.

2.1 企业内部人际情报网络

组成企业内部人际情报网络的节点是由来自于企业内部的员工构成。具体来说,企业内部的员工主要包括:一般工作人员、基层和中层管理人员和企业高层领导等。企业内部的每一位员工都是企业重要的情报源。由于他们各自的教育背景、从事的工作的不同,使得他们各自所拥有的知识或情报的类型也不尽相同。然而,由于自身能力的局限性,企业内部任何员工都很难拥有工作需要的全部知识,这就使得他们产生对知识或情报的各种不同需求。为满足企业员工的不同的知识需求,就需要企业员工之间共享自己的知识,以便于需求者能够及时获得该知识。然而,由于企业员工的知识或情报通常以隐性的状态存在于他们的头脑之中,这给充分共享和利用这些隐性知识或情报带来了不小的困难和阻碍。由隐性知识管理的人格化模式可知,要充分发掘企业内部员工中的这些隐性知识或情报,这就需要构建企业内部的人际情报网络,通过节点之间直接的、面对面的交流,来达到这些隐性知识或情报共享的目的。合理利用企业内部的人际情报网络,充分挖掘企业内部员工所拥有的各种隐性知识或情报,可以采用以下几种方式:首先,建立一个知识共享的企业文化,使得企业员工具有共享自身所拥有的隐性知识或情报的习惯;其次,可以采取各种激励措施(包括物质激励和精神激励)调动企业内部员工的积极主动性,使得他们自愿主动的共享自己所拥有的隐性知识或情报;接着,通过各种培训,提高企业内部员工的情报意识,使他们充分意识到自身所拥有的知识或情报的价值,注意搜集相关的知识或情报;而后,企业要通过组织各种活动(正式或非正式),如专题研讨会等,为组织内部员工之间的相互交流提供平台;最后,企业要为内部员工提供各种知识共享的硬件条件,如网络设备等。企业内部人际情报网络一般是由强关系连接起来的协调紧密型的人际情报网络,网络中各节点之间的关系比较紧密,信任度高,因此有利于节点之间隐性知识的共享。

2.2 企业外部人际情报网络

企业外部人际情报网络的节点从宏观上来看有与企业相关的政府部门、法律咨询机构、中介机构、科研机构等;从中观上来看包括与企业生产经营相关的分销商、供应商等;从微观上来看包括与企业内部员工有咨询关系的企业外部各类人员,如外部同行、相关领域专家等。对于企业外部的人际情报网络,企业可以通过各种途径如电话、电子邮件、面谈等多种方式获取企业所需要的知识或情报。随着企业之间的竞争越来越激烈,当前,企业也越来越重视企业外部人际情报网络的构建和维系。企业外部的人际情报网络一般是由弱关系构成的松散型人际情报网络。网络中节点之间的关系比较松散,交往不是非常频繁,信任度较低,因此企业外部的人际情报网络不利于知识的转移和共享。但由于企业外部人际情报网络中节点拥有的知识具有较高的异质性,因此有利于企业对新知识的获取。

3 人际情报网络的作用

人际情报网络作为企业竞争情报活动中的重要平台,在企业竞争情报活动的整个过程中都发挥着重要的作用。具体来说人际情报网络的作用主要体现在竞争情报搜集、竞争情报分析和竞争情报服务等的过程之中。

(1) 在竞争情报搜集阶段中的作用

在竞争情报收集阶段,人际情报网络发挥着其他情报搜集方法或手段不可比拟的优势和作用。通过人际情报网络进行竞争情报的搜集,是一种借助人际情报网络中节点之间的直接交互的方式来获取所需知识或情报方法,如竞争情报中的"四分卫法"就是人际情报网络在情报搜集中的一种典型应用。与其他情报搜集方法相比,采用人际情报网络进行情报搜集的作用和优势主要体现在以下几个方面:首先,借助人际情报网络有利于获取高价值的隐性知识或情报。隐性知识或情报通常以内隐的形式存在于人们的头脑之中,很多都难以外化,只能通过直接的、面对面的交流和观察才能获得,因此,这些知识难以为其他企业所获取。正因为如此,这些隐性知识或情报通常是企业的核心竞争力之所在,具有较高的价值。其次,通过人际情报网络进行情报搜集,有利于提高情报搜集的及时性和效率。这是因为,借助人际情报网络这一非正式渠道搜集的知识或情报通常是存储在人们头脑之中的尚未被外化的零次知识或情报,与正式情报搜集渠道相比,省去了情报或知识的出版、发行和流通阶段,节约了大量的时间,因此可以有效地提高情报搜集的及时性和效率。例如,一个新的知识从科研人员在实验室里发现到通过期刊出版发行然后与读者见面通常都需要两年左右的时间,而通过人际情报网络则可以省去这些出版发行的时间,使得情报搜集的及时性大大地提高。接着,借助人际情报网络进行情报搜集能够提高情报搜集的全面性。这是由于通过人际情报网络进行情报搜集可以获得诸如人的表情、语气、情感等方面的情报,这些是很难通过其他情报搜集渠道获得的。在实践中,通过人际情报网络进行情报搜集的方式有多种,例如:借助内部人际情报网络获取企业内部员工头脑中的隐性知识或情报;通过参加各种会议,从中搜集行业或竞争对手的情报;直接或间接地与竞争对手的分销商、客户、供应商进行交互,获取有关竞争对手的产品、原材料等的相关情报;雇用竞争对手企业的员工等。

(2) 在竞争情报分析阶段中的作用

人际情报网络在竞争情报分析阶段同样也起着非常重要的作用。竞争情报分析是对收集到的各类知识或情报进行加工、整理,形成对企业有用的竞争情报的过程。该过程需要融入较多的智力活动,需要整合各方面的情报和知识,进而产生企业所需情报。由此可见,情报分析的过程事实上也是一个知识创新的过程,而知识创新需要人的智能的广泛参与,因此,在该过程中需要企业内部分析人员彼此之间密切配合,各抒己见,集思广益,将各类相关知识进行有机集成才可能出色地完成竞争情报分析的任务。人际情报网络无疑将在竞争情报分析过程中发挥至关重要的作用。这主要是由于,人际情报网络作为一个基于业缘关系的人际网络,网络中节点所拥有的知识之间具有相关性,借助于人际情报网络中形成的融洽的关系,在竞争情报分析的过程中,可以有效地将相关分析人员和知识集中起来,进而实现对竞争情报的有效分析。

(3) 在竞争情报服务阶段中的作用

人际情报网络在竞争情报服务阶段也起着重要的作用。竞争情报服务是指将竞争情报分析阶段得到的竞争情报产品及时提供给企业各级决策层和其他一般用户,并根据需要对企业外部实现适当共享的过程。随着信息技术的发展,虽然信息网络在竞争情报产品传递过程中发挥了重要的作用,然而,仅依靠信息网络无法实现竞争情报产品供需双方的有效沟通,因此也就不能很好地实现竞争情报产品的有效提供。这一方面是由于在情报产品制作的过程中,情报分析人员不可能充分地将自己的意思完全表达出来;另一方面,由于竞争情报产品供需双方知识背景的差异,同一语句可能会产生不同的理解。为此,这就需要竞争产品双方面对面的沟通交流,而人际情报网络为此提供了一个重要的交流平台,它将竞争情报网络所涉及的所有人员统筹在了一起,既有情报产品的生产者:情报专家;又有情报产品的推销者:说服专家;还有情报产品供需双方的联系人:人际专家;等等。他们在人际情报网络中发挥着不同的作用,处于不同的网络位置之上,彼此相互协作和互联,共同构成人际情报网络,借助该网络能够及时将情报产品提供给需求者,从而达到提高竞争情报传递的速度和效果,实现竞争情报服务的目的。

4 人际情报网络的基本理论

当前人们主要从三个视角来认识和把握人际情报网络,并形成了三种基本的人际情报网络理论:人际情报网络的构成论、资源论和平台论。

4.1 人际情报网络的构成论

人际情报网络的构成论主要是从人际情报网络的构成元素和人际情报网络的模式两个方面来把握人际情报网络。构成要素是从微观上对人际情报网络进行把握,而模式则是从宏观上对人际情报网络进行理解。

就人际情报网络的构成元素来看,人际情报网络是由节点、节点之间的关系构成,它们在总体上决定着人际情报网络的性质和功能。人际情报网络中的节点既是情报源又是情报的需求者,在人际情报网络中,节点通过自己所拥有的联系与网络中的其他节点不断交互,互通有无。每个节点都具有自身的属性,如节点所拥有的知识的类型、数量和水平等,节点的这些属性在一定程度上决定了节点在人际情报网络中的位置和作用。例如,当某节点拥有较多的 know–what 或 know–how 类型的知识时,他在人际情报网络中往往起到知识源的作用,是人际情报网络中的知识专家。而当某节点拥有比较丰富的 know–who 类型的知识的时候,他在人际情报网络中就起到知识桥的作用,是人际情报中的人际专家。节点之间的关系是连接节点的纽带,是节点之间进行知识交流的渠道。在人际情报网络中,节点之间建立联系的动机是对知识或情报的需求,建立联系的目的是获取知识或情报。节点之间的关系有强弱之分。强关系往往形成于节点属性较为相近的节点之间,由于具有强关系的节点之间存在较强的信任关系,因此与弱关系相比更有利于隐性知识的转移;而弱关系往往形成于属性差异较大的节点之间,虽然这种弱关系不利于节点之间隐性知识的转移,但由于节点具有较大的属性差异,即节点所拥有的知识具有较大的差异性,因此,与强关系相比,弱关系更有利于节点对异质知识的获取。

就人际情报网络的模式而言,它可以由结构模式和内容模式两种类型构成。人际情报网络的结构模式是指人际情报网络节点之间的联系方式。依据节点之间联系方式的不同,人际情报网络的结构模式又主要可以分为:强关系—弱关系模式、结构空洞模式和闭合—开放模式三种类型。强关系—弱关系模式揭示的是人际情报网络中点对点的成对关系的紧密程度,而不涉及网络本身或网络之间的关系。在强关系—弱关系模式中,由强关系连接的节点之间关系比较密切,因此节点之间的信任度比较高,这就有利于节点之间知识或情报的扩散与传播,但由于强关系链接的节点之间的相似度也往往较高,因此容易造成知识或情报的冗余。而由弱关系连接的节点之间关系比较疏远,相互之间接触较少,信任度比较低,交流的阻碍较大,成本较高,因此不利于节点之间知识或情报的交流和共享。但由弱关系连接的节点通常拥有异质知识或情报,因此,弱关系有利于节点对异质知识或情报的获取。结构空洞模式是对强关系—弱关系模式的发展。该模式主要是用来分析网络本身或网络间存在的各种非直接联系,进而揭示人际情报网络中这些非直接联系的意义和价值。通常来说,拥有结构空洞较多的节点通常占据着重要的位置优势,具有较多的知识或情报的控制权利。闭合—开放模式是企业常采用的一种人际情报网络模式。在该模式中,节点之间互有联系,交往比较频繁的网络结构称为闭合型结构。在闭合型结构中,节点之间相互信任度高,因此交流的成本比较低,有利于节点之间知识或情报的转移或共享;然而该结构模式中其结构洞比较少,冗余联系较多,网络的广度也比较有限,因此,查找的范围比较窄。而在闭合—开放模式中,节点之间联系相对较少,交往不密切的网络结构称为开放型结构。该网络结构的网络规模相对比较大,因此具有较大的搜索范围,往往能够提供一些异质的知识或情报;然而其缺点也比较明显,对于开放型网络结构来说,其控制难度比较大,投入也相对较多。人际情报网络的内容模式是指人际情报网络联系的内容。依据联系内容的不同,通常人际情报网络的内容模式又可以细分为信任网络、咨询网络等几种类型。信任网络通常是在长期的交往与合作中建立起来的基于互利关系的人际情报网络,在信任网络中节点之间的关系相对比较稳固,而且合作具有长效性的特点。咨询网络是节点为了更好地完成组织中的工作而建立起来的以传递与工作有关的知识或情报的网络。咨询网络主要受到个人所拥有的知识和能力等方面因素的影响。

4.2 人际情报网络的资源论

人际情报网络的资源论认为,人际情报网络是一种人际网络资源,一种社会资本,该资本为人际情报网络的人力资本的利用提供了外部条件,如果没有这些社会资本,网络中人力资本也难以发挥作用。因此,企业中的社会资本越丰富,越能发挥人力资本的作用,其回报率也就会更高。也即是说,社会资本在一定程度上决定了人力资本实现的可能性。有关人际情报网络的资源论主要有三种论述:关系强度理论、网络闭合理论和结构空洞理论。

关系强度理论认为,人际情报网络中节点之间的强关系和弱关系在节点之间发挥着不同的作用。强关系起着维系人际情报网络存在的作用,而弱关系则在群体、组织之间起着纽带和桥梁的作用。由于具有强关系的节点之间具有较高的相互信任度,因此有利于知识或情报在节点之间的传播和共享,但由于强关系所连接的节点之间相似度较大,因此不利于异质知识或情报的获取;相反,由弱关系连接的节点的相似度较低,知识的异质性较大,因此有利于节点对异质知识或情报的获取,但由于弱关系联系的节点之间相互信任度低,因此在知识或情报的转移上存在一定的困难。

网络闭合理论认为,人际情报网络的网络密度与社会资本成正相关的关系。这是由于人际情报网络中,网络密度越大,节点之间相互关联越多,节点之间的信任度也就越高,因此也就越有利于节点之间知识或情报的转移。相反,在人际情报网络中,网络密度越低,网络节点之间的联系越少,节点之间的信任度就会相对较低,从而不利于节点之间知识或情报的交流和传播。此外,网络闭合理论还认为,网络中心度与网络的社会资本成负相关的关系。这是由于,在人际情报网络中,网络的中心度越大,网络对中心人物的依赖性也就越强,因此节点之间交流的风险也就越大,如当中心人物离开人际情报网络时,其他节点就很难再相互交流,或者说,如果中心人物自身能力有限,传递了错误的知识或情报等,这些都会造成网络社会资本的降低。

所谓结构空洞是指:"非冗余联系之间的分割"。①某节点拥有的结构空洞的数量可以通过该节点拥有的单线联系的节点的数量来确定。结构空洞理论认为,节点拥有的结构空洞越多,其拥有的社会资本就越多;节点拥有的结构空洞越少,其所拥有的社会资本也就越少。因此,在人际情报网络中,拥有结构空洞越多的节点其关系优势就越大,获得利益回报的几率也越高,因此,其竞争力就越大。因此,依据该理论,任何节点要想在竞争中获胜,保持自己的竞争优势,就需要尽可能地与其他节点建立广泛的关系,以取得获取知识或情报的相对优势,从而提高自己的竞争能力。

4.3 人际情报网络的平台论

人际情报网络的平台论认为,组织的竞争情报和知识管理等工作都是内嵌在组织的人际情报网络之中的。因此,该理论认为,人际情报网络不仅是一种社会资本,也是竞争情报活动和知识管理活动得以顺利开展和进行所依托的平台。

人际情报网络作为竞争情报活动的重要平台,在竞争情报收集、竞争情报分析和竞争情报服务等竞争情报活动的各个流程阶段中都发挥着非常重要的作用。在情报搜集中,通过人际交流,可以充分获取、挖掘正式交流中难以获得的隐性知识或情报(如情感信息),可以实现隐性知识的有效转移和传递;在情报分析中,竞争情报分析人员通过相互配合、协调、各抒己见、取长补短,可以出色地完成情报分析任务;在情报服务中,通过人际情报网络可以及时有效地将情报提供给知识或情报的需求者。由于人际情报网络在竞争情报活动中起着如此重要的作用,当前人际情报网络已与信息网络、组织网络一同成为竞争情报系统的三大支持网络之一,在隐性知识或情报的收集、分析和服务中发挥着重要的作用。由此可见,组织竞争情报活动的整个流程都是内嵌在人际情报网络之中的,人际情报网络是竞争情报活动得以实现的重要平台。

人际情报网络作为知识管理的平台,在知识尤其是隐性知识的收集、转移和利用过程中起着非常重要的作用。关于知识管理通常采取两种模式:编码化

---

① Burt R S. Structural Holes: *The Social Structure of Competition* [M]. Cambridge: Harvard Business School Press, 1992.

模式和人格化模式。编码化模式通常是将知识与知识的创造者分离,对知识进行编码后进行管理,因此该模式适用于显性知识的管理;而人格化模式则是将知识与知识的创造者紧密结合在一起,通过对知识的创造者的管理来达到对知识创造者所拥有的知识的间接管理,知识通过知识创造者的直接交互实现共享,因此该管理模式比较适合对隐性知识进行管理。在采用人格化模式进行知识管理时,通常是绘制一张"谁认识谁"和"谁知道什么"的知识地图,而这也恰恰是人际情报网络构建的目的。由此可见,人际情报网络作为一个人际资源地图,从根本上来说是一种采用人格化模式对隐性知识进行管理的方式。因此,我们可以说人际情报网络是对知识进行管理的一种重要平台。

5 人际网络研究现状

5.1 国外人际网络研究现状

人际网络又称社会网络(Social Network),这一概念由英国人类学家拉德克利夫·布朗(Radcliffe Brown)于20世纪30年代首次提出。之后,有关人际网络的研究得到快速的发展。1957年,伊丽莎白·鲍特(Elizabeth Bott)使用结(Knit)这一测量工具对人际网络结构进行研究,她的著作《家庭与社会网络》也一直被认为是人际网络研究的经典著作之一。1967年,美国社会心理学家斯坦利·米尔格拉姆(Stanly Milgram)在试验的基础上,提出了著名的"六度分离"理论(也即小世界理论)。随着有关人际网络的研究的不断深入,"人际网络"一词也逐渐进入学术殿堂。1978年,"国际社会网络分析学会"成立,并出版发行了相关的学术刊物《关系》(*Connections*)和《人际网络》(*Social Networks*)。而后,随着研究的深入,逐渐形成了人际网络研究的两个学派:社会计量学派和网络结构学派。社会计量学派遵循计量学的传统,研究社会体系中角色关系的整体网络结构。该学派在对人际互动和交换模式进行分析时,构建了一系列诸如紧密性、中距性和中心性等整体网络分析概念。该学派的主要代表人物有林肯·弗里曼(Linton Freeman)。网络结构学派继承了英国人类学家的传统,把人际网络中的各种纽带关系看做是一种客观的社会结构,并研究这些纽带关系对人际网络中节点的影响。该学派的主要代表人物有哈里森·怀特

（Harrison C. White）、马克·格拉诺维特（Mark Granovertter）、林楠（Nan Lin）和罗纳德·博特（Ronald Burt）等。以上两个学派的学者从不同的角度论述了人际网络的思想，接下来，本文将对这些学者中比较有影响的观点和思想加以详细阐述。

哈里森·怀特从人际网络的角度提出了自己关于市场内涵的理解，认为市场社会网络发展的产物，市场中存在的各种秩序是由市场参与者网络内部通过不断的相互交互而产生的各种暗示、规则的反映。马克·格拉诺维特作为弱关系理论的创始人认为，人际网络中的弱关系在网络成员之间起着非常重要的作用。与维系组织的强关系不同，弱关系的作用主要体现在其是建立组织成员之间联系的纽带上。此外，他还指出，人类的各种经济行为都是嵌入在人际网络之中的，核心的社会结构是人们在社会实践的过程中形成的社会网络结构，嵌入的网络机制是信任。与马克·格拉诺维特的弱关系理论相对应，克拉克·哈特（David Krachhards）提出了强关系优势理论。强关系是人际网络中的个体经过长期多次交流形成并发展起来的密切的关系。人际网络中经常发生的知识交流通常也是在强关系中发生的。由于强关系通常是建立在高度的信任的基础之上的，因此，通过人际网络中的强关系能够传递一些高质量的、比较复杂的隐性知识和信息。社会资本理论的创始人林楠认为嵌入在个人人际网络中的权利、财富、声望等社会资源并不是为个人所直接拥有，而是需要个人通过各种社会关系直接或间接地去获取。基于马克·格拉诺维特的弱关系理论，林楠指出了社会资本理论的三个基本假设：地位强度假设、弱关系强度建设和社会资本效应假设。地位强度假设是指在人际网络中个体的社会地位越高，其获取人际网络中的社会资源的机会也就越多；弱关系强度假设是指在人际网络中个人拥有的异质关系越多，其通过该弱关系获取社会资源的机会也就越多；而社会资本效应假设则是指在人际网络中个人的社会资源越丰富，其社会活动也就越顺利。理性选择理论的提出者科尔曼（James Coleman）将马克·格拉诺维特和林楠等学者的有关人际网络的观点集成到理性选择理论之中，认为，社会资本由社会结构的各个要素构成，嵌入在人际网络的结构之中。为了更好地把握社会资本的内涵，科尔曼对人力资源和社会资本进行了区分。他认为，人力资源与社会资本的区别在于：人力资源是人际网络中的各节点所拥有的各种资源，而社会资本则是存在于连接各节点的线段之中；两者之间的联系在于：社会资本是获取和积累人力资源的途径。在以上分析的基础上科尔曼分析了在个体人际网络中什么样的社会关系才是对个体有用的社会资本。罗纳德·博特于1992年在其著作《结构洞》一书中开创性地提出了人际网络的结构洞理论。他认为个体在人际网络中的社会资源与关系的强弱没有必然的联系，而是与个体在人际网络中所处的位置高度相关。他指出，在人际网络中处于桥位置的个体，其拥有的"结构洞"比较多，处于结构洞上的节点都需要通过他进行联系，因此该节点在该人际网络中拥有的社会资本也就越多。邓肯·瓦茨（Duncan Watts）等学者在对小世界网络的特征进行研究的基础上，提出了网络动力学理论。该理论指出，网络结构对系统的集体动态行为有着重要的影响作用，网络结构的细小变化将会导致系统动态行为的巨大变化。该研究具有重要的意义和价值：该理论首次从动态分析的视角来研究人际网络的结构与集体行为的互动过程。后来，随着网络技术的发展，有关在线人际网络的研究也得到人们重视，并取得大量的研究成果。比较有代表性的作者有安德鲁斯（Dorine C. Andrews）、巴拉布（Sasha A. Barab）等，他们将人际网络的相关理论应用到虚拟社区的设计中，将两者结合起来进行研究。马克·诺艾曼（Marco Neumann）也同样借助人际网络的相关理论对人际网络门户进行了分析，首次提出了"语义人际网络"的概念，并指出语义人际网络将成为第二代人际网络。

近年来，随着人际网络，尤其是在线人际网络的研究的不断深入，人们越来越深刻地认识到人际网络的动态本质，有关动态人际网络的研究逐渐进入人们的视野，并成为当前人际网络研究的一个热点。当前，有关动态人际网络的研究主要从宏观和微观两个方面进行。研究的内容主要集中在人际网络的动态演化过程的分析上。在宏观方面，主要是采用统计力学的方法对动态社会网络进行分析，它将社会网络看做是一个复杂的物理系统，将社会网络中的节点看做是物理系统中的一个粒子，借助统计学方法来揭示社会网络动态演化的宏观规律，这方面的主要代表人物有R. Albert、A. L. Barabasi等学者。在微观方面，主要是借鉴多代理（智能体）系统的思想，将社会网络中的节点看做是具有认知能力的个体，而不是简单地认为是无差别的物理系统中的粒子，通过对个体以及个体之间的交互过程的分析（如博弈分析），来计算各种网络结构出现的可能性，进而实现对动态社会网络演化过程的微观分析。这方面研究的代表人物有K. Carley等学者。

5.2 国内人际网络研究现状

与国外相比,虽然国内有关人际网络的研究相对比较滞后,但也取得了一些让人欣慰的研究成果。归纳起来,国内在人际网络方面的研究成果主要集中在三个方面:国外先进理论的引入、与我国国情相适应的人际网络研究、以国外理论为基础的实证研究。

在国外先进理论的引入方面,国内相关研究主要是介绍国外人际网络研究的动态,引进国外先进的人际网络研究成果。方卫华先后翻译了格拉诺维特的著作《经济社会学的理论日程》和林楠的《建构社会资本的网络理论》,前者较为全面地阐述了弱关系在人际网络中的重要作用;后者主要论述了人际网络社会资本的概念、测量和社会资本模型的构建等问题。后来,中国人民大学信息学院经济科学实验室于2005年翻译并出版了邓肯·瓦茨的《小小世界:有序与无序之间的网络动力学》。接着,上海交大出版社也于2006年出版并发行了琼·沃纳(John Warner)的《人际网络》一书。2007年重庆大学出版社翻译并出版了约翰·斯科特的《社会网络分析法》一书。以上这些引入的研究成果,为起步较晚的国内人际网络的研究提供了重要的参考,在推动国内人际网络的研究方面起到了非常重要的作用。

在与我国国情相适应的人际网络研究方面,我国学者从我国实际情况出发,开展自主研究,探索针对我国国情的人际网络理论。这方面研究的代表学者有费孝通、边燕杰等。他们立足中国社会文化,探索并提出了与中国国情相适应的人际网络理论。如边燕杰通过实证研究,发现强关系理论在中国城市职业流动中具有比弱关系更为重要的作用,这与马克·格拉诺维特的弱关系理论是相悖的,其主要原因就在于我国国情与西方国家不尽相同。此外,丁浩和杨小平等设计并开发了支持人工生命建模的能够模拟社会网络中节点的相互作用关系的平台。以上这些研究成果对于推动我国人际网络研究的深入和人际网络理论的应用具有重要的意义和价值。

在以国外理论为基础的实证研究方面,国内研究主要是根据要验证的人际网络理论,设定研究对象和方法,通过对调查数据的收集和分析达到对理论的科学性和适用性等进行检验的目的。例如国内学者张其仔就通过实证研究检验了范德普尔的社会支持网发现法的科学性和适用性,并探讨了弱关系理论对于非就业领域是否具有同样的适用性等问题。再如，张文宏通过实证研究，在对人际网络不同层次上的社会资本进行分析的基础上，解释了阶层地位对网络结构特征的影响方式和程度。通过研究他发现，阶层地位对网络结构的影响与个人特征无关，而主要是受个人在阶层结构中所占据的位置的影响。此外，贺寨平、罗家德等学者也在该领域做了相应的研究。这些研究成果为促使国外人际网络研究成果在我国的应用提供了重要的帮助和指导。

6 人际情报网络研究现状

6.1 国外研究现状

人际情报网络是应情报工作的需要而构建的人际网络。人际网络与情报工作密不可分，自情报工作开展以来，人们就注意到人际网络在情报工作中的重要作用。但是，在初期，由于人们对人际网络在情报工作中的作用重视不够，因此，虽然很多学者如美国的佩尔兹(Pelz)、安德鲁斯(Andrews)、明茨伯格(Mintzberg)和艾伦(Allen)等都发现人们在获取情报时通常都会先咨询其他人，而不是直接查找情报本身，但他们未能在此基础上做进一步的深入研究。直到20世纪90年代中后期开始，有关人际情报网络的研究才得到重视，并形成了一系列的研究成果。最早将人际网络相关理论和方法引入到竞争情报工作中来的是以艾米·伯杰(Amy Berger)、约翰·普赖斯科特(John E. Prescott)、菲利普·戴维斯(Philip N. Davies)等为代表的学者。此后，他们以及相关领域学者也先后在《竞争情报评论》等杂志上发表了各种有关人际情报网络的研究成果，探讨了人际网络在竞争情报工作中的重要作用、人际情报网络的构建等，一个新的有关人际情报网络的研究领域就此开辟。由于国外有关人际情报网络的研究时间也不是很长，因此，研究成果也相对不多，且较为集中。比较有代表性的研究成果有约翰·普赖斯科特等人出版的《竞争情报：最佳实践过程指南》一书，在该书中他们探讨了人际情报网络的作用、两种主要的类型和五种人际情报网络的构建方法等。此后，奥格斯特·杰克逊(August Jackson)和埃伦·梅勒(Ellen Naylor)等也分别报告了题为《竞争情报视角的社会网络分析》

和《合作情报:超越网络开发竞争情报领导才能以及评估网络效果》的研究成果。

6.2 国内研究现状

在我国,20世纪90年代人际网络的基本原理开始逐渐地被引入到情报研究领域。1998年,包昌火研究员首次提出将人际网络作为竞争情报系统的三大支持网络(人际网络、组织网络、信息网络)之一的构想。随后,于2000年12月,包昌火研究员主持并完成了国家自然科学基金资助的项目:企业竞争情报系统的模式和运行机制研究。与此同时,他完成并出版了《竞争情报解决方法》和《企业竞争情报系统》两本著作。在这两本著作中,他全面系统地提出了建立人机结合、一个中心、六大功能、三大系统、三个网络组成的企业竞争情报系统的构想。再后来,在2001年举办的清华峰会上,国内外学者对有关人际情报网络的研究进展进行了充分的交流,进一步推动了我国对人际情报网络研究的发展。接着,2005年由各相关领域专家参与的我国首届人际情报网络高层研讨会在京召开。这次会议对当时人际情报网络研究的前沿动态:人际情报网络的理念、操作与管理等进行了探讨。例如,包昌火研究员在与会期间作了题为"人是竞争情报活动的灵魂"的报告。此外,其他专家如王康乔和武秋等也分别作了题为"人际情报研究中的几个新趋势"和"人际情报网络在商业竞争中的应用"等的演讲。随后,北京大学秦铁辉教授主持并完成了题为"竞争情报活动中的人际网络研究"的自然科学基金项目,进一步推动了人际情报网络研究的发展。近年来,我国有关人际情报网络的研究也逐渐深入,发表了一系列相关的论文,并从基础理论层面的研究开始向人际情报网络构建、实施等可操作层面迈进。如王秀玲提出的依据业务需求构建人际情报网络的方法,王曰芬等学者提出的基于知识管理的人际情报网络构建的方法,芦方琪和马晓慧提出的基于竞争情报活动流程的人际情报网络构建等。

从国内外人际情报网络研究的现状可以看出,有关人际情报网络的研究主要集中在三个领域:人际情报网络基本理论的研究、人际情报网络分析的应用研究、人际情报网络构建与管理研究。就人际情报网络基本理论的研究而言,包昌火研究员将其概括为三个方面:构成论、资源论和平台论。构成论主要从组成人际情报网络的节点、节点间的联系以及网络结构上来探索人际情报网的性质和功能;资源论主要从社会资本理论、关系强度理论、结构空洞理论等方面来研究人际情报网络的资源属性;平台论主要是将人际情报网络与竞争情报工作的流程结合起来进行研究,探索人际情报网络在竞争情报活动中的平台作用。人际情报网络分析的应用研究概括起来主要体现在两个方面,一是人际情报网络分析方法在对人际情报网络科学有效性和竞争能力的评价方面的应用,以在评价的基础上达到对人际情报网络结构进行优化的目的;二是人际情报网络分析方法在竞争战略与战术情报分析上的应用。人际情报网络构建与管理方面的研究,通常是结合竞争情报系统的建设展开的。这方面的研究成果相对较少,从构建流程上来看,现有的这些人际情报网络构建方法基本上也都遵循了包昌火研究员总结的人际情报网络构建的基本流程:需求分析—确定网络模式—识别网络成员与关键联系—建立联系—网络管理与拓展。

7 展 望

综观人际网络和人际情报网络的国内外发展现状可以发现,当前有关人际情报网络的研究具有以下两个方面的特征:首先,人际情报网络的研究相对落后于人际网络的研究。从人际网络的研究进展可以看出人际网络的研究已经发展到动态的层面,而人际情报网络作为一种特殊的人际网络,当前对它的研究仍停留在静态的层面,有关它的动态特性以及动态演化机理的研究少有人论及;而人际情报网络在本质上又是动态变化的,因此,为深化对人际情报网络的认识,提高人际情报网络研究的科学性,更好地满足企业对人际情报网络的需求,加强对人际情报网络的动态特性及其演化机理的研究势在必行,它必将成为人际情报网络研究的一个发展方向。其次,人际情报网络的研究继承了人际网络研究的成果和传统。与人际网络基本相同,人际情报网络研究的内容和成果也主要集中在网络的基本理论和分析方法上,主要研究了人际情报网络的基本理论和分析方法在竞争情报工作中的应用,而有关人际情报网络构建的研究成果相对较少。而且通过对人际情报网络构建的国内外研究现状的分析,本文发现:当前已有的这些人际情报网络构建方法也仅仅反映了组织某一时刻的人际情报网络的自然状态,没有考虑人际情报网络的动态属性,构建的也往往只是一个"静态人际情报网络"。而人际情报网络的构建作为人际情报网络应用的基础,对于企业来说具有重要的意义和价值,为此,加强对人际情报网络构建的研究,尤其是动态人际情报网络构建的研究将成为人际情报网络研究的又一个难点和重点。

参考文献

[1] 晏创业. 竞争情报活动中的人际网络研究[D]. 北京:北京大学,2005.

[2] 徐登峰. 基于社会网络的集群企业创新机制研究[D]. 天津:天津大学,2010.

[3] 王倩. 社会网络对创业机会识别的影响:信息获取的中介作用[D]. 长春:吉林大学,2011.

[4] 张淑华. 基于人际网络的营销员隐性知识共享路径研究[D]. 沈阳:沈阳师范大学,2011.

[5] 包昌火,李艳,王秀玲,等. 人际情报网络[J]. 情报理论与实践,2006,29(2):129-141.

[6] 包昌火等. 人际网络分析[J]. 情报学报. 2003,22(3):365-374.

[7] 吴晓伟,徐福缘. 基于人际网络节点中心度的竞争对手分析[J]. 情报学报,2006,23(1):121-128.

[8] 胡蓉,邓小昭. 基于结构洞理论的个人人际网络分析系统研究[J]. 情报学报,2005,24(4):485-489.

[9] 艾丹祥,张玉峰. 利用主题图建立概念知识库[J]. 图书情报知识,2004(2):48-50,53.

[10] 丁晟春,李飞,王曰芬等. 竞争情报活动中人际网络构建的一般模型与聚类分析[J]. 情报科学,2008,26(5):712-717.

[11] 吴鹏,李思昆. 社会网络信息的本体论建模与可视化[J]. 计算机辅助设计与图形学学报,2009,21(4):518-525.

[12] 吴淑燕,许涛. 知识管理中的人际网络[J]. 图书情报工作,2003(10):59-63.

[13] 秦铁辉,刘宇,杨薇薇. 竞争情报与人际网络研究述评[J]. 情报科学,2007,25(12):1761-1768.

[14] 秦铁辉,刘宇,仝丽娟. 竞争情报网络中的人际网络研究综述[J]. 情报探索,2007(11):3-6.

[15] 李映洲,王晓冬. 论竞争情报的效用[J]. 兰州大学学报(社会科学版),2003,31(1):126-129.

[16] 庄玮. 竞争情报的效用评估之我见[J]. 情报杂志,2004(6):51-55.

[17] 秦铁辉,吴菁. 基于节点关系的企业人际网络解析[J]. 情报科学,2006,24(12):1761-1765.

[18] 魏勇军. 企业隐性知识线性化的路径分析[J]. 湖南师范大学,2005(4):27-38.

[19] 罗会华.企业知识状态:企业竞争优势的一种理论解析[J].中国软科学,2005(11):125-127.

[20] 李江,和金生,王会良.基于情景管理的隐性知识管理方法研究[J].科学学与科学技术管理,2008(8):77-81.

[21] 秦铁辉,杨薇薇.社会网络视角下的知识管理研究[J].情报科学,2009,27(8):1121-1125.

[22] 翟金金,刘敏榕.竞争情报活动中的人际网络研究综述[J].图书与情报,2007(4):82-84.

[23] 余以胜,张洋,丘均平.知识管理中的人际情报网络研究[J].图书情报工作,2008,52(7):79-83.

[24] 吴才唤.社会网络分析在隐性知识地图构建中的应用[J].图书馆,2010(1):48-51.

[25] 懂智文,张旭.使用人际情报网络解决企业研发中的问题[J].图书情报工作,2008(2):101-104.

[26] 仝丽娟,秦铁辉.试论企业人际情报网络的构建[J].图书情报工作,2009,53(16):69-73.

[27] 秦铁辉,汪琼.试论专家型隐性知识地图的构建[J].国家图书馆学刊,2007(2):58-62.

[28] 张旭,张嵩.隐性知识转移中的社会网络因素研究综述[J].情报杂志,2009,28(12):42-47.

[29] 陈强,廖开际,奚建清.专家知识地图的关键技术与设计[J].计算机工程与科学,2008,30(2):96-114.

[30] 丁晟春,李飞,王曰芬,等.竞争情报活动中人际网络构建的一般模型与聚类分析[J].情报科学,2008,26(5):712-717.

[31] 秦铁辉,周嘉彦.人际情报网络的结构模式研究[J].山东图书馆,2006(4):7-11.

[32] 李文华.企业知识地图构建分析[J].科技咨询,2006(1):117.

[33] 王国弘,陈士俊.企业隐性知识的分类与外化模式研究[J].科学管理研究,2008,26(3):79-82.

[34] 赵超.企业人际情报网络中知识共享障碍及其克服[J].图书情报工作,2007,51(9):37-61.

[35] 任红娟.企业人际情报网络的构建与管理[J].情报科学,2006,24(6):839-842.

[36] 王曰芬,黄加虎,王海丹.竞争情报中的知识流及转化机制研究[J].情报学报,26(3):415-421.

[37] 周朴雄,余以胜,胡昌平.竞争情报系统与人际情报网络关系探讨[J].情报杂志,2008(6):117-119.

[38] 蔡翠盟. 基于知识管理的图书馆人际情报网络构建[J]. 情报探索,2009(7):126-129.

[39] 潘松华. 基于定量分析的竞争情报人际网络研究模式构建[J]. 情报杂志,2008(2):34-36.

[40] 芦方琪,马晓慧. 基于竞争情报活动流程的人际情报网络构建[J]. 晋图学刊,2008(1):35-38.

[41] 辛晴,杨蕙馨. 基于社会网络视角的知识转移研究述评[J]. 图书情报工作,53(14):92-96.

[42] Burt R S. Structural Holes: *The Social Structure of Competition*[M]. Cambridge: Harvard Business School Press,1992.

[43] Krackhardt D. *The Strength of Strong Ties: the Importance of Philos in Networks and Organizations.* See: edited by Nitin Nohria, Robert G. Eccles. Networks and organizations[M]. Cambridge: Harvard Business School Press, 1992:216-241.

[44] Barrett Chris, Hunt Harry Blll, Marathe Madhav V. *Modeling and analyzing social network dynamics using stochastic discrete graphical dynamical systems*[J]. 2011, 412(30):3932-3946.

[45] Zhao Kun, Stehle Juliette, Bianconi Ginestra. *Social network dynamics of face-to-face interactions*[J]. Physical review E, 2011, 83(5):1-18.

[46] Li Qingjun, Cui Wentian, Sun Xiaoming. *A growth model of social network based on individual selection*[J]. Information-aninternational interdisciplinary Journal, 2011,14(2):361-372.

[47] Granovetter M S. *The Strength of Weak Ties*[J]. American Journal of Sociology, 1973(78):1360-1380.

[48] Coleman J. *Social Captial in the Creation of Human Capital*[J]. American Journal of Sociology, 1998:95-120.

[49] Brian skyrms, Robin Pemantle. *a dynamic model of social network formation*[J]. PNAS, 2000, 97(16):9340-9346.

[50] Tanya Y. Berger-wolf, Jared Saia. *A framework for analysis of dynamic social networks.* In Proc. KDD'06, 2006:523-528.

[51] A.-L. Barabasi, R. Albert. *Emergence of Scaling in Random Networks*[J]. Science, 1999,286:509-512.

[52] A, Parker, L. Prusak, S. Borgatti. *Knowing what we know: Supporting knowledge creation and sharing in social networks*[J]. Organ, Dynam, 2001, 3(2):100-120.

[53] Gao, L., Liu, J., Zhang,S., Yang, J. *Discovering the Dynamics in a Social Memory Network.* 2008 IEEE/WIC/ACM *International Conference on Web Intelligence and Intelligent Agent Technology*, 2008:200-2003.

[54] Yang, B., Liu, J. *Discobering global network communities based on local centralities* [J]. ACM Transactions on the web, 2008, 2(1): 1-32.

[55] Carmi, S., Cohen, R., Dolev, D. *Searching Complex Networks Efficiently With Minimal Information* [J]. Europhys. Lett., 2006, 74(6): 1102-1108.

[56] Holme, P. *Efficient local Strategies For Vaccination and Network Attack* [J]. Europhys. Lett., 2004, 68(6): 908-914.

[57] Davidsen J, Ebel H, Bornholdt S. *Emergence of a small world from local interactions, modeling acquaintance networks* [J]. Physical Review Letters, 2002, 88(18): 128-151.

[58] Zhang S, Liu J. *Autonomy-orinented social networks modeling: discovering the dynamics of emergent structure and performance* [J]. International Journal of Pattern Recognition and Artificial Intelligence, 2007, 21(4): 611-638.

[59] Huberman B A, Ledyard J O. *Information dynamics in the networked world* [J]. Information Systems Frontiers, 2003, 5(1): 7-8.

[60] Kuperman M, Abramson G. *Small world effect in an epidemiological model* [J]. Phys Rev Lett, 2001, 86(13): 2909-2912.

[61] Newman M E J. *The structure and function of complex networks* [J]. SIAM Reriew. 2003, 45(2): 167-256.

[62] Roopnarine P D. *Extinction cascades and catastrophe in ancient food webs* [J]. Paleobiology, 2006, 32(1): 1-19.

[63] Valdis E. Krebs. *Mapping Networks of Terrorist Cells* [J]. Connections, 2002, 24(3): 43-52.

[64] Peter D. Hoff, Adrian E. Raftery, Mark S. Handcock. *Latent space approaches to social network analysis* [J]. Journal of American Statistical Association. 2002, 97(460): 1090-1098

[65] Peter D. Hoff, Michael D. Ward. *Modeling dependencies in international relations networks.* Political Analysis, 2004, 12(2): 160-175.

[66] Valdis E. Krebs. *Mapping networks of terrorist cells* [J]. Connections, 2002, 24(3): 43-52.

[67] Prunamrita Sarkar, Andrew W. Moore. *Dynamic social networks analysis using latent space models* [J]. ACM SIGKDD Explorations, 2005, 2(2): 31-40.

[68] Koka. B. R, Madhavan Ravindranath, Prescott. J. E. *The evolution of interfirm networks: Environmental Effects on Patterns of Network Change* [J]. Academy of Management Review (USA), 2006, 31(3): 721-738.

[69] Kristien Van Laere, Aime Heene. *Social networks as a source of competitive advantage for the firm* [J]. Journal of Workplace Learning, 2003, 15(6): 248-258.

[70] Jose Maria Viedma Marti. *Social capital bench marking system: Profiting from social capital when building network organizations* [J]. Journal of Intelectual Capital 2004, 5(3):426-442.

[71] Jay Liebowitz. *Linking social network analysis with the analytic hierarchy process for knowledge mapping in organizations* [J]. Journal of knowledge Management. 2005,9(1):76-86.

[72] Min Jun-Ki, Cho Sung-Bae. *Mobile Human Network Management and Recommendation by Probabilistic Social Mining* [J]. IEEE Transactions on Systems Man and Cybernetics Part B-Cybernetics, 2011, 41(3):761-771.

[73] Huett Alan, Ng Aylwin, Cao Zhifang et al. *A Novel Hybrid Yeast-human Network Analysis Reveals an Essential Role for FNBP1L in Antibacterial Autophagy* [J]. Journal of Immunology, 2009, 182(8):4917-4930.

[74] Tanimoto J, Fujii H. *A study on diffusional characteristics of information on a human network analyzed by a Multi-Agent Simulator* [J]. 2003, 40(3):479-485.

[75] Demchenko Oleg. *Social Network and Occupational Mobility: A Mathematical Model* [J]. Social Science Quarterly, 2011, 92(4): 1118-1132.

[76] Miller Greg. *The Brain's Social Network* [J]. Science, 2011, 334(6056):578-579.

[77] Stoykova Ralitsa, Matharan Fanny, Dartigues Jean-Francois. *Impact of social network on cognitive performances and age-related cognitive decline across a 20-year follow-up* [J]. International Psychogeriatrics, 2011, 23(9):1405-1412.

[78] Kim Sungjin, Suh Euiho, Jun Youngjoon. *Building a Knowledge Brokering System Using Social Network analysis: A Case Strudy of the Korean Financial Industry* [J]. Expert Systems With Applications, 2011, 38(12): 14633-14649.

Technological Innovation and Scenario Analysis seen from Competitive technical Intelligence

Yoshio Sugasawa[①]   Fumiyuki Takahashi[②]

Abstract

Competitive Technical Intelligence (CTI) is an important driver for enterprise competition, playing a signification role in technological innovation. This research focuses on 1) the role of CTI, 2) the analysis of product life cycle through a case study of radio controlled watches and 3) scenario planning using case study of the Japanese broadband service.

This paper introduces the discontinuous strategy observed from CTI to encourage research and development (R&D) and innovation. This paper also emphasizes the importance of CTI in new product and technology development.

Keywords

Technological Innovation, Technology Mature, R&D, Competitive Technical Intelligence, Product Life Cycle, Scenario Analysis, Discontinuous Strategy

Introduction

Due to globalization and intense market competition, the business environment is changing rapidly, due to numerous technological innovations and the shortening of the product life cycle. When a mature market is filled with competitors using the same technology, technological innovation is necessary to generate larger profits.

---

① Graduate School of Japan University of Economics, Tokyo, Japan, sugasawa@tk.jue.ac.jp
② Japan University of Economics, Tokyo, Japan, taka@tk.jue.ac.jp

Unfortunately, innovation does not happen at the snap of a finger. Innovation demands detailed coordination of adequate technical knowledge and excellent market judgment.

In the development of a new product or new technology, management must evaluate the discontinuous technological development apart from the saturated market. Competitive Technical Intelligence is playing a significant role in technology innovation. It is important to consider the Product Life Cycle (PLC) and to ensure the state of technology maturity. In addition, given the future of the market condition is unknown. We need to conduct a scenario analysis.

This paper will describe the role of CTI in technological innovation and discuss in detail the role of CTI in each PLC stage. Afterwards, we will look at two case studies, one on PLC analysis and another scenario analysis.

1　TWO IMPORTANT TOPICS IN CTI

Competitive technical intelligence [1], or Technology Intelligence (TI) [2],[3], as a subset of Competitive Intelligence (CI) [4], is the process of collecting and analyzing information related to products and technology of competing firms. It plays an effective role in avoiding threats from competing firms or avoiding premature technology investments.

There are two important Topics in CTI. The first topic is that the future can be foreseen. If management could foresee the future, they would know the precise product development strategy. However, since the future is unpredictable, management can forecast the future by technology forecasting and technology scouting. Management can know the business, the customer, the supply chain or the technology in the present and the future by competitive analysis.

The second topic is innovation. When CTI is employed, the possibility of innovation increases. The key is how to arrange the information. A company may use CTI to collect, analyze and evaluate information on the technology needed to enhance competitiveness. It is important, of course, for the company to take action based on the results of the analysis. CTI can be used as a source of intelligence to develop better technology.

2 ROLE OF CTI IN TECHNOLOGICAL INNOVATION

In this section we will discuss how to encourage innovation, especially how intelligence is generated from superior information.

Creativity is the new combination of existing elements. Innovation is a new combination that adds value. Schumpeter describes innovation as a "creative destruction" [5] and defines five different kinds of innovation. Figure 1 is one of the most important technical innovation models constructed by Myers & Marquis. [6] This concept is very easy to understand. The model addresses the needs and technology, how they generate new ideas and turn this idea into a commercialized product.

For instance, regarding information on technology and customers' needs, information is collected and arranged by order of important. As a result, a new technology may emerge to meet customers' needs. It is extremely important to understand the concept and process of CTI before collecting, analyzing, and evaluating the information.

Understanding the necessary of technological innovation is the first step for an enterprise to enhance its innovative ability. Technological innovation such as disruptive innovation defined by Christensen [7] based on the market needs and driven by advanced technology is designed to improve enterprise performance and enhance en-

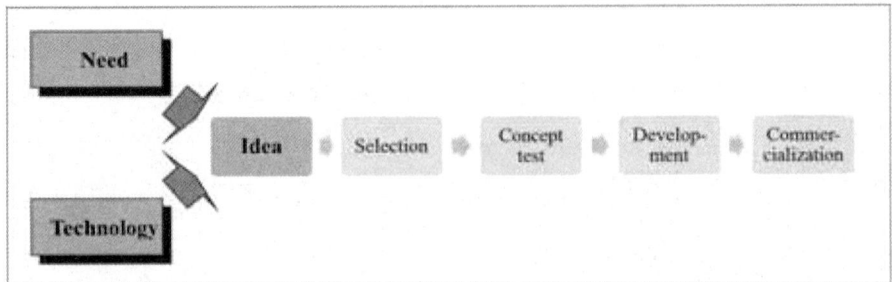

Figure 1. Successful Industrial Innovation model, Adapted from Myers and Marquis, 1969

terprise competitiveness. The role of CTI is to identify the needs and the technology to meet those needs. Thus, this CTI process leads the birth of new ideas.

3 DISCONTINUOUS DEVELOPMENT IN MATURE MARKET AND INNOVATION

Most pricing strategies for product and technology are formulated and implemented in mature markets. Innovation is most likely to occur in a mature market. [8]

When products in the market have matured and profitability falls to a certain level, it is very important to find the next area of new development and enter the new market quickly. CTI is useful in analyzing the state of products of product maturity and industry maturity.

Understanding the present state of PLC can improve the efficiency of R&D. It is important to consider the PLC of a new technology which may appear in the discontinuous curve.

3.1 Product Life Cycle

Using a biological analogy, the PLC describes the evolution of sales as a function of time. This model asserts that, similar to all living organisms, a product pass through four stages: Introduction, Growth, Mature and Decline stages. PLC describes the product in terms of its business/commercial costs and sales. There are four main stages of a product's life cycle, each stage specific characteristics. However it is difficult for marketing management to accurately identify where a product is located on its PLC graph.

3.2 Technology Maturity

Most new technologies follow a similar technology maturity lifecycle. The technology maturity lifecycle differs from a product life cycle, and applies to an entire technology or a generation of a technology. Technology adoption typically occurs in an S-curve. Depending on whether technology is in its emerging, growing, or maturity stage, the sort of management challenges varies significantly. The importance of understanding technology maturity cannot be underestimated. It is possible to construct S – curves for the technologies under examination. It is more important to understand how mature the technology is, and then to explore the management implications.

The relative level of technology maturity is only part of the technical intelligence required. Where is the owned company? Where is the rival? When does the technology mature? Or, are there choices of technology? Is there a superior new technology? When will the new technology be commercialized? How fast is the technology evolving and who is driving the technology evolution?

If the market switches to a new technology prematurely, investing in new technology is only a waste of money. It is important for management to make the right decisions and switch to new technology at the right time. Failure to foresee these changes may lead to serious mistakes. Figure 2 illustrates the key topics of technology intelligence.

3.3 Role and importance of CTI corresponding to each stage of PLC

Since the business environment changes rapidly, the construction of the intelligence framework plays an important role in each stage of PLC. For the enterprise,

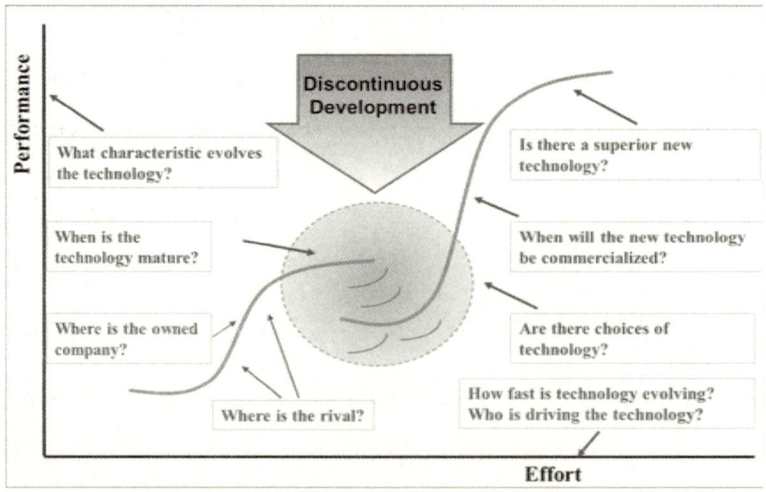

Figure 2. CTI Topics on Technology Mature

Table 1. Major problems concerning CI at each PLC stages

Emerging stage
Who is the rival in a new market?
What is the rival's strong point and weakness?
When did this rival gain access to the market?
What should we do to prepare for rival entry? (SWOT analysis)
Is the rival from other industries or a foreign country?
Is the phase of competition predictable? (Market analysis)
If we introduce a new product, how can we manage it?
Can we become a pioneer? Why?
How will the competition be affected if we don't introduce this product?
What is our dominant market share?
What is the cost of becoming the pioneer of the next new product? (Competitive market and external marketing analysis)
Will there be an increase of market-share if our product is improved? (Strategic product improvement)
Is there a clear market forecast?
Is this market clearly defined? (Market forecasting)
What long-term view do we have for the market? (Definition of market)

Growth and Maturity stage
Is the change induced by customer preferences or revision in rival's strategy?
Are there changes with the competition? (Intensification of shape, the amount or the competition) seen at stages of growth? (Market scanning)
How has competition changed the makeup of the industry?
Which strategy is the rival using to increase market share? (Growth measure and competitive analysis)
Is there a substitute for the product in the market? Is there a way to expand the market? (Extra-market assessments)
Growth potential of the market (Length and depth at period) (Market forecasting)
Is the new rival a threat?
How do you identify the rival from another industry?
Does an alternate industry introduce new threats? The possibility of the entry and time? (SWOT and market scanning)
What positioning policy does a strong rival adopt in this stable market?
What is the strategy to maximize profit during times of market stability?
What is an effective strategy that intimidates rivals? (Market monitoring, SWOT and progressing of strategy)
Does its enterprise have enough information on market circumstance?
How is collected information used for the future market and a new product? (System that evaluates study in enterprise)
Until when does such a stability period continue?
How should we respond to an too early decline of the market? (Market forecasting, Evaluation for positioning of the market)
How is its own domination positioned in the decline stage?
How is sales at this stage secured? (Strategic positioning)
Does it search for the new market, and is the preparation for the future market completed?
Do we pay attention to information sent from the market? (Market forecasting and strategic planning)

Decline stage
In the absence of sustainable profits, how long should we remain in this market?
Should we remain in this market? Should we withdraw? (Market forecasting, Rate of profit and evaluation for comparison)
Does it have the vision needed to be going to recognize the market in the future?
Can we prepare for the competitive market in the future?
Does the rival withdraw from the market? Why do they withdraw? Why do not they withdraw?
Does rival move on to another industry? Why?
Is there an enterprise that plays the role as the leader? What kind of enterprise is it? (Market insight, Positioning and market scanning)
How much market share can we obtain? Do we connect with the market of the future?
Are there existing parts that can be applied to another product and the market?
Can the product be reused for other markets after modifications or in a new application? (Experimental curve, Reconfirmation and evaluation in enterprise)

forecasting or predicting the future and catching the trend promptly and accurately are very important.

During the initial stage of market introduction, the role of CTI is to identify and monitor potential competitors. It is necessary to identify alternate products and rival enterprises accurately. Once potential competition is identified, strategic planning is needed to assess the situation and to implement appropriate strategies.

During the advanced stages of growth and maturity, competitive threats may change in quantity and/or quality. During the growth stage, it is important for the enterprise to make certain adjustments. For example, if it is facing severe competition, it must restructure its marketing strategy.

During the seemingly inevitable decline stage, the CI professional will need to prolong profitability and to prevent as much market loss as possible. As a product life cycle draws to a close, the profit period can be extended by using alternate products or exploring new markets. CI practitioners can gather the acquired market knowledge. These can be useful in future markets.

In summary, the role of the CI is to gather, analyze, and disseminate intelligence. The intelligence helps the enterprise to maintain its competitive advantage throughout all stages of the product life cycle. Gleaning from our practical experience, the major CI problems at each PLC stages are shown in table 1.

3.4 Case Study on PLC Analysis of CASIO Radio Controlled Watches

As an example of the PLC in application, we will discuss the case of Casio watches.

Since its establishment in 1957, Casio Computer Co., Ltd., made "Creativity and Contribution" its mission. In fiscal year 2003, Casio promoted and developed three strategic businesses: timepieces, digital cameras, and Mobile Network Solutions (MNS). MNS includes electronic dictionaries, and TFT LCDs as strategic businesses. The Company continues to strengthen its management structure to expand business through innovative products and to maintain stable, long – term profitability.

From the historical perspective, timepiece technology evolved from sundials to mechanicals, from mechanicals to quartz, and from quartz to digital watches. Casio's radio controlled watches are the most accurate watches in the world. These watches can catch radio waves from a transmitting station and display accurate time.

However, a radio controlled watch is effective only in the area where it can receive a time calibration signal. The infrastructure is essential to this technology. The infrastructure was made available nationwide in 2001 in Japan. The infrastructure was also available in Germany and the United States, so the radio controlled wristwatches are sold in these two markets as well. In 2003, 1.5 million units of Radio Controlled watches were sold. In fiscal 2003, the global economic environment remained challenging. Casio was leveraging on its core technology to develop unique products.

The line of popular G – Shock watches is in a class by itself. The G – Shock has high shock resistance and its wave functions are solar powered. So what is the PLC stage of Radio Controlled watches? Does an alternative product exist? Should the company continue to focus on Radio Controlled watches?

As per the PLC analysis performed in 2004, the growth stage of radio controlled watches was predicted on the PLC curve. (Ref. Figure 3) The market share is expected to increase in the future. There was an industry rumor that there would be a reformation of the quartz product. Despite these rumors, the company continued to incorporate cutting – edge technologies into the radio controlled watches in 2004. To further expand this market and offer a wider product selection, the company is currently developing all – metal and multi – band models. Additionally the company made plans to increase the sales of women's watches as well. Besides Japan, data transmissions are also available in other areas, such as the U.S., Europe, and China in the near future.

At the end of 2006, Casio claimed the No. 1 worldwide market share in these markets by launching competitive radio controlled watches. As a result of these ef-

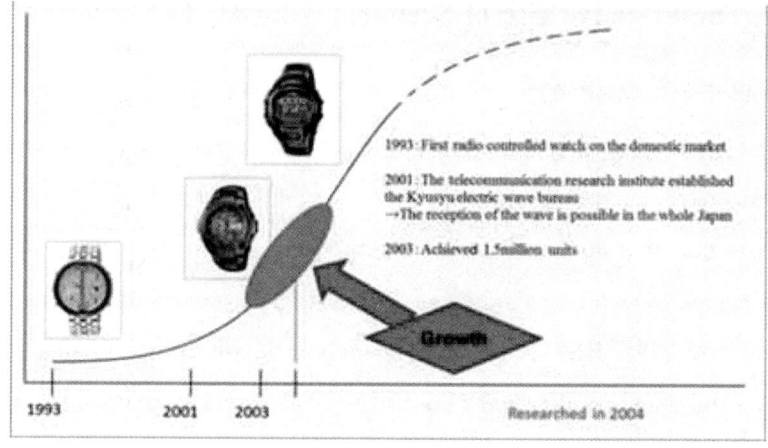

Figure 3. PLC (S Curve) Analysis on Casio Radio controlled Watches (2004)

forts, the Company achieved sales of 2.5 million unites of radio controlled watches sales, with 45% net sales among a total of 33 million unit watches showed in figure 4.[9]

Figure 4. Radio Controlled Watches Sales Volume in(2006)

4 MAKING SCENARIO OF STRATEGIC DEVELOPMENT

The purpose of R&D is to enhance a company's products and services. This means improvements to current products or the introduction of completely new products. Good R&D is necessary to meet customer needs. A scenario analysis allows diverse stakeholders to explore the uncertainties involved in an open way. Ultimately, it can provide exciting new insight, deepen the shared understanding of R&D decision – making, and build cross organizational relationships.

4.1 The Effective Use of Scenario Analysis to Support R&D

A scenario is a detailed, internally consistent description of what the future may look like. It is based on a set of assumptions that are critical for the evolution of the economy, industry, or technology.

Scenario planning and analysis are a structured way of developing multiple scenarios that compensate for two common decision – making errors. Scenario analysis can enhance and guide R&D efforts by engaging a broader range of stakeholders and leveraging on their experience and knowledge. This creates divergent scenarios that highlight future risks and opportunities. It also provides an approach to evaluate existing and potential strategies in an uncertain world. This analysis makes uses of approaches that define and project several alternative futures. [10] Ultimately, scenario analysis can enrich an organization's ongoing strategic conversation about the purpose and value of forward – looking research, development, and innovation.

The first step of the scenario analysis is to understand the company's strategy, organizational positioning, vision and corporate culture. Otherwise, it will be an unrealistic projection, or it will have no effect. In developing scenarios, it is useful to establish the framework by isolating two highly uncertain but very important variables create a large impact in the final analysis.

During the past few years, we had conducted CTI researches on several companies. Scenario analysis was conducted on their R&D plans over the medium to long – term (generally 5 to 10 year timeframes). Based on our experience, we have identified a number of best practices that produce the most useful results. The following is one of analysis results on Japan Optical broadband service industry done in 2004.

4.2 Case study on Japanese Optical Broadband Service Industry

The Japanese government has set up a goal to "become the world's most advanced IT nation" by 2005, according to the e – Japan Strategy formulated in January 2001. So far, some goals have been achieved, such as the provision of low cost broadband services and optical fiber services, and being the leader in the mobile communications field such as mobile Internet. According to the 2003 White Paper on Telecommunications published by the Ministry of Public Management, Home Affairs, Posts and Telecommunications, the population of Internet users in Japan at the end of 2002 was estimated to be 69.4 million. This was an increase of 13.5 million (or 24%) over the previous year. The Internet saturation rate stood at 54.5%, exceeding half of the population for the first time. Moreover, the shift from narrowband to broadband continues to increase.

In the study completed in 2004, we made market survey for the Japanese broadband services (FTTH, ADSL, Cable, Mobile phone). We analyzed the marketing activities and strategies, especially for the three major optical broadband access carriers (NTT, TEPC, USEN) in Kanto area, Japan. A Scenario of broadband service industry was analyzed.

According to scenario construction process, the STEEP (Social, Technological, Economic, Ecological, Political) analysis is first conducted to evaluate external factors affecting the business. The scenario approaches are included in table 2. The final scenario is exhibited in table 3. This scenario approach is facilitates broadband companies' decision – making for R&D and business strategies.

5 Summary

This paper describes the role of CTI in technological innovation, especially in each PLC stages through PLC analysis. It also ensures technology maturity for the discontinuous technological development. In addition, it describes the content of CTI in scenario planning. In conclusion it presented the discontinuous strategy observed from CTI using two case studies. It is our hope that these case studies will encourage further research and development and new innovation ideas.

CTI analysts have impressive tools for R&D decision – making support. Areas that warrant further research include technology scouting and monitoring to seek weak signal of emerging technology.

Table 2. Scenario Space Analysis in Broadband Service Industry

	Name of scenario	Possibility	Optical fiber liberating obligation of NTT		Appearance of application that can be done only because of optical		Spread of super-high-speed wireless access technology	
			Obligation	Non obligation	Appear	Not appear	Spread	Not spread
1	Only NTT is a victory.	Y		●	●			●
2		Y	●		●			●
3	The competition intensifies by the entry of many telecommunications providers	Y	●		●			●
4	Oligopoly of 3 companies	Y		●	●			●
		Y		●		●		●
5	Age of wireless	Y	●		●		●	
		Y	●			●	●	
		Y			●	●	●	
		Y		●		●	●	

Table 3. Extracted Scenarios of Broadband Service Industry

Scenario 1: Only NTT is a Winner
NTT makes use of the fiber and the brand power of independence. The FTTH market is monopolized
Scenario 2: Because a lot of entrepreneurs enter, it becomes a severe competition.
Liberating the optical fiber that NTT owns is required. Consequently becomes competitive, and price competition occurs.
Scenario 3: It becomes monopoly by 3 companies
As a result, the 3 optical fiber construction traders form an oligopoly. (NTT, TEPCO, USEN)
Scenario 4: Age of wireless
A wireless technology that enables a super-rapid access at the optical fiber level is developed. Wireless technology dominates the market and the optical fiber and ADSL are disappears.

REFERENCES

[1] Coburn, M. M. 1999. *Competitive Technical Intelligence, A Guide to Design, Analysis and Action*, Oxford University Press.

[2] Lichtenthaler, E. 2003. *Third generation management of technology intelligence processes*, R&D Management, Vol. 33, No. 4, pp. 361-375.

[3] Savioz, P. 2004. *Technology Intelligence: Concept Design and Implementation in Technology Based SMEs*, Hampshire, UK: Palgrave Macmillan.

[4] Prescott, J. and Miller, S. H. 2001. *Proven strategies in competitive intelligence lesson from the trenches*, Society of Competitive Intelligence Professionals (SCIP), John Wiley & Sons, Inc.

[5] Schumpeter, J. 1992. *Capitalism, Socialism and Democracy*, contributors, p81, Routledge, London.

[6] Sumner Myers and Donald G. 1969. *Marquis, Successful industrial innovations*, National Science Foundation.

[7] Clayton Christensen, 1997. *The Innovator's Dilemma: When New Technologies Cause Great Firms to Fail*, Boston, MA: Harvard Business Press.

[8] Y. Sugasawa, A. Okamura. 2010. *Technical Marketing and Intelligence*, Corona.

[9] *CASIO Corporate Report*. 2003-2006.

[10] Coates, J. F. 2000. *Scenario planning, Technological Forecasting and Social Change*, V65, pp. 115-123.

[11] Fleisher, Craig S. Bensoussan, Babette. 2003. *Strategy and Competitive Analysis: Methods and Techniques for Analyzing Business Competition*, Pearson Prentice Hall.

[12] Fleisher, Craig S. 2010. *The Tools CTI Analysts Use: An Overview*, Competitive Technical Intelligence, pp. 113-124.

Evaluation and Selection of Competitive Intelligence Software

陶庆久(Qingjiu Tao)[①]

Abstract

Competitive Intelligence Software is a critical part of any firm's CI function. This paper attempts to provide a practical approach to evaluate CI software packages and help CI practitioners select the appropriate package for their specific needs. A tool has been developed to combine qualitative and quantitative approaches to evaluate capabilities of CI software along the entire CI process/intelligence cycle.

Keywords

Competitive intelligence software, Evaluation and selection, CI process

Introduction

Competitive Intelligence software serves an important role in the intelligence cycle and provides much needed support in resource acquisition, storage, analysis and dissemination processes. It frees up precious time of CI practitioners and provides a platform for them. The current generation of CI software has made great progress in secondary source acquisition, especially through web. However, the shortage in intelligence analysis still leaves much to be desired. This paper tries to identify the roles CI software can play in the intelligence cycle and provides suggestions on how to evaluate and select appropriate software to enhance CI function in modern firms.

---

① 陶庆久, Ph. D., College of Business, James Madison University, Harrisonburg, VA 22801, U.S.A.

1 CI process—The Intelligence Cycle

To evaluate the effectiveness of different CI software, we need to develop a framework that incorporates the entire CI process/the intelligence cycle, see Figure 1. We will then discuss how different software fare against each other in each stage of the entire intelligence cycle.

The overarching process in CI is the intelligence cycle. It is an iterative process that begins with identifying key topics that are at the heart of the decision – maker's intelligence request. Collection identifies the best available research to support the project, and outlines how to gather the raw data. The available data is then organized to form a coherent basis for analysis. The team then analyzes the data using a variety of methods, striving to present an insightful and value – added view into market and competitive environmental conditions, as befits the initial intelligence request. The analyzed information is then packaged according to the decision – maker's needs, and is delivered for review. Throughout this process, the CI team engages the decision – maker for both feedback and to identify new questions that the group's deliverable may have generated. New key topics are then identified, and the process is off on another cycle. It is important that the decision – maker be engaged throughout the cycle to ensure that the project remains both on track and in synch with the original request. Using the cycle's discrete steps is a great start to building a simplified

Information Technologies Used in CI process and the Developmental Stages of a CI Function

Figure 1. CI process and the Intelligence Cycle

framework for identifying and evaluating where technology can have significant impact. [See Figure 1.]

The advance of information technology has provided CI practitioners a wide range of techniques and tools along the entire CI process/intelligence cycle (see table 1). We are now well equipped with modern means of project management, data acquisition, information organization, basic intelligence analysis, intelligence dissemination. Information technology has freed up large amount of time for CI practitioners and enable them to accomplish much more than they could ever before the readily available information technology. Among all the software packages developed for business professionals, vast majority of them are intended for Business Intelligence rather than Competitive Intelligence purposes. We define CI software as those packages that cover at least two stages of the CI process/intelligence cycle and were developed with CI usage at the very beginning.

Table 1. Information Technologies and CI process

CI Process	Technology
Planning and request	Project management
Collection of Information	Profiling/push technology, filtering/intelligence agent technology, web searching, project management
Data Organization, Storage and retrieval	Document and content management, text discovering, text analyzing and structuring, analyzing and reporting data, BI and e – business applications
Intelligence Analysis and CI product development	Text summarizing, text/graph analyzing and structuring, visualizing data, analyzing and reporting data
Dissemination	Groupware, Multipurpose portals, information services/vendors

2 The functions and limits of CI Software

Before we get to evaluating and selection of CI software, we need to be aware of the functions and limits of all the CI software on market today and talk about some common myths regarding CI software among CI practitioners. While CI software has made significant progress over time in terms of helping practitioners improve their efficiency and effectiveness in CI process, it still cannot replace a seasoned analyst in analyzing all the pieces of information/data and turn them into actionable intelligence. In the following section we will discuss several wide – spread myths about CI software.

1. Software or software package is not Competitive Intelligence

Some people think a firm's CI function should be constructed around their CI software/platform. This notion will lead to an over emphasize on information technology and deviate from the core function of intelligence.

2. Search engine is not Competitive Intelligence, web search is critical but far from complete

Many new practitioners of CI think a good search engine with great web search capability will lead to successful CI operation (Rocker and Roncaglia, 2002). This can't be further from the truth. While more and more information and data are available on the web; it is still critical to rely on human intelligence and primary sources to acquire/verify the most important pieces of the puzzle.

3. What software does well and where it is still weak

Current generation of CI software has come a long way in secondary information search, data organization, visualization of data relationship, as well as dissemination of intelligence products. However, it still lacks in ability to develop strategic insights from integrating industry experience, knowledge, multiple sources of data, business intuition like a established analyst.

4. Software capability is just part of the whole picture

Successful implementation of a CI software system requires more than just identifying its capabilities at each different stage of the CI process/intelligence cycle. We need to check its level of customizability, training provided, maintenance cost, client acceptance, etc.

3 The most commonly used CI software

Based on our definition of CI software packages, we listed eight developers and provided some brief information about these firms in table 2. Furthermore, we listed more CI software packages in use and their different functionalities in table 3 for reference.

Table 2. Brief description of prominent CI software packages

Software	Vendor	Web address	Product description
Knowledge Works`	Cipher Systems, U.S.	www.cipher-sys.com	Supports entire CI process
Strategy!	Strategy Software, U.S.	www.strategysoftware.com	Enterprise CI system, strong in analysis
Viva Intelligence Portal	Viva Business Intelligence, Finland	www.vivaintelligence.com	CI solution based on web environment
Wincite	Wincite systems, U.S.	www.wincite.com	Intelligence portal
Wisdom Builder	Wisdom Builder, U.S.	www.wisdombuilder.com	Comprehensive analysis and report
Digimind	Digimind, U.S.	www.digimind.com	CI management platform
Autonomy	Autonomy, U.S.	www.autonomy.com.cn	Meaning based solutions
TRS	TRS, China	www.trs.com.cn	Enterprise CI system

Table 3. CI software packages and their key functions

Software	CI Tool	Content Analysis	Visualization	ERP	ASP	Customization	Market Intelligence
Autonomy		X					
Biz360		X	X		X	X	X
Brimstone	X	X		X			
Cipher	X	X	X	X	X	X	X
Clear Forest		X	X				
Coemergence	X	X				X	X
Comintell	X			X			
Cymfony		X	X		X		X
FirstRain	X	X			X		
Intelliseek	X	X					X
Netro-City	X		X				
Strategy Software	X						
Wincite	X						

Source: Fuld& Company 2008–2009.

4 Evaluating and Selecting CI Software

Evaluating and selecting a CI software package for one's organization can be a very challenging job. It should typically involve the following 9 steps (Cipher, 2010).

1. Define strategic objectives and targets

Ask yourself what are the most important objectives you plan to achieve with the help of CI software package and define explicit target in terms of efficiency improvement, productivity gain, faster response to client requests, etc.

2. Determine timeline and milestones

When do you need the package? How are you planning to incorporate it into your daily work? Who will be involved in the implementation?

3. Define technical requirements and weight on different dimensions.

Be very specific in your technical requirement when you talk to different vendors. Do you need to install/host everything in house? Or you are planning to utilize the cloud service some vendors can offer? Develop your specific weight system for different dimension of the CI process and use it to calculate total score for each package.

4. Define expected outcomes/deliverables

What will be your desired CI output/products? How do you plan to communicate/disseminate your products to your potential clients?

5. Compare current CI practice and expected future practices

Conduct a systematic survey of your current CI process within your organization and determine what aspects need to be sustained and what aspects should be replaced by the software and how to integrate them together well.

6. Define security requirement

Security requirement is always critical for CI related processes in any organization. Determine who will have access to what content at what time. Determine what content/part of the process need to be kept inside the organization and what part/capability can be placed via cloud computing.

7. Define user interface requirements

How user-friendly should the interface be? Do your clients ask for or prefer certain means of communication? Should the system allow customization of different views?

8. Demo sessions

Ask for a software demo and try to invite key potential clients sit through the session. Also walk through the software evaluation tool (table 4) with salesman from the vendor.

9. Biding process

It is also very important to invite multiple independent vendor to the final bidding. This will give you great leverage in asking for more customization for your specific needs and lower overall cost.

The most critical step in selecting a CI software for one's CI function is to develop a framework/tool to compare different packages before the final purchase decision.

Primarily based on Bouthillier and Shearer's pioneering work (2003, see table 2), we further developed a framework for CI software evaluation and selection. The framework covers all 5 stages of the CI process/intelligence cycle and assesses important aspects of the software capability in fulfilling different tasks in hand. A CI practitioner can use this tool to evaluate and compare different software packages and develop a total score for each package based on predetermined weighting system for his/her firm. The first column covers critical questions to ask in assessing the capabilities; the second column is used to record if a specific software has or has not that capability; the third column is used to quantify the degree of effectiveness of the capability if it is available. Bouthiller and Shearer's model used the second column to tally the number of yes and no in a software package and then used the total number to compare and contrast all the available packages. We think it is critical to go further and evaluate the actual effectiveness of each capability; otherwise, practitioners/buyers would not be able to really evaluate different packages quantitatively.

Table 4. A framework for CI software evaluation and selection

Planning and request (P)	Evaluation		Score Subtotal
1. Does the software help to identify CI clients within the organization?	Yes	No	0 1 2 3 4 5 6 7 8 9 10
2. Does the software help to identify key intelligence topics?	Yes	No	0 1 2 3 4 5 6 7 8 9 10
3. Does the software help to identify information sources?	Yes	No	0 1 2 3 4 5 6 7 8 9 10
4. Does the software help to identify/recommend analysis tools?	Yes	No	0 1 2 3 4 5 6 7 8 9 10
5. Can KITs and tools be changed?	Yes	No	0 1 2 3 4 5 6 7 8 9 10
6. Does the software have CI project management capability?	Yes	No	0 1 2 3 4 5 6 7 8 9 10

Collection of Information (C)	Evaluation		Score Subtotal
1. Does the software help to identify external information sources?	Yes	No	0 1 2 3 4 5 6 7 8 9 10
2. Does the software help to identify internal information sources?	Yes	No	0 1 2 3 4 5 6 7 8 9 10
3. Does the software relate information sources with specific topics?	Yes	No	0 1 2 3 4 5 6 7 8 9 10
4. Does the software have the capability to monitor content changes within information sources?	Yes	No	0 1 2 3 4 5 6 7 8 9 10
5. Does the software have the capability to monitor changes regarding information sources?	Yes	No	0 1 2 3 4 5 6 7 8 9 10
6. Does the software have the capability to find specific pieces of information in particular sources?	Yes	No	0 1 2 3 4 5 6 7 8 9 10
7. Does the software Have the capability to filter information to meet minimum CI needs?	Yes	No	0 1 2 3 4 5 6 7 8 9 10
8. Does the software Have the capability to import information in different formats?	Yes	No	0 1 2 3 4 5 6 7 8 9 10
9. Does the software Have the capability to import information in different formats?	Yes	No	0 1 2 3 4 5 6 7 8 9 10

Data Organization, Storage and Retrieval (S)	Evaluation		Score Subtotal
1. Does the software offer an indexing function?	Yes	No	0 1 2 3 4 5 6 7 8 9 10
2. Does the software allow for hierarchical linking?	Yes	No	0 1 2 3 4 5 6 7 8 9 10
3. Does the software allow for cross – topic linking?	Yes	No	0 1 2 3 4 5 6 7 8 9 10
4. Does the software store a variety of formats?	Yes	No	0 1 2 3 4 5 6 7 8 9 10
5. Does the software store a variety of formats?	Yes	No	0 1 2 3 4 5 6 7 8 9 10
6. Does the software offer an internal search facility?	Yes	No	0 1 2 3 4 5 6 7 8 9 10
7. Does the software allow for browsing?	Yes	No	0 1 2 3 4 5 6 7 8 9 10

Intelligence Analysis and CI Product Development (A)	Evaluation		Score Subtotal
1. Does the software Offer relevant analytical techniques?	Yes	No	0 1 2 3 4 5 6 7 8 9 10
2. Does the software allow for varying levels of analysis?	Yes	No	0 1 2 3 4 5 6 7 8 9 10
3. Does the software Synthesize (summarize) information in any way?	Yes	No	0 1 2 3 4 5 6 7 8 9 10
4. Does the analysis result in recommendations for action?	Yes	No	0 1 2 3 4 5 6 7 8 9 10

Product Development and Dissemination (D)	Evaluation		Score Subtotal
1. Does the software Offer a variety of formats for viewing the final product?	Yes	No	0 1 2 3 4 5 6 7 8 9 10
2. Are the formats effective in conveying CI?	Yes	No	0 1 2 3 4 5 6 7 8 9 10
3. Can one format be easily adapted to another format?	Yes	No	0 1 2 3 4 5 6 7 8 9 10
4. Does the software help identify potential CI consumers in light of particular product?	Yes	No	0 1 2 3 4 5 6 7 8 9 10
5. Does the software offer a function for distributing intelligence?	Yes	No	0 1 2 3 4 5 6 7 8 9 10

Total = pP + cC + sS + aA + dD
p—weight assigned for Planning
c—weight assigned for Collection
s—weight assigned for Storage
a—weight assigned for Analysis
d—weight assigned for Dissemination

The weight is customized based on different stages of CI system development and on different needs of each individual firms/units. Heavier weight will be given to what the firm need the most at time of consideration or what the firm intend to improve in the future.

5 Summary

Design, development and implementation of competitive intelligence information system is a long term process that needs to be carefully planned. Meanwhile, it is necessary to develop administrative procedures, intelligence management procedures, management of human resources and necessary technical resources. But that kind of a system is necessary in order to collect and prepare data for analytical tools and Intelligence Analytical Software. Evaluating and selection of CI software should be an integral part of the whole process and should not be treated as an independent technical/IT decision.

REFERENCES

[1] Bouthillier, F. and Shearer, K. 2003. *Assessing competitive intelligence software—a guide to evaluating CI technology.* Information Today, Inc.

[2] Cipher Systems. 2007. The 10 steps in selection the right CI software. July/August edition of Competitive Intelligence. SCIP member publications.

[3] Fuld& Company. 2009. The intelligence software report 2008 – 2009.

[4] J. Rocker and G. J. Roncaglia. 2002. Using the web for competitive intelligence gathering. AIAA 2002 – 2182.

网络人物观点识别研究

陆伟①　雷声伟②　张晓娟③

[摘要]　本文在前人的研究工作基础之上,利用相应的算法对文章进行预处理,通过文章句子中的词汇、词性标注和词汇之间的距离关系实现了观点指示动词识别和观点持有者识别,从而实现网络人物的观点识别。实验结果表明,通过对网络人物进行指代消解和观点持有者扩展能有效地提高观点识别的准确率。

[关键词]　观点　观点识别　观点持有者　观点指示动词

Study on Recognizing the Opinion of People in the Network

[Abstract]　This paper firstly preprocesses the article by applying corresponding algorithm, and then realizes the opinion – bearing verb recognition and opinion holders recognition through the words, the POS tagging of word and the distance between the words in the sentences of article, which it can make we can realize recognizing the opinion of people in the network, based on the previous research. The final results of experiment show that the precision of opinion recognition will be effectively improved by resoluting the anaphora and expanding the opinion holders.

[Keywords]　Opinion, Opinion Recognition, Opinion Holder, Opinion –

---

① 陆伟,教授、博士生导师,武汉大学信息资源研究中心,reedwhu@ gmail. com
② 雷声伟,武汉大学信息管理学院 2008 级信息管理与信息系统本科生,武汉大学信息资源研究中心,945433924@ qq. com
③ 张晓娟,武汉大学信息管理学院 2011 级情报学博士研究生,武汉大学信息资源研究中心,zxj0614@ yahoo. cn

Bearing Verb

1　引　言

随着 web 2.0 的出现,用户不再只是网站内容的浏览者,也是网站内容的制造者。用户除可以从网络上获取更多的信息外,还可以通过产品评论网站、个人博客、社区、论坛等传递自己的观点。于是,以网络评论为代表的主观性网络文本迅速增加。针对这些网络文本的观点分析能为政府舆情监控、厂家或商家获取产品用户反馈意见以及获取竞争对手相关信息等方面提供帮助,具有潜在的实用价值。因此,学术界也对该研究领域给予了极大的关注。

早期的观点分析研究主要是从整体角度来判断句子或评论的情感倾向[1],自 Kim 等[2]将观点细分为主题、持有者、陈述和情感四个元素后,学者们分别从持有者识别、主题抽取、情感分析等子任务来对观点分析加以探讨。[3]本文主要是通过对观点指示动词和观点持有者的识别来对观点句进行检测和抽取。针对该子任务,国外的相关研究主要是针对英文文本,基于句法分析来识别观点持有者从而进行观点句的检测和抽取,如 Bethard 等人[4]结合词法和句法特征,通过对语义分析技术进行扩展来抽取出建议性观点和这些观点的持有者;Choi 等[5]利用条件随机场和模式匹配来识别观点持有者;文献[6]采用基于规则的方法简单地进行观点持有者识别;文献[7]采用最大熵来获得观点持有者的句法特征,并识别出观点持有者。而基于汉语的观点分析相关研究仍处于起步阶段。由于中文在自然语言处理方面还不太成熟,准确率不高,使得句法分析在观点识别中的作用并不明显,国内的部分学者在探讨中文文本的观点识别问题时,尽量减少对句法分析的依赖。如郭巍等[8]首先通过建立观点分析相关的观点指示动词集,然后利用 SVM 与距离加权计算的方法来对观点和持有者进行识别,对句法分析的依赖性很小。宋瑞等[9]将观点持有者的识别看成一个序列标注的任务,通过 ChunkCRF 模型对观点表达句中的观点持有者进行识别。

本文在总结前人研究工作的基础上,基于词性分析,通过对观点指示动词和观点持有者的识别来对观点句进行检测和抽取。其中,文中所指的网络人物为网络文本如网络新闻等中所出现的人物,将观点界定为文档中观点持有者直接发表的观点,对于借用他人陈述的观点,如:李白说:"杜甫说明天要考试"中杜甫的观点作为间接表述的观点,不在本文的探讨范围内。因此,本文主要抽取两种类型的观点:(1)包含观点持有者和观点指示动词的观点;(2)包含人物语言的观点。

2 词汇资源建立

一个完整的观点句应包括一些重要的词汇特征,如观点词、观点指示动词,以及观点持有者。因此,为了弥补中文分词工具所存在的缺陷,有效地进行观点自动检测、抽取以及观点持有者自动抽取两项任务,本实验建立了相关词汇资源。

(1) 观点指示动词

观点指示动词是指用以指示观点的动词,如"认为"、"指出"、"批评"、"说"等。考虑到一些观点指示动词本身带有情感倾向,情感词的引入可能会使观点句抽取不全,本实验的观点指示动词是通过语料查找加人工搜索方法获得,共有观点指示动词106个,其中包含中性观点指示词65个,如"阐述"、"论述"、"回答"等;消极词观点指示动词11个,如"反对"、"否认";积极观点指示动词30个,如"赞赏"、"赞扬"、"鼓励"等。

(2) 人物词汇

人名、地名、某个组织机构、团体、区域、某些新闻中经常出现的模糊指代的集合人物(如有关部门、专家等)、人称代词(包括他、她、他们、她们)及其他部分普通名词都可作为观点持有者的候选词。该实验为了克服分词器的分词效果不能满足网络人物识别需要的困难,人工将一些新闻中常见的一些能够指代人物的词汇添加到用户词典中。其中,笔者总结了两种人物词汇,其一是新闻中经常出现的一些模糊指代的词汇,如消费者、顾客、组织者等;其二是表示职业或者人物关系的词汇,如专家、父亲等。本实验向用户词典中添加了24个第一种词汇和33个第二种词汇,且第一种词汇标注为defnr1,第二种词汇标注为defnr2。

3 预处理

本实验对文章进行观点分析之前,经过以下步骤对文章进行预处理。

（1）分句

观点句识别是在文章分句的基础之上进行的,故分句的效果在很大程度上影响着观点抽取的完整性。本文分句的主要思想:将引号内的内容视为不可拆分的部分,而对引号之外的内容采用"。"、"?"、"!"三种分句标点符号和文档本身存在的回车换行符号作为句子界限,进行分句处理。

（2）分词

本实验采用中科院的分词工具 ICTCLAS2010 进行分词与词性标注。为了提高观点识别的查全率和准确率,实验中还添加了两种词性(defnr1,defnr2)。如上文所述,defnr1 表示网络文章或新闻中经常出现的一些模糊指代的集合人物(如人士)名词,defnr2 表示能够联系到其他人物的关系属性的词汇(如父亲、继母等)和一些职业相关的名词(如专家、律师、记者等)。

（3）文章解析

文章经以上两步预处理后,将其解析成模拟树 List < Sentence < Word > > 的形式;其中 Sentence 是文章中的句子实体,包含句子的编号、词语的数量、词性标记后的句子的字符串;Word 是词语的实体,包含词语、词性标记、在句子中的编号、所在句子的编号、词语在所在句子中的起始索引位置、特殊标记(如人名标记:1;人称代词标记:2;观点指示动词标记:3)等。

4 相关算法设计

4.1 观点指示动词识别

在本文中,笔者认为观点指示动词具有如下特征:(1)观点指示动词不在引号内;(2)观点指示动词一般比较接近观点持有者;(3)观点指示动词一般比较接近标点符号如冒号、引号等。观点指示动词识别主要基于如下思想:抽取出某句话的所有候选观点指示动词,若该句话中只有一个观点指示动词,该候选词默认观点指示动词;若该句中包含两个或者两个以上的观点指示动词,则根据公式1来计算每个候选词的权值,从而识别出最终的观点指示动词。

$$S_{verb} = w_{ne} * dis_{ne} + w_{ne} * dis_{pu}$$ （公式1）

其中,dis_{ne} 表示观点持有者与最近动词之间的距离;w_{ne} 表示 dis_{ne} 的权值,实验中取值 0.4;dis_{pu} 表示观点持有者与最近标点符号之间的距离;w_{pu} 表示 dis_{pu} 的权值,实验中取值 0.6;S_{verb} 表示动词的最终权值,S_{verb} 值越大,这个动词作为观点指示动词的可能性越小。

4.2 观点持有者识别

在本实验中,笔者假设观点持有者具有以下特征:(1)观点持有者不在引号内;(2)观点持有者一般距离观点指示动词比较近;(3)观点持有者一般接近句首或句尾;(4)在第二种观点句中,若句中无相关的观点指示动词,则观点持有者一般接近引号;(5)不同类型的观点持有者具有不同的权值,其中人名权值最高,其次分别是人称代词、地名、机构名等其他普通名词或者专有名词;基于以上五个特征,本文采用公式 2 和公示 3 计算候选持有者的权值。

$$S_{ne} = (1 - (w_{vp} * dis_v + w_{se} * dis_{se}/_{sen})) * w_p \quad (公式 2)^{[8]}$$

$$Dis_{se} = Min\{dis_{句首}, * dis_{句尾}\} \quad (公式 3)^{[8]}$$

其中,dis_v 在第一种观点中表示候选词与最近动词之间的距离,而在第二种观点中表示候选词与最近引号之间的距离,若观点持有者在引号之前,则表示它和左引号之间的距离,若在后,则表示和右引号之间的距离;W_{vq} 在第一种与第二种观点中分别表示候选词距离动词的权值或候选词距离引号的权值;dis_{se} 取值为 $dis_{句首}$ 与 $dis_{句尾}$ 二值之中的较小值,其计算公式参见公式 3,其中,$dis_{句首}$ 为候选词与句首之间距离,$dis_{句尾}$ 为候选词与句尾之间距离。w_{se} 表示候选词与句首或句尾之间最近距离的权值;len_{sen} 表示句子的长度;w_p 为该候选词本身作为观点持有者的权值(特征 5);S_{ne} 表示该候选词的最终权值,某候选词的 S_{ne} 值越大则该候选词是观点持有者的概率越大。

为了提高观点持有者识别的准确率,本实验进行了简单的指代消解和观点持有者扩展。

(1)简单指代消解

本文进行的指代消解界定为对人称代词进行指代消解,其中,处理的人称代词包括他、她、他们、她们四种,且对指代单复数的情况作了简单的处理。其方法是:如果是前两个代词,向前查找单数类型的人物名词(如 nr,nr1),如果是后两个词语,则查找集合性质的人物名词(如 defnr1 等),查找范围局限在向前一定阀值的句子内一定数量的人物中,选择最优的候选词作为照应词。

（2）观点持有者扩展

本文并没有依赖句法和语法规则,而是根据词性规则并总结一些常见的模板来拓展观点持有者,其主要思想是:采用向前向后连续查找词汇,一旦有其他词性,则停止扩展。本文假设已得到可参考的人物名词,通过以下几种情况对观点持有者进行扩展:

1）一位中国地震局的专家:前边为量词、名词、形容词等;
2）李白的妻子:后边为"的"、单数名词、集合名词等;
3）李女士的丈夫张某:前边为"的"、单数名词等,后边为名词、后缀词等;
4）其他情况。

5 实验过程及结果分析

5.1 实验过程

本实验整个流程如图 1 所示。其中,本实验中所指观点具有如下要求:(1)第一种观点,需要有观点指示动词,允许观点持有者和观点指示动词间的距离在一定的阈值之内,以产生照应;(2)第二种观点,必须有人物语言出现;(3)这两种观点句中都必须有观点持有者出现。整个算法参见图2。

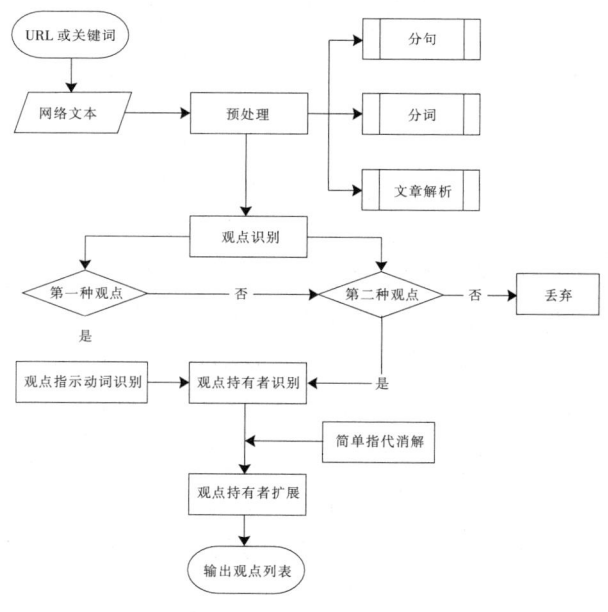

图 1 实验总体流程

> 1) 预处理,将文章解析成 List < Sentence < Word > > 的形式;
> 2) 按照句子进行循环,针对每一句,做如下操作:
> 3) 根据句中词语的 tag 属性识别出该句中包含的观点持有者和观点动词的候选词的列表;
> 4) 第一次观点判断:如果该句中没有观点持有者词语,认为这句话不是观点句,进入下一个循环;
> 5) 如果句子包含观点指示动词,则根据观点指示动词识别算法(参见表1)识别得到本句的观点指示动词,并进入下一步,否则进入9);
> 6) 如果根据5)中算法得到了观点指示动词,则根据观点持有者识别算法(参见表2)获取观点持有者;
> 7) 如果根据6)中算法得到了观点持有者则进入下一步,否则进入9);
> 8) 第二次观点判断的依据:其一,若动词和人名之间距离很远,则不是观点句,返回 false;其二,若人名和动词之间有断句符号(如逗号等),且两个词语的距离超过一定权值,则不是观点句,返回 false;否则返回 true,并进入10);
> 9) 对于前面观点判断失败的句子,进行第三次观点判断:依据是,如果该句中包含人物的说话内容,则是观点句,然后根据观点持有者算法获取观点持有者,如果没有得到,则不是观点句,否则进入10);
> 10) 根据简单指代消解方法对人称代词进行指代消解,并将指代消解的结果作为观点持有者词语;
> 11) 对最后得到的观点持有者,根据观点持有者扩展方法,进行观点持有者的扩展,进入12);
> 12) 将得到的相关属性赋给观点实体 View,然后添加到观点列表中。

图 2 观点识别算法

5.2 实验结果分析

(1) 观点句自动抽取

本实验总共选取了 9 个关键词,并在百度新闻搜索中进行关键词检索,每个关键词检索得到 40 篇新闻,最后得到 360 篇文章作为实验语料。依据标点符号将这 360 篇文章进行句子划分,共得到 9497 个句子,然后对这些句子进行观点句人工标记,共得到观点句 1491 个,最后将这些人工标注的语料作为测试集。本实验采用准确率(precision)和召回率(recall)来评价观点自动抽取的效果。

$$Precision = \frac{机器识别的正确观点数}{人工标记的观点总数} \times 100\% \quad (公式4)$$

$$Recall = \frac{机器识别的正确观点数}{机器识别的观点总数} \times 100\% \quad (公式5)$$

在本实验中,判断一句话是否是观点,首先判断这句话中是否存在潜在的观点持有者,若存在,则判断这句话中是否有观点指示动词,将该方法作为一次判断,即作为 Baseline;在一次判断的基础上,对潜在的观点持有者和观点指示动词之间的距离限制在一次的范围之内,即二次判断。然后对于剩下来的句子,如果句子中有引号,且引号内是一句话,就将其视为观点句,即作为三次判断。针对以上三种情况进行实验,得到的实验结果如表 1。

表 1　　　　　　　　　三种情况的评测结果

	判断条件	Recall(%)	Precision(%)
一次判断	潜在观点持有者 + 观点指示动词	73.0	65.7
二次判断	潜在观点持有者 + 观点指示动词 + 距离限制	69.2	70.3
三次判断	二次判断或引号成句	75.7	70.5

由表 1 中的实验结果可得:在一次判断的基础上,对潜在观点持有者与观点指示动词的距离加以限制,可以在一定程度上提高准确率,而召回率有所下降,二次判断的实验效果不是很好;在二次判断的基础上进行三次判断,准确率和召回率都有所提高。

(2) 观点持有者的自动抽取

本实验在抽取观点持有者时,将人工标注的 1491 个观点句通过机器抽取得到正确的观点句 1128 个,并将这 1128 个观点句作为观点抽取的实验语料。对于观点持有者的自动抽取结果的评价,本实验将机器抽取结果与人工标记结果进行对比,把平均相似度作为评价指标。其中,平均相似度(AVE_SIM)表示单句抽取结果的相似度的平均值,是机器抽取结果与人工标记相匹配的字串长度与抽取结果和标注结果字串长度中的较大者之比,如公式6:

$$SIM(Extractor, Marked) = \frac{\sum SIM(Extractor, Marked)}{totalNumber} \quad (公式6)^{[8]}$$

其中,Extractor 和 Marked 分别表示机器抽取结果和人工标记结果。在获得单个句子的相似度的基础上,平均相似度的计算方法如公式7:

$$AVG\_SIM = \frac{LengthofMatchedCharacter}{Max\{LengthofExtractor, LengthofMarked\}} \quad (公式7)^{[8]}$$

在 Baseline 的基础上,本实验分别进行短语扩展和指代消解,三组实验结果如表 2:

表 2　　　　　　　　　　短语扩展和指代消解的评测结果

实验方法	实验结果			
	完全匹配数	部分匹配数	不匹配数	平均相似度(%)
Baseline	389	527	212	48.6
短语扩展	756	163	209	73.8
指代消解+短语扩展	781	167	180	76.1

由表2的实验结果可以看出,在Baseline实验的基础上,再进行短词扩展,可以在很大程度上提高观点持有者的识别效果,平均相似度提高了近25%,而在短语扩展的基础上,再进行人称的指代消解,虽然效果不是很明显,但平均相似度有略微的上升,这也是本实验的一大进步。总体来说,短语扩展将大量部分匹配的观点持有者变为完全匹配,使得观点持有者的机器抽取结果更加完整,较大程度地提高了实验效果。而指代消解,主要是将不匹配的观点持有人(一般是一些人称代词如他、她等等)转化为正确的结果,即将这些人称代词转化为正确的观点持有者,从而进一步提高了实验结果的准确度。

6　总　结

本文在总结前人的研究工作的基础之上,根据自己的研究实践,针对中文文本,进行网络人物的观点识别。本文在分词和词性标注的基础之上,利用词性分析和词汇之间的距离提出了观点指示动词识别算法和观点持有者识别算法。为了进一步提高识别的效果,本文还考虑到利用指代消解和观点持有者扩展。从实验结果来看,总体上取得了比较理想的结果。而本文在对观点句进行检测和抽取时只是从观点指示动词和观点持有者这两者的角度,未对观点主题和观点极性进行探讨,这是本实验所存在着不足之处,这也将是笔者以后研究工作中需要进一步深入的地方。

参考文献

[1] 周杰,林琛,李弼程. 面向网络评论的观点主题识别研究[J]. 情报学报,2010(5):858-863.

[2] S M Kim,E Hovy. *Determining the sentiment of opinions*[C]. *Proceedings of the 20th interna-*

tional conference on Computational. Switzerland,2004:1367-1373.

[3] 姚天昉,程希文,徐飞玉,等.文本意见挖掘综述[J].中文信息学报,2008(3):71-80.

[4] Bethard S, Yu H, Thornton A, et al. *Automatic Extraction of Opinion Propositions and Their Holders* [C] // Proc of AAAI 04 Spring Symposium on Exploring Attitude and Affect in Text , 2004.

[5] Y Choi, C Cardie, E Riloff, et al. *Identifying sources of opinions with conditional random fields and extraction patterns* [C]. *Proceedings of the conference on Human Language Technology and Empirical Methods in Natural Language Processing*, 2005.

[6] L Lee. *A study of opinion summarization* [D]. *Department of computer science and information engineering*, National Taiwan Universtiy, 2005.

[7] SM Kim, E Hovy. *Identifying Opinion Holders for Question Answering in Opinion Texts* [J]. *American Association for Artificial Intelligence*, 2005.

[8] 郭巍,宋锐,林鸿飞.基于SVM与距离加权计算的观点和持有者识别机制[J].计算机工程与科学,2008(10):125-128,146.

[9] 宋瑞,洪莉,林鸿飞.基于ChunkCRF的观点持有者识别及其在观点摘要中的应用[J].小型微型计算机系统,2009(7):1462-1466.

Exploring the Unknown Unknows – Advanced Computer – Linguistic Methods for Social Media Analysis

Martin Grothe[1]   Hanna Huber[2]

Abstract

What companies have to be aware of is that social media is there, it is growing, and it is influencing people's decisions. But not only is social media omnipresent and common usage nowadays, it is also a growing phenomenon that is here to stay. This paper aims to show that there are powerful methods to extract relevant issues from chatter through social media analysis and that CI professionals should pay more attention to this phenomenon. Computer – linguistic and semantic tools help to explore the unexpected.

Keywords

Social Media, Social Media Analysis, Social Media Monitoring, Social Network Analysis, Semantics, Computer – Linguistics, Information Extraction, Topic Map, Decision Tree, Pattern Matching, Complexity

1 THE RELEVANCE OF SOCIAL MEDIA FOR COMPETITIVE INTELLIGENCE

"It is pardonable to be defeated, but never to be surprised."

– Frederick the Great

---

[1] complexium GmbH, Berlin, Germany, CEO, grothe@ complexium. de
[2] complexium GmbH, Berlin, Germany, COO, huber@ complexium. de

All over the world practitioners in the field of Competitive Intelligence (CI) are still quite reluctant to utilize the potential of social media to gain insights into the business of their competitors or their customers. This paper aims to show that there are powerful methods to extract relevant issues from chatter through social media analysis, and that CI professionals should pay more attention to this phenomenon. Of course, it is not a magical wonder tool, and the raw data needs extensive filtering and analysis, but the results are worth the effort.

David Sifry, the CEO of technorati – one of the first social media aggregation portals – said that "*In the world of the Internet, you don't own your brand. Your customers and your users own your brand. You're lucky if you get to shepherd it. That loss of control is very scary*". This key element of social media can be a little uncomfortable for corporations sometimes, but it also opens a new window of opportunities, especially when searching for information about competitors.

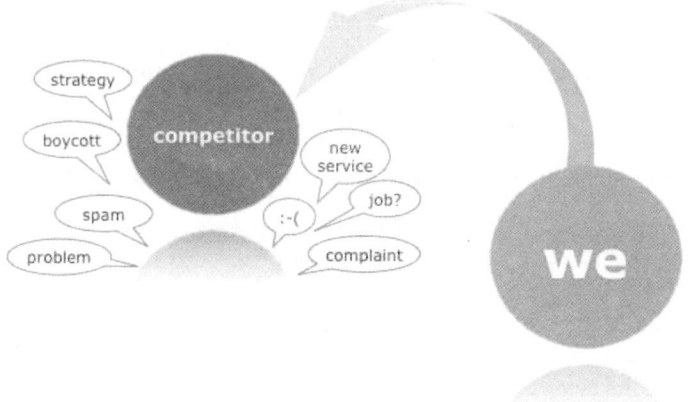

Figure 1. Social Media Buzz is mirroring your competitor's eco – system

Collective intelligence can become competitive intelligence with the right approach and the right tools. Tapping into the raw, unfiltered, and uncensored discussions of users can provide some of the most timely and accurate insights into competitive issues that you can find. The buzz is already there, but most companies and CI professionals still see social media only as a colorful marketing hype. Others start to listen, identify, and analyze emerging patterns, from which they learn about consumers and competitors – finally and reduce the "unknown".

2 UNDERSTANDING SOCIAL MEDIA

What companies have to be aware of is that social media is there, it is growing, and it is influencing people's decisions. But not only is social media omnipresent and common usage nowadays, it is also a growing phenomenon that is here to stay.

According to the Nielsen report of April 2010, three of the world's ten most popular internet brands are social media brands. Those are facebook, which is used by 54% of the world's internet population, YouTube (used by 47%), and Wikipedia, which is visited by 35% of all global internet users. But the report also shows that the usage of social networks and blogs combined ranges from 86% of the population in Brazil to 59% of the population in Switzerland, indicating that the usage differs immensely from country to country.

The GlobalWebIndex, an extensive survey that researches the world's key internet markets, shows that the social web is used quite differently around the globe. Comparing the data from China and the USA it becomes quite clear that while the mass adoption of social networks takes place in both countries, the Chinese population also uses microblogs (twitter), blogs, and especially forums extensively and tends to contribute way more.

Another survey from Forrester Research separates users into groups due to their online behavior and concludes that – while the percentage of inactive persons is about the same in both countries, users in China are much more engaged when it comes to producing content. This development becomes more and more important for businesses, since the Nielsen report also found out that 41% of all users worldwide are willing to share negative experiences with businesses and products on the internet, and Chinese users are most likely to share negative experiences with products on social media sites.

Social media is made up of a variety of different platforms and channels. Each has its own features und subsequent uses.

- **Social networks** are secured platforms for registered users who can to build networks by forming "friendships" with others. They can discuss topics or post photos and videos on their own profile pages, in groups, or on institutional accounts such as brand or company pages. Worldwide, facebook is clearly dominating, but in China, QZone is the most used social network.

- **Blogs** are regularly updated by one author or a small group of authors. They offer content in the form of long text, pictures, or videos mostly regarding only one certain topic. Bloggers are often the first to comment on new trends or phenomena. Due to the large amount of cross – linkage between blogs new topics can spread fast through the blogosphere and not seldom reach the mass media.

- **Microblogs** like twitter allow only texts with length of about a standard SMS and are mainly used for spreading news and messages extremely fast.

- **Forums** offer detailed and extensive discussions about specific topics or questions and can usually be read by everyone. Opposed to social networks users usually do not register under their given name but use pseudonyms. Accordingly a lot of interesting discussions are found here. The longevity of the some threads is another notable characteristic of forums.

- **Review portals** are especially important in regard to brands and products, because users can leave positive or negative reviews, which other users can comment on.

- **Media Sharing communities** are platforms whose main purpose is publishing or receiving multimedia content like YouTube and flickr. Generally those communities resemble social networks in a lot of ways since they offer most of the same functions such as generating accounts, networking, and commenting on the published media. The platforms are usually differentiated by the type of content that is published such as videos, photos, music, or even presentations and papers.

It's all those differences that have to be taken into account by companies who want to participate and use social media for their business. Very different information can be derived from the different channels. And all have their own set of rules that have to be taken seriously.

3 SOCIAL MEDIA IN CI SCENARIOS

In a 2002 U.S. Department of Defense press briefing the former United States Secretary of Defense Donald Rumsfeld stated several facts that do not only apply to the work of the Department of Defense but also to the work of every CI professional: "*There are known knowns; there are things we know we know. We also know there are known unknowns; that is to say we know there are some things we do not know. But there are also unknown unknowns — the ones we don't know we don't know*". ①

Systematically one should add the "unkown knows" and receive a matrix showing four different intelligence scenarios.

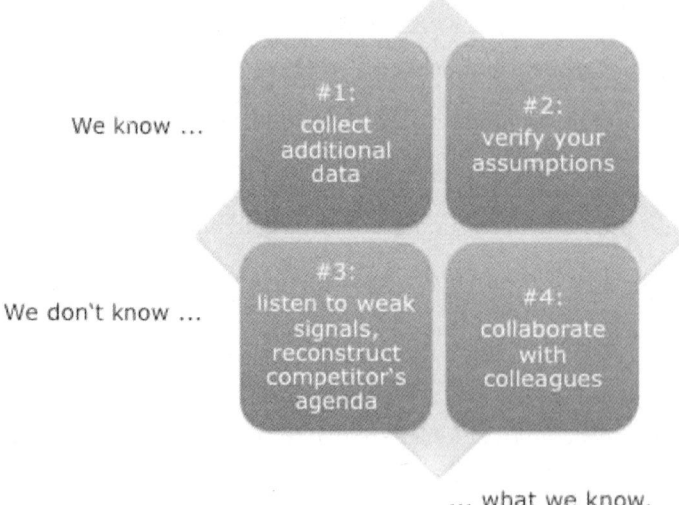

Figure 2. Intelligence Scenarios

---

① U.S. Department of Defence (2002). DoD News Briefing – Secretary Rumsfeld and Gen. Myers. http://www.defense.gov/transcripts/transcript.aspx? transcriptid = 2636

For example, if you know that you don't know something (#1), then the obvious solution is to collect additional data so that you will gain the missing knowledge. One of the ways to gather such data is through social media analysis, which is also a way to find unknown unknowns (#4) and to verify some kinds of assumptions (#3).

There are three major applications for CI where social media analysis is helpful:

- **A focus analysis** (also status quo analysis) is used to analyze forums, communities, networks, and blogs in order to reveal the content of user discussions like questions, experiences, recommendations, or arguments. A good social media focus analysis goes far beyond just counting articles. The results enable the CI professional to create overviews of discussions or reconstruct decision processes in order to profile competitors or industry sectors. Social media analysis is a way to profile action groups and key influencers. Opinion leaders and other relevant authors might be identified. Through semantic analysis top topics are deduced, top channels ranked, and profiles of the most important channels are created.

  Through social media analysis competitor's agendas can be reconstructed by mirroring the competitor's eco-system. An appropriate analysis reveals relevant information about the competitor, its stakeholders, and the current issues. A focus analysis may concentrate on topic analysis or on author profiling or a combination thereof.

- Through a regularly performed **monitoring** changes and trends can be identified. Changes in the top sources, sentiment concerning certain issues, and new weak signals are revealed. Additionally specific Key Performance Indicators (KPI) measure the development over time. A monitoring helps the CI professional to keep track of competitors or trends in the industry sector. It is suggested to perform a focus analysis prior to a monitoring, in order to evaluate the topics and relevant points of interest as a status quo. The monitoring KPI then enable a company to adjust its own behavior to the changes in the strategic positioning of competitors or industry trends.

- A special form of social media analysis is the **sonar**. This form of social media information extraction does not aim to show all conversations regarding a brand or issue in the social web, but to find those few critical issues that may arise and threaten the reputation, safety, or strategic positioning of a company. Reports show the online activities of stakeholders, activists, or general public opinion. Weak signals can be detected through semantic methods, and alarm terms can be defined that will automatically alert the company in cases of crisis or specific events. The management is therefore given more time and more opportunities to react to any incidents that may arise. A sonar prevents surprise.

4 ADVANCED COMPUTER – LINGUISTIC METHODS

For social media analysis the first step is to collect vast amounts of data on the social web in social networks, blogs, forums, or other channels, which afterwards have to be scanned, identified, and categorized. Especially for Competitive Intelligence it is essential to use a hypothesis – free approach by not limiting searches to a predefined list of sources. Instead, all detectable sources on the internet have to be accessed to find those weak signals and scattered bits of information that will allow to form a picture of the competitor's strategies.

The overall process combines several advanced methods:

1. **A hypothesis – free approach** finds information that could not be anticipated before, but it also means that a lot of articles and information without relevance are found. This huge amount of hundreds or thousands of articles (depending on time – frame and topic) has to be scanned and categorized further in order to deliver good results.

2. **On a first filtering level** spam, advertisements, and editorial content are eliminated through software algorithms. The remaining articles are have to be checked again in order to include only thematically relevant articles in the analysis. This can be achieved by combining several computer – linguistic methods of which some have

proven very effective in practice.

3. **Pattern Matching** is a method used in social media analysis to reduce the large numbers of articles by eliminating irrelevant content. Patterns are sets of keyword combinations, complex expressions, and other available meta data that help to automatically categorize articles. Irrelevant information can be detected and sorted out, whereas relevant information is kept and aggregated with semantic topic maps in the next step.

4. **Semantic Topic Maps** open up significant issues without having to read thousands of articles individually. By matching hundreds or thousands articles (previously identified in step 1) with the linguistic reference corpus of the accordant language, important aspects and contexts are being identified. Editorially colored labels highlight topical focal points ("What are the central topics in the discussion?").

The advantages of Semantic Topic Maps are firstly, that issue clusters and connections can be easily identified by simply looking at the map. It secondly shows significant topics like weak signals and hidden issues without presets, and therefore avoids a bias that most methods in the social sciences have to deal with. Finally, the identified categories can be assigned to articles automatically after a training phase for recurrent monitorings.

The technology behind semantic topic maps combines Social Network Analysis (SNA) with an identification of the semantic significance frequency of certain words that are used in the discussion. The most significant terms are displayed as boxes and connecting lines show a strong coherence between topics. This allows, for example, to view a discussion about an industry sector as a topic map in which companies respectively the competitors are positioned.

5. **Information Extraction** is a technique for deriving information in a structured form out of unstructured documents. Since information and discussions on the social web are scattered over different channels, the form in which they are presented differs a lot. Some channels like twitter allow only short texts, blog articles range from extremely short sentences combined with videos or photos to extended articles, and in forums long and short comments alternate. The automatic classification of

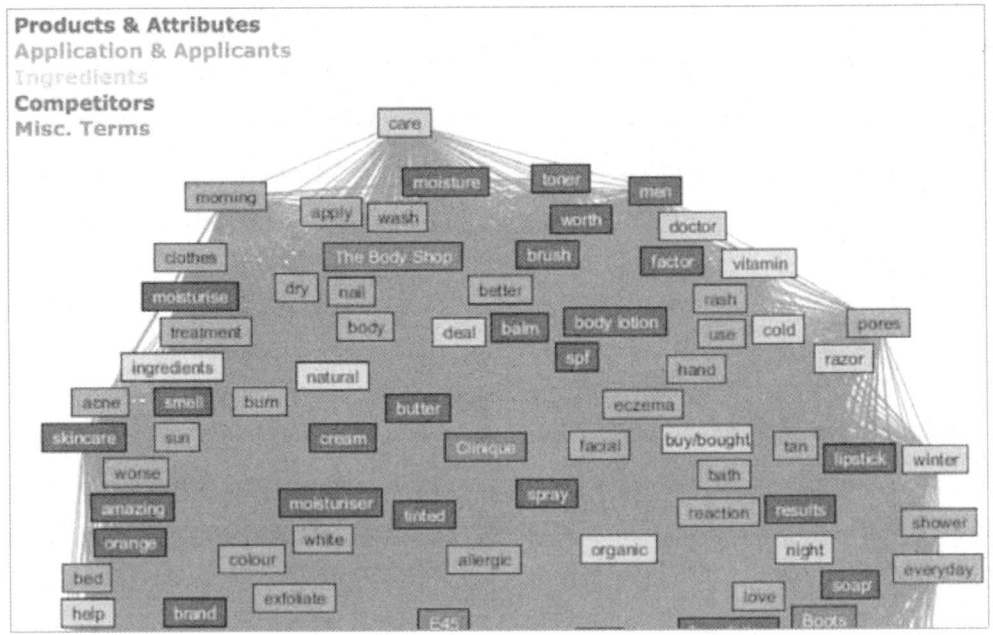

Figure 3. Semantic Topic Map

(Example: Industry Sector Skin Care / Source: complexium analysis)

texts into categories (industry, competitor, product, etc.), which is essential for CI insights, is usually very difficult because of the missing comparability of documents.

Information Extraction condenses texts from different sources by using clustering, onthologies, and automatical sentiment analysis. Especially for monitorings a speedy automatic classification is needed, and structured information is required for the measurement by Key Performance Indicators. If Information Extraction is then enhanced by the usage of so called "Decision Trees", automatic classification of huge amounts of articles becomes possible.

6. **Decision Trees** "learn" how to categorize articles by using a sample that has been manually sorted by analysts. The algorithm then searches for underlying patterns in the selected articles and builds complex "paths". These paths make it possible for the software to decide from now on, if an article contains, for example, information about a new competitor strategy or merely a customer complaint. The paths (sometimes hundreds or thousands of different conditions for a single category) allow the software to categorize the remaining articles with a very high probability. The

software practically learns what to do for itself.

5 CONCLUSION

Social media analysis is not a solution for every question. But in the face of "known unknowns" and "unknown unknowns" it can deliver very fast additional insights. Computer – linguistic and semantic tools help to explore the unexpected – human analysts have to deduce an interpretation.

It is expected that CI professionals will spend much more time on social media analysis to gain a competitive edge. It is simply irrelevant whether you show enthusiasm about social media, because the competitors certainly will.

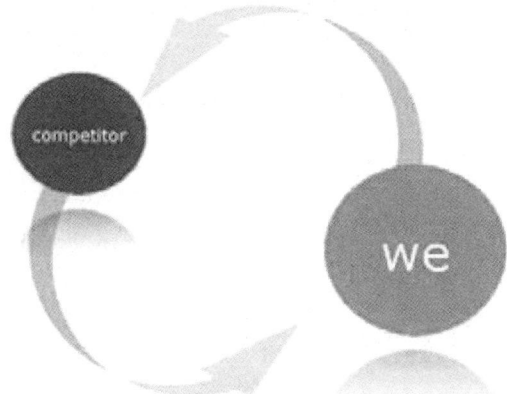

Figure 4. Social Media: A new arena of competitive analysis

The social web is not (yet) representative, but it is fast, diverse, and a growing source of information of all kinds: Users are voicing their opinions, and footprints in the social web show current and arising topics concerning businesses or brands. The role of the CI professional is to **identify** relevant information, **interpret** it and **integrate** the findings into CI reportings. Two scenarios will become more and more common practice:

1. Deep – dive **Social Media Analysis**: The important factors for an CI social media analysis are the integration of all social media channels, a set of methods that can help extract the unexpected, and an understanding of network dynamics. Such

an deep – diving analysis let CI professionals identify core topics, crucial items, and key influencers.

2. Continuous **Social Media Monitoring**: For subsequent monitorings or sonars it is important to focus on information about the changes in topics of competitors or action groups, listen to "weak signals", and to find the right KPIs for your CI reporting.

After integrating social media analysis into everyday CI work the next step towards an integrated enterprise 2.0 is to develop a social media management process model.

REFERENCES

[1] Forrester (2010). Social Technographics Defined 2010 [EB/OL]. http://www.forrester.com/empowered/ladder2010.

[2] Forrester (2011). What's the Social Technographics Profile of Your Customers? [EB/OL]. http://www.forrester.com/empowered/tool_consumer.html.

[3] Nielsen. Social Media Dominates Asia Pacific Internet Usage [EB/OL]. http://blog.nielsen.com/nielsenwire/global/social – media – dominates – asia – pacific – internet – usage/. [2012 – 7 – 9].

[4] Scott, John. 2000. Social Network Analysis. A Handbook [M]. London: SAGE Publications Ltd.

[5] The GlobalWebIndex. Annual Report 2011 [EB/OL]. Welcome to Social Entertainment. http://globalwebindex.net/explore – the – data/data/annual – report – 2011/.

Automatic Patent Analysis – Technological Strategic Dependence

Henri Dou[①]　Jean Marie Dou J[②]　Getachew Mengistie Alemu[③]

Abstract

The concept of strategic dependence in patent strategy is a relatively new point of view and is seconded by the large increase of Chinese priority patents, not extended to other countries. The concept is relatively simple, when a large number of patents are extended in other countries than the priority country, or when they are the designated states which are concerned (European Patents, and PCT) this means that the country in which all the patents are extended become dependent for the applications and technologies of these patents. A contrario, and specially for developing countries, if a patent has not been extended in this country, this patent can generally be used in this country without constraint. The restriction is the following, if the patent concerns objects or a machines, the exportation of these products in countries covered by the former patent is not possible The modern tools which perform APA (Automatic Patent Analysis) and the increasing number of patents available, pushed to the scene this strategic dependence.

Keywords

Patents, APA Automatic Patent Analysis, Technological Dependence, OAPI, China

---

① Atelis, Strategic Intelligence Workroom, Goupe ESCEM, France, douhenri@yahoo.fr
② Chamber of Commerce and Industry, Marseille Provence, France jeanmariedou@yahoo.com
③ Intellectual Property Consultant & Attorney, Ethiopia, getachewal@gmail.com

1　INTRODUCTION

Many works concern the use of patents to determine technologies or to analyze the strategies in patents of different firms. Recently the patent information has been used in the WIPO program of innovation for the SME and in this context the strategic dependence has been pointed out by various consultants. In Indonesia, Michael Porter pointed out recently the very weak activity of the country in patenting and a recent work presented at the 3rd European Symposium of Competitive Intelligence pointed out the strategic dependence on technologies of certain countries. Analysis of Patent dependence in Science for China has also been studied recently. In innovation a publication of the Carnegie council pointed out that in domains such as the wind energy, the solar power, the biofuels most of the patents are concentrated in United States and OECD countries, which means that these countries develop the technology and that the gap with the developing countries, which need these technology increase[1]. But nevertheless the aspects of technology dependence linked to the number of patents extended to developing countries has not been underlined. Other study of the technology dependence according the count of the cited patents to determine the key patents[2] has also be performed.

In this paper, we wish to develop another view of the problem: not really the way that a country must be dependent of a technology, but how the increasing extension of patents in another country from various countries may create technology dependence. [3]

2　THE CONTEXT

There are different routes to secure patent protection for inventions. These include national, regional and international routes. An inventor may apply for and secure patent protection by filing with a patent application in a national patent office. It is also possible to file a single patent application with a regional intellectual property office and secure a patent. At present there are two approaches in this regard. There are regional patent systems that provide for filing of single application but the granting of a patent may be made by a regional organization with or without involving member states. An example of the former is the regional patent cooperation agreement administered by the Organization Africaine de la Propriété Intellectuelle (OAPI), where a single and uniform patent system, which has the same effect as a national patent system in each of the member states, is implemented[①]. Examples of the latter include the regional patent cooperation agreements administered by the European Patent Office (EPO)[②] and the African Regional Intellectual Property Organization (ARIPO).[③] Under this system, patents granted by the regional organization will only be valid in designated member states when there is no objection against the granting of a patent and the validity of the regional patent is governed by national patent laws of the member states. In addition to the national and regional route, there is an international route. The Patent Cooperation Treaty that was concluded in 1970 provides for filing a single application, performing international prior art search and international publication of patent applications. The Treaty also provides for international preliminary examination that is made optional to member countries. An applicant may file a single PCT application with his own country patent office or the World Intellectual Property Organization (WIPO). It should be noted here that there is no system that grants world patent.

The purpose of this article is not to examine the different routes available for pa-

---

[①] These countries are Benin, Burkina Faso, Camerron, Central African Republic, Congo, Cote dIvoire, Equatorial Guinea, Gabon, Guinea, Guinea Bissau, Mali, Mauritania, Niger, Senegal, Chad and Togo.

[②] EPO consists of Albania, Austria, Belgium, Bulagria, Croatia ,Cyprus Czech Republic, Denmark, Estonia, Finland, Former Yugoslav Republic of Macedonia,France, Germany, Greece, Hungary, Ireland, Iceland, Italy , Liechtenstein , Lithuania, Luxembourg, Latvia, Malta,Monaco , Netherlands, Norway, Poland, Portugal, Romania, San Marino,Serbia, Slovenia, Slovakia,Spain , Sweden, Switzerland, Turkey? and United Kingdom.

[③] ARIPO, which was established in 1985, consists of eighteen countries as members, namely: These are Botswana, the Gambia, Ghana, Kenya, Lesotho, Liberia, Malawi, Mozambique, Namibia, Rwanda, Sierra Leone, Somalia, Sudan, Swaziland, Tanzania, Uganda, Zambia and Zimbabwe.

tent protection but examine patent applications filed with OAPI and China to demonstrate the issue of technological dependence arising from extended patents and the opportunity of using non extended patents.

After the first filing of a patent application with a national or regional patent office, not using the PCT route, the applicant will have a period of 12 months to file patent application in other countries. The first filing date will give rise to a right of priority that will be recognized in the countries where later applications are made. The different patent applications extended to other countries and patents granted by different countries will constitute a family of patents. There is a possibility of having national patents, a European Patent (EP) that is valid in designated member states or an OAPI patent that is automatically valid in the 16 French Speaking African countries, which are members of the organization. As a result of the different routes of patent protection and the concept of prior right, it is common to find a certain invention protected in a number of different countries. For instance the following patents cover various countries:

A coconut de – husking apparatus, is an Australia Priority Patent PR = AU1997PO05061 10 – 02 – 1997 which has been extended to Indonesia PN = ID20936A 01 – 04 – 1999. Then, the Indonesian country will be dependent of this patent for this type of application.

Blade with empennage of vertical – axis windmills, is a Chinese priority patent PR = CN20092052708U 16/03/2009 which had not been extended in other countries. Then if another country want to extend or to cite China as a country of extension or deposit, the foreign patent will be facing the technology already patented by the Chinese.

These two patents explain the mechanism of the technology dependence for the first one and of technology protection for the second. With these two aspects in view we are going to show some aspects of the technology dependence and of the technology protection in useful or useless cases.

3 MATERIAL AND METHOD

Issues involved in technology dependence and technological protection can be highlighted taking OAPI member states as example using patent data bases and patent search tools.

To demonstrate the technological dependence we use the OPS VI① database from EPO (European Patent Office) which is equivalent to the world patent database available online via Internet. ② To be able to handle a large number of patents which will be downloaded from this database we used the Matheo – Patent software already described in various publications. [4,5] This software plays the role of an interface between your computer and the OPS VI database. It also allows the automatic processing and analysis of patents.

To refine the analysis further, a more powerful software called Matheo – Analyzer③ is used The data downloaded from the OPS VI database via Matheo – Patent are transferred into Matheo Analyzer for further processing (names treatments, lemmatization, groups of patents finalization, etc.).

3.1 The method used

The query is the following: search for patents number beginning by OA (this will allow the creation of the local database by downloading the patents from the OPSVI database.) When this database will be created, a rapid examination of the results will be done with the Matheo – Patent functionalities and if the corpus appears to be suitable for further analysis, the database will be transferred in the Matheo – software analyzer. Then, different treatments to select the OA priority countries from other will be done as well as the analysis of the extended Patents (Patents numbers

---

① This database allow the query by robots and the downloading of a large number of patents.

② http://gb. espacenet. com/search97cgi/s97_cgi. exe? Action = FormGen&Template = gb/EN/home. hts.

③ http://www. matheo – patent. com.

with the exclusion of the priority patents).

It is possible, that not all the patents from the OAPI office are present in the OPS database, but this is not very important for what we want to demonstrate. It is only necessary to extract a significant numbers of patents to validate the demonstration.

Results:

The query PN = OA leads to the following patents retrieval:

Table 1. Number of Patent retrieved

All OAPI Patents : 2411 (about 10% are missing due to downloading problems)

2006	2005	2004	2003	2002	2001	2000
1138	176	200	300	365	227	5

This search was performed by one of the author (Henri Dou) during a workshop[1] organized in Cameroon by the WIPO and the Cameroon Patent Bureau. Further analysis of the results show that the number of patents granted by OAPI countries is the following:

Cameroun = 54; Sénégal = 45; Côte d'Ivoire = 31; Mali = 24; Benin = 17; Niger = 13; Mauritanie = 13; République du Congo = 12; Gabon = 9; Guinée = 8; Tchad 6; Burkina Faso = 6; Togo = 5; Niger = 3; Guinée Equatoriale = 2 ; République Centre Africaine = 2

A total of 250 patents from , 2411 granted by OAPI during the period between 2000 to 2006, were made to residents of member states of the organization. This means that 10.4% of the patents are from OAPI states, with a priority OAPI[2]. The remaining patents are foreign patents which have been extended to OAPI countries. One remark can be done about it: if the concept of OAPI (a global protection) seems good at first sight, it greatly facilitates the extension of patents to all the member states.

3.2 Further analysis of the downloaded patents

With the help of the Matheo Patent software, we created several groups of pa-

---

[1] Competitive Intelligence et Information Stratégique L'Innovation et l'Information brevet au coeur de la stratégie Dou H, WIPO, OMPI, Cameroun, Yaoundé, 5 – 6 May 2011.

[2] At the RIC meeting of Competitive Intelligence in Burkina Faso (Ouagadougou, September 12 – 13, 2011). A presentation from a Burkinabe attorney indicates percentage of OAPI Patents around 7, percentage of marks around 24%.

tents, according the priority country. We stopped at the frequency 30 (30 patents per country). Then the data were transferred from Matheo Patent to Matheo Analyzer (which performs more powerful analysis), the groups created have also been transferred. The following table gives the number of patents selected in each group (countries). For the group PR = OA (Patent with a priority OAPI) we put the patents which originated from the member states of OAPI.

Forms	Frequency
USA	754
France	272
Empty Field	270
PR=OA	207
UK	153
Netherland	143
Germany	72
switzerland	58
Belgium	44
Australia	36
Italy	31
Canada	30

Figure 1. Numbers of patent per groups (countries)

3.3 The technological dependence of the OAPI countries

We have now the possibility to work on each groups separately and to examine all the patent extended to OAPI, the different International Patent Classification present in each of the group. This can be done either globally using the 4 digits IPC or in depth by using the full IPC. A comparison between the different classes present in each of the groups of countries will indicate if a special strategy to extend to OAPI countries is noticeable. If a more precise analysis is necessary, the full IPC can be used. The result is indicated in table 2.

Table2. Partial view of the matrix country's groups versus IPC 4 digits

	A61K	A61P	C07D	E21B	C07C	A01N	C07K	C12N	B63B	C07H	F16L	A23L	B01D	G01V	G01N	B65D	B01J
USA	495	458	356	44	103	26	51	45	32	43	10	14	17	11	25	14	14
France	62	53	43	36	9	22	14	6	16	4	34	3	6	17	3	8	3
UK	82	74	54	7	13	16	5	8	4	6	2	1	1	1	5	4	12
PR = OA	40	13	2	0	1	3	0	2	0	0	0	21	4	0	2	1	1
Netherland	3	2	0	85	1	0	2	5	9	0	4	2	2	9	10	2	2
Germany	34	32	24	1	6	17	2	2	0	2	0	0	2	0	1	3	1
switzerland	9	8	5	3	3	7	2	5	2	1	0	13	4	0	1	1	3
Belgium	23	21	11	6	2	0	5	4	0	1	0	0	1	0	0	4	0
Canada	11	10	6	0	1	1	3	2	0	3	0	1	5	1	1	0	1
Italy	14	14	9	1	2	2	3	2	1	2	2	0	0	0	0	4	0
Australia	4	4	1	0	0	4	0	2	0	1	0	0	0	1	0	2	0

When the patent number in one cell is not following the general pattern (decreasing order), this indicates a different strategy within the group. These cells are indicated by a grey color. The comparison with the PR = OA line, allows to see the degree of strategic dependence of OA countries versus foreign technologies and also to see in which domain the OA countries take the maximum of patents. (IPC A23L: Foodstuffs and non alcoholic beverages)

To obtain a more synthetic view of this dependence, we build a network with the IPC 3 digits and the country groups the result is indicated in figure 2. The interval of frequency used was from 539 to 15. In this network the figures in the squares box indicate the numbers of patents of the country groups and the figures in the circles indicate the frequency of the patents dealing with the linked IPC.

This network indicates that the IPC B65, C09, C12 concerning US Patents are original compare to the other patents present. Same remark for the IPC F16 concerning the French patents.

If we build up a synthetic matrix using the IPC 3 digits with the country groups, we can design a strategic matrix which will underline the main concern of each country, in patent extension to OAPI.

If we except the two first rows where most of the patents are concentrated (ex-

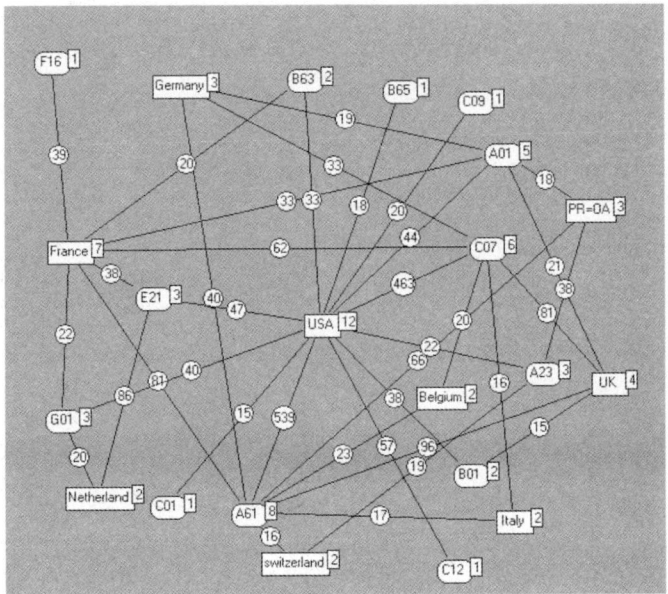

Figure 2. Network of country croups and IPC 3 digits (frequency between 539 and 15)

cept for Netherland), and also the USA which are present almost everywhere it is possible to underline the main trends of this matrix: orange where the strategy of patent deposit is important, green when there is no strategy since no patents have been extended and blue when there is a "behavioral difference" with other countries is noted.

One remark could be done concerning the most important group of countries analyzed. China, which makes a great effort in patent deposit (Chinese Priority and Chinese extensions) is not present in spite of the commercial and also cooperative presence of China in Africa (for instance the center for rice technology transfer in Cameroun near Yaoudé).

	A	B	C	D	E	F	G	H	I	J	K	L
1		USA	France	UK	PR=OA	Netherland	Germany	switzerland	Belgium	Canada	Italy	Australia
2	A61	539	81	96	66	3	40	16	23	12	17	6
3	C07	463	62	81	11	3	33	13	20	12	16	3
4	E21	47	38	8	5	86	1	3	6	0	1	0
5	A01	44	33	21	18	3	19	10	1	2	2	4
6	C12	57	7	10	9	5	4	7	5	3	2	2
7	G01	40	22	6	5	20	1	1	1	2	0	2
8	B01	38	13	15	8	4	3	7	2	7	0	1
9	A23	22	4	3	38	2	1	19	0	1	0	0
10	F16	13	39	5	4	6	1	0	0	0	2	6
11	B63	33	20	4	3	11	0	2	0	0	1	0
12	B65	18	12	5	3	5	3	3	6	0	4	2
13	C09	20	6	2	2	9	6	2	10	0	0	1
14	C02	14	3	1	5	1	5	1	1	4	0	1
15	C01	15	6	7	2	1	0	1	1	2	0	4
16	C10	11	3	10	4	4	1	2	0	0	2	0
17	H04	11	5	4	2	2	3	5	1	0	1	0
18	E02	13	10	1	0	6	0	1	1	1	0	0
19	H01	6	11	1	3	2	0	0	0	0	1	0
20	C08	8	5	1	1	3	9	1	0	1	0	0
21	G06	13	10	1	1	0	2	0	1	0	0	0
22	B29	10	2	0	4	1	6	0	0	1	0	3
23	A47	1	3	0	13	0	1	6	0	0	1	0
24	C22	12	1	1	2	0	0	0	1	6	0	2
25	F25	14	4	1	2	4	0	0	0	0	0	1

Figure 3. Strategic trends in patent extension in OAPI countries

4 THE CASE OF CHINA

4.1 Overview

A recent study published by La Tribune[①] and which made reference of a work from Thomson Reuters indicates that the trend of increase in patent applications and granted titles make china the largest country in the world based on the volume of applications and number of granted patents. The figure 4 indicated the trend in the patent deposit in China. This projection is based on an analysis of the total volume (nationals and foreigners) of the patents deposited in China, in Europe, in Japan,

---

① La Tribune December 10th 2010. http://www.latribune.fr/actualites/economie/international/20101012trib000559284/comment – la – chine – va – devenir – la – championne – du – monde – des – brevets – .html.

in Korea and in the United States. Thus, between 2003 and 2009, this volume grew with the annual percentage of 26.1% in China compared with 5.5% for its direct competitor the United States. Consequently in 2013 China will take over the United States and Japan and will be the leading country in the world in terms of the number of patents deposited.

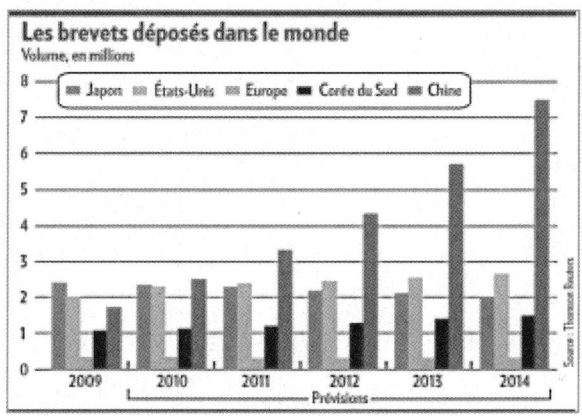

Figure 4. **Number of patents granted in China per year**

Attaining the above mentioned goal started from the incentive initiated by the Chinese Prime Minister Wen Jiabao in 2003, during the launching of the national innovation program. But, the global amount of patent gives after analysis a contrasted. In 2010, 814,825 patent have been approved by the Chinese patent office, out of which only 12,337 are international requests which places China in the 4th place after the United States (44,855), Japan (31,156) and Germany (17,171). Remaining Chinese priority patent not extended, are moreover done for about 40% of them of utility certificates which give a protection for about 6 years instead of the 20 years for a classical patent[1].

It seems relatively clear that China is leaving as soon as possible the "copying" system, to move to innovation. This is interesting because most of the experts estimate that this path is a strong differentiation between China and India which will be

---

[1] Que Vallent les brevets Chinois, L'Usine Nouvelle, February 23rd, 2011. http://www.usinenouvelle.com

remaining in the state of low technology products for a longer time①. It is also necessary to note the tremendous effort② made by China in the domain of information not only in the field of patens, but also in the field of Scientific Information. The growing number of Chinese patents makes a full coverage of the country buy Chinese technologies even if, according to the director of the Research center of the intellectual property of the University of Jiaotong (Shanghai), Chen Naiwei③, "most patents granted in China do nothing but change appearance or propose new models, which does not require a great innovating technique". Then the Technology dependence as described by H. Dou[6] will no longer occurs. Portals[7] such as the CNKI have been also developed in China, they provide a way to access to Scientific Information.

4.2 Taking advantage of Chinese Innovation and ideas

As we saw, that most of the Chinese patents are not extended to other countries and are only Chinese priority patents. Then, it is interesting to note that all these patents can be used in all other countries but China. This is important for developing countries because often simple ideas, models or other features are available from Chinese patents and can be used to build up new ideas and then promote innovation. The following extracts of various research made in different subjects will demonstrate how Chinese ideas may be used in particular in low income developing and least developed countries.

4.2.1 *Example solar panel*

The search conducted on Solar panel using Matheo patent search software revealed the following:

Quick report:

---

① Conference of Alain Juillet (High Responsible of Competitive Intelligence near the Prime Minister in France) Aix en Provence (Technopole de l'Arbois), November 20, 2007. See also http://www.ciworldwide.org.

② Intérêt et méthode d'extraction de l'information scientifique chinoise Guenec N, Dou H Cahiers de la Documentation Belge, n°4, Décembre 2008.

③ La Tribune op. cited.

solarpanel [761 Families – 1017 Patents]

Search : [EPO world patent database] : solar and panel(TI in titles of the patents);

941 Applicants; 1443 Inventors; 131 IPC4; 555 IPC; 363 ECLA;

PD Year : 2010 [387] 2009 [299] 2011 [144]

App. : empty field (– –) [106] hitachi high tech corp (– –) [23] iwabuchi minoru (– –) [14]

Inv. : empty field (– –) [19] araki masaki (– –) [18] iwabuchi minoru (– –) [14]

IPC4 : h01l [391] f24j [224] e04d [77]

IPC7 : h01l31 [382] f24j2 [223] e04d13 [73]

We selected the Chinese patents extended to other countries or WO or PCT, and the Chinese priority patents not extended. The results are presented in table 3.

Table 3. Number of Chinese patents extended

Total number of patents	PN = China global	PN = China WO and other extensions	PR = CN with no extension
	180	13	167

The above table clearly shows that the majority of the patents granted in China are not extended to other countries outside of China there by providing with the opportunity of exploiting technologies that are patented in China but not in other countries. Patent protection is territorial in its nature. Countries where a technology is not validly protected will be considered as falling in the public domain and can be freely used.

4.2.2 *Taking advantage of Chinese ideas*

We extracted from the 167 Chine patents, some of them which may be used to get ideas or implement innovation programs. The results (in part) is the table 4.

Table 4. Example from various patents with Chinese priority not extended

S	C	D	Pertinence	Number	Title
				CN201429008Y	POROUS MULTI-ANGLE SOLAR PANEL BRACKET
				CN201425247Y	LED STREET LAMP WITH SOLAR PANEL
				CN201422085Y	GROUP SUPPORT FOR SOLAR ENERGY PANEL
				CN201422084Y	SOLAR ENERGY PANEL FLAT-ROOF SUPPORT STRUCTURE
				CN201412871Y	LIGHTER WITH SOLAR ENERGY PANEL
				CN201412759Y	DECORATION TABLE LAMP WITH POWER CELL HAVING AMORPHOUS SILICON SOLAR PANEL
				CN201409100Y	SOLAR PANEL FOR WINDOWS
				CN201398158Y	SOLAR PANEL
				CN201397231Y	MECHANICAL LOAD TESTING EQUIPMENT OF SOLAR PANEL
				CN201393184Y	MOUNTING FRAME OF SOLAR PHOTOVOLTAIC PANEL
				CN201391051Y	SOLAR PANEL BRICK AND MOUNTING PART THEREOF
				CN201389535Y	ULTRASONIC SOLAR PANEL CLEANER
				CN201388175Y	DOUBLE SHAFT ROTARY SOLAR PANEL RACK
				CN201388169Y	SOLAR ENERGY PHOTOVOLTAIC PANEL MOUNTING BRACKET
				CN201382598Y	SOLAR CONDENSATION PANEL WATER HEATER
				CN201382592Y	MULTIFUNCTIONAL SOLAR PANEL WATER HEATER
				CN201378813Y	FISH SCALE-SHAPED SOLAR PANEL BRACKET
				CN201368344Y	TORCH WITH BUILT-IN SOLAR PANEL STRUCTURE
				CN201367685Y	SOLAR POWER GENERATION HEAT PRODUCTION ENERGY-SAVING ROOF PANEL
				CN201364902Y	SOLAR PANEL FOR IMPROVING OPTICAL ABSORPTIVITY

Patent CN2013895Y Ultrasonic solar panel cleaner

Abstract: An ultrasonic solar panel cleaner is used for solving the problem of the cleaning of a solar panel. The technical scheme of the ultrasonic solar panel cleaner is as follows: the ultrasonic solar panel cleaner consists of a motor, a water pump and an ultrasonic oscillator, wherein the water pump is driven by the motor a water inlet of the water pump is connected with a cleaning liquid source by a water inlet pipe a water outlet of the water pump is connected with a liquid outlet pipe and an energy converter of the ultrasonic oscillator is arranged in a pipeline, through which cleaning liquid flows. The ultrasonic solar panel cleaner not only can conveniently and efficiently clean the installed and fixed solar panel, but also has simple structure and low cost.

Patent CN 201382598Y Solar condensation water panel heater

Abstract: The utility model discloses a solar condensation panel water heater, belonging to the field of water heaters. A solar condensation panel is arranged below a water storage tank at the top of a water heater bracket a heat collector is arranged at a condensation focus the top of the heat collector is provided with a communicating pipe connected with the lower part of the water storage tank and a one-way valve is arranged inside the communicating pipe at a connecting end of the communicating pipe and the water storage tank. Just like a solar cooker, the solar condensation panel water heat can boil water in the heat collector within a short time and heat energy can be transmitted to the water storage tank through heat convection to enable the water temperature in the water storage tank to reach a very high value, therefore, the utility model has the advantages of high heating speed, high water supply temperature, greatly increased hot water supply amount and long service life.

Note that the use of the expression "utility model" in the abstract may be used to select the utility model: over the 167 patents with Chinese priority and not extended, 69 are a utility modesl.

4.3 Translation problems

It was noted above that the Chinese technologies that are protected as a patent or utility model in China and not extended in other countries can be freely used. However, there is a serious problem that may be encountered in making use of technological information contained in Chinese patent documents. The problem relates to language. Technological or patent information that is related to a Chinese technology that is extended to other countries and made available, for example, in WO patent can easily be accessed as there is a requirement of translation and can made available in different languages such as English and French. This is not the case regarding technologies protected in China using a patent or utility model as the technological information will only be available in Chinese. This could be explained in the table below.

The table 5 show part of the patent (Ultrasonic solar panel cleaner) after downloading:

Table 5. First page and second page of the former patent

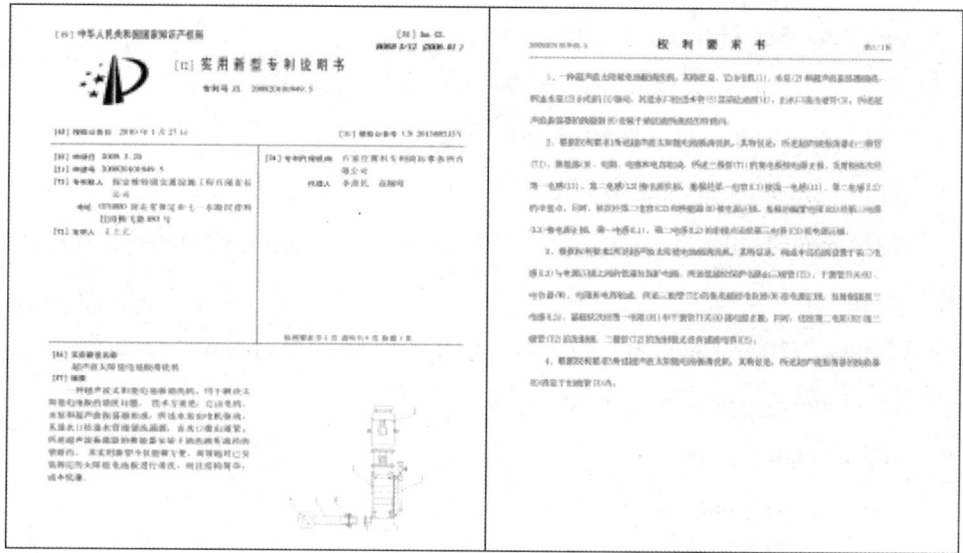

Most of the people have no access to Chinese translation at low cost there by making the technology inaccessible. There is therefore need to develop a simple method to translate automatically the patent, at least to get a basic information. Off course if a further use of this patent must be done, it will be necessary to refine the translation.

The process is the following:

The patent is downloaded as a pdf. This is an image and no translator may be used. Further processing of the technological information can be made using the steps below:

- Use on OCR (Optical Character Recognition) which is able to recognize chine simplified (for instance the OCR used in Adobe professional).
- Made a cut and paste of the parts submitted to OCR.
- Paste in Word for instance and translate (Systran for example) but other translator may be used.

This process will result in the following:

[19] People's Republic of China State Intellectual Property Rights Office [51] Int. Cl.

B08B3/12 but 106.01)

[12] patent of utility model instruction booklet

Patent number ZL 200920101949.5

[45J was authorized to announce the date on January 27, 2010

[22J string i blue days 2009.3.20

[21J application number 200920101949.5

[73J patent holder Baoding Terui traffic equipment process limited liability Company

Address. 71000 Hebei Baoding 71 east road privately operated branches Technique garden soaring road 893rd

[72J inventor Wang Shiyuan

[Various 54J model utility names

Ultrasonic wave solar cell board clearer

[57] abstract

One kind of ultrasonic wave solar cell board clearer, for solving too

The positivity can volta cell board clean question. The technical program is: It by electrical machinery, Water pump and ultrasonic oscillator composition, states water pump by motor – driven, The water inlet meets cleaning liquid source after the water inlet pipe, the water outlet leads the fluid tube:

Stated the transducer installment of ultrasonic oscillator to flow through in the cleaning liquid In pipeline. Not only this model utility can settle to oneself conveniently and highly effective Installs the fixed solar cell board to carry on the clean. Moreover the structure is simple, The cost is inexpensive.

[11] are authorized to announce number CN 201389535Y

[74] patent agency Shijiazhuang Hebei branch patent trademark transaction all Limits the company

Proxy Li Xianmin Gao Ximing

Claim of right book 1 page of instruction booklet 4 pages of attached figure 1 pages

4

200920101949.5 the claim of right book 1/1st page

1st, one kind of ultrasonic wave solar cell board clearer, its characteristic is, it (2) and ultrasonic oscillator is composed of electrical machinery (1), water pump,

Stated the water pump (2) by the electrical machinery (1) actuation, its water inlet (5) met the cleaning liquid source after the water inlet pipe (4), the water outlet led the fluid tube (3); Stated ultra

The transducer (B) installment of hammerbox in the pipeline that the cleaning liquid flows through.

2nd, basis claim of right 1 stated the ultrasonic wave solar cell board clearer, its characteristic was, states ultrasonic oscillator by triode

(T1), transducer (B), resistance, inductance and electric capacity composition, states the triode (T1) collecting electrode receiving a telegram source positive electrode, the emitter electrode passes through in turn

The first inductance (L1), second inductance (L2) receiving a telegram source cathode, the base electrode (C1) meets the first inductance (L1), second inductance after the first electric capacity (L2)

The series connection point, meanwhile, passes through the second electric capacity in turn (C2) and transducer (B) receiving a telegram source positive electrode, the base electrode bias resistance (R3) passes through the third inductance

(L3) receiving a telegram source positive electrode, first inductance (L1), second inductance (L2) series connection also passes through the third electric capacity (C3) receiving a telegram source positive electrode.

3rd, basis claim of right 2 stated the ultrasonic wave solar cell board clearer, its characteristic was, in the framing also included the setting in the third electricity

Feeling (L3) low fluid position protection circuit with power source positive electrodes, states low fluid position protection circuit by triode (T2), dry reed pipes switch (Omega,

Potentiometer (, resistance and electric capacity composition, states triode (T2) collecting electrode after potentiometer (W) receiving a telegram source positive electrode, the emitter electrode meets second

Inductance (L3), the base electrode passes through the first resistance in turn (R1) and does the reed pipes switch (K) receiving a telegram source positive electrode, meanwhile, but also passes through the second resistance (R2) to meet three

Manages (T2) emitter electrode extremely, the triode (T2) emitter electrode is also equipped with eliminates the Polish electric capacity (C5).

4th, basis claim of right 3 stated the ultrasonic wave solar cell board clearer, its characteristic was, states ultrasonic oscillator's transducer (B) fixes in leaving the fluid tube (3).

It is clear that the translation is not optimal but the use of specific dictionaries which can be improved will lead to a better translation. Nevertheless the translation is sufficient to give to the "homme de l'art" some useful information.

5 CONCLUSION

We saw that strategic dependence may occur in certain countries if the most important technologies are not covered by "national patents". The example of developing countries such as the OAPI countries indicated that the dependence exists, but according to the level of knowledge and technical knowledge in the member countries it may be difficult to address the problem. One way of dealing with the problem of inadequate technological capacity is attracting and promoting the activities of foreign firms in the country, and to consider them as part of the national firms if they made their research and development in the country and if they patent (priority patent) in the country also[①].

The Chinese experience shows that they recognized the problem of technological dependence and engaged in building local technological capacity earlier than 200 . They put in place an incentive scheme that stimulate Chinese firms and Universities to move to the patent field. This gives a tremendous push to the number of Chine patents granted. However, the technologies that are protected using patents and utility models may not be that sophisticated. The large number of Chinese technologies that are protected in China but not extended in to other countries can be freely used, for example, as the starting point of new ideas or innovative processes in other countries. The problem, however, is the technological information disclosed in patent and utility model documents are made in Chinese. Most of the time, people are reluctant to use them because of the translation problem or the cost involved in translation. However, this should not be a problem. Thanks to the development made in translation software, people that may want to use Chinese technologies will be in a position to use them. The facilities offered by various software including Google help

---

[①] This question rose in France in the context of the poles of competitiveness. Does for instance IBM France be considered as a French firm? We considered that if the research is done in France as well as the applications and if the patent IBM France is taken in France, we can consider this firm as French.

to translate and use technological information made available in the different languages. The title and the abstract of an invention can be used for the initial query (for instance for the world patent database) and further to the selection of the more useful patents.

REFERENCES

[1] Nirmalya Syam, Carnegie council. Rush for Patents May Hinder Transfer of New Climate – related Technologies. http://www.policyinnovations.org/ideas/briefings/data/000162/:pf_printable.

[2] Xian Zhang, Shu Fang, Chuan Tang, Guohua Xiao, Zhengyin Hu, Lidan Gao. 2009. Study on indicator system for core patent documents evaluation. The Chinese Academy of Sciences.

[3] Dou H, Manullang S, Dou JM Jr. 2009. Strategic Dependence of a Developing Country - Vision from Patents. Third Euroepean Competitive Intelligence Symposium, June 11 – 12th. Editor Malardalen University, Box 883, Vastera Eskitsina, Sweden(Web of Science).

[4] H Dou, V Leveillé, S Manullang, JM Dou Jr. 2005. Patent Analysis for Competitive Technical Intelligence and Innovative Thinking. Data Science Journal, Vol. 4, pp. 209 - 236.

[5] Karadsah Suryadi, Agus Salim Ridwan, Henri Dou, Andrian Purnama. 1999. Technology Forecasting in Competitive Intelligence: The use of Patent Analysis. http://isdm.univ-tln.fr/articles/num_archives.htm.

[6] Dou H, Manullang S, Dou JM Jr. 2009. Strategic Dependence of a Developing Country - Vision from Patents. Third Euroepean Competitive Intelligence Symposium, June 11 – 12th. Editor Malardalen University, Box 883, Vastera Eskitsina, Sweden.

[7] Guénec N, Krumeich C, Paoli C, Dou H. 2010. Knowledge Building in the field of STI (Strategic Technical Information) and Geopolitics for Competitive Intelligence: a Strategic Application for the Chinese Market in the field of Agricultural Biotechnologies in the People Republic of China (PCR). Data Science Journal (CODATA), January 13.

面向企业技术创新的关键竞争情报课题构建

刘细文① 熊 瑞②

[摘要] 构建关键情报课题是企业开展竞争情报研究的重要过程,是一种程序化的、正式的竞争情报需求识别与管理。明确关键情报课题的内涵、组成要素和构建原则,有助于关键情报课题的成功构建。本文分析了关键情报课题的管理目标、关注内容、情报任务三个要素。通过对比分析 Herring 和 Porter 的关键情报课题框架、关键技术创新管理框架的构建过程,提出了一个"好"的"关键情报课题"应当满足"面向管理决策(Decision-oriented)、目标性(Focus)、课题可执行(Executable)、信息粒度适当(Appropriate)、稳定性(Stability)、优先级(Priority)"六大原则。以企业技术创新为切入点,建立包括58个课题和64项情报任务的"企业技术创新的关键情报课题内容框架"。

[关键词] 关键情报课题 企业技术竞争情报 竞争情报 技术创新管理

Construction of Key Intelligence Topics for Enterprise Technology Innovation

[Abstract] Constructions of KIT are important processes of enterprises competitive intelligence service, and also are programmatic and formal recognitions and managements of competitive intelligence needs. So it is helpful to the constructing a good KIT frameworks to clear up the content and parts and principles of the KIT. The paper analyses the three factors of KIT, such as the managing goal, main content, CIT task. The paper compares Hering's and Alan Porter's on the construction

---

① 刘细文,研究员,中国科学院国家科学图书馆,liuxw@mail.las.ac.cn
② 熊瑞,商业分析师,百度时代网络技术有限公司,xiongrui@baidu.com

of KIT framework and management of key technology innovation, and claim the six principles of the "good" KIT, a good KIT should mandate the decision – oriented needs and strongly focus and executable programme and appropriate information granularity and topic stability and rank priority. Then the paper set up a KIT framework of enterprise technological innovation, which includes the 58 topics and 64 intelligence tasks.

[**Keywords**] Key Intelligence Topic, Enterprise Competitive Technical Intelligence, Competitive Intelligence, Technological Innovation Management

20世纪80年代中期,J. P. Herring离开美国政府部门加入摩托罗拉公司,将政府情报部门的"国家情报课题"(National Intelligence Topics,NITs)运用于企业,提出"关键情报课题"(Key Intelligence Topics,KITs),用于识别和优先考虑高层管理者以及整个公司的关键情报需求。通过多年的竞争情报服务实践,J. P. Herring发现,尽管不同行业不同企业的情报需求各有不同,但却大致可归为三类:(1)战略决策和行动;(2)早期预警课题;(3)对公司所处市场的主要参与者的监测。[1]

J. P. Herring认为情报需求识别有两种基本模式[2]:第一种为被动式(Responsive Mode),意味着企业情报组织做好应对用户各种需求的准备,当情报组织接到用户请求,如果该情报请求得到确认,便将递交必要的情报报告;第二种为主动式(Proactive Mode),情报人员主动询问决策者(用户),识别和确定他们的情报需求,并予以满足。Herring将这种主动模式称之为"KIT"流程,在这个流程中,情报人员通过日常会议与主要情报用户接触,确定和修正用户需求,更有效地协调和满足整个组织的情报需求。

1 关键情报课题的内涵演进

关键情报课题流程的提出,引起了竞争情报理论研究者和实践者的关注。J. P. Herring认为,关键情报课题是一种程序化的、正式的管理需求识别过程,用于识别和优先考虑高层管理者的关键情报需求[3],大部分从事KIT研究人员都认同了这种想法。[4]

David Francis、Jan Herring 合作为美国生产力促进中心进行了大规模的 KITs 实证研究。[5]他们根据对组织各类 KITs 数量进行统计,认为三类 KITs 的理想比例是:战略决策和行动(＞35%),早期预警课题(＞20%),关键参与者描述(＜30%),并在此基础上提出了"KITs 值"这一概念。将一个企业的 KITs 值与理想比例的差异,以及与该企业当前的竞争境况分析、过去的竞争经验联系起来,可以对企业的竞争态势进行一种简单的定量分析。Hussey & Jenster 认为,KITs 反映了组织中的情报优先权,常被定义为"将对公司价值产生显著影响的产品或解放方案",将为情报搜集与分析的关注焦点提供一个可操作性的框架;他们补充提出了 KITs 的第四种功能——反情报课题,即 KPR(Key Protection Requirement)。[6]

在国内,戴侣红(2002)最早根据 Herring 的专论文章将"关键情报课题"研究引入我国[7],北京大学硕士黄英(2003)在其学位论文中从"KIT 内容、KIT 流程、KIT 文化"三层框架对关键情报课题进行了较为集中的论述。[8]北京市科技情报所夏晨曦(2009)对关键情报课题提出一种比较创新的想法,即建立一种关键情报课题管理模型。该模型由任务模块、任务要素、情报模块、情报要素、情报元素、元素值等部分构成。[9]其中,任务模块对应情报需求;情报模块代表情报类型;情报元素是竞争情报中的一些关键要素(如产品、竞争对手、销售价格、时间等),分别说明任务要素和情报要素;元素值则表示枚举的情报元素。该模型可应用于竞争情报软件的关键情报课题模块,但稍显抽象、复杂,有待进一步提升实用性。

J. P. Herring 在 2005 年又发表了一篇文章:*KITs Revisited: Their Use and Problems*,对"关键情报课题"存在的问题和一些错误理解进行澄清与评论。他指出[10]:

(1)KITs 并不是简单的问题和答案。不是简单地回答管理层提出的问题(需要一定的显性信息),而是一个持续的情报需求识别的过程。同样重要的是,它需要一系列规划、搜集、分析活动。最后,提供的 KIT"答案"能否应用于一定的商业活动是对整个过程的检验。

(2)KITs 不是关键情报问题。John Nolan 等(2009)发展出对 KIT 内容进一步细化、具体化分析的工具——关键情报问题(Key Intelligence Questions,

KIQ),以促进 KIT 的可实施化。[11] Herring 认为,KIQs 可用于分析 KIT,形成对 KIT 课题关键要素的理解,它在制定 KIT 行动计划、决定采取何种情报活动中非常有用。但它并不是与 KIT 用户进行交互的方式,列出一长串有趣的问题通常不能形成一套转化为情报行动的 KIT 方案。

(3)KITs 需要行动计划。KIT 识别需求只是第一步,需要进一步分析 KIT,理解决策者将如何应用得到的情报,从而决定如何搜集、分析和提供产品。在开始任何情报活动之前,必须确保 KIT 是正确的,并让决策者了解将做些什么、可能的结果。

(4)KITs 的数量要控制。KITs 数量依情报组织规模所定,要将 KITs 数量控制在组织能够充分处理的范围内,并按时间紧急性、优先级来执行。KIT 是 CI 经理识别、规划并同时实施一系列情报活动的工具。一些搜集活动经过规划不只满足一个 KIT,各 KIT 之间是相互联系的。

综上所述,关键情报课题可以从狭义与广义两个方面来理解。狭义的关键情报课题更加关注于内容,广义的关键情报课题则能为未来的情报需求识别、课题目标锁定、情报成果分享复用提供重要的基础。狭义地讲,关键情报课题是情报人员凭借一定的知识、经验和方法,了解分析管理者要面临的决策、关心的问题,从中识别和捕获情报需求,并将其转化成若干个重要的、可执行的、具有优先次序的情报研究课题,有效提高竞争情报研究工作的效率;广义地讲,关键情报课题是贯穿竞争情报需求识别、规划、执行、反馈与共享的一个循环往复过程,包括了指导制定情报活动执行规划(如配置情报资源、选择信息源、分析方法),根据用户对情报成果的反馈完善需求,最终实现情报课题成果共享、复用的整个过程机制。

2 企业技术创新的竞争情报需求

C. Freeman(1986)认为,技术创新是新产品、新过程、新系统和新服务的首次商业化转化。[12] S. Myers 和 D. G. Marquis(1969)认为,技术创新是一个复杂的活动过程,从新思想和新概念开始,通过不断地解决各种问题,最终使一个有经济价值和社会价值的新项目得到实际的成功应用。[13] 傅家骥教授(1998)则认为,技术创新是企业家抓住市场的潜在盈利机会,以获取商业利益为目标,重新组织生产条件和要素,建立起效能更强、效率更高和费用更低的生产经营系统,从而推出新的产品、新的生产(工艺)方法、开辟新的市场、获得新的原材料或半成品供给来源或建立企业的新组织,它是包括科技、组织、商业和金融等一系列活动的综合过程。[14]归纳起来,"技术创新"区别于"发明创造"、"研究开发"、"知识创新"等,即"技术创新"包括:(1)发明构思、产品设计、试制生产到商业应用等所有环节;(2)它是技术成果的商业化应用,以产生新产品、新工艺、新服务为结果;(3)技术创新强调以新的技术创造出尽可能多的经济效益,并获得最大的企业利润。

2.1 企业技术竞争情报需求研究

美国的技术竞争情报专家 W. Bradford Ashton 和 Richard A. Klavans(1997)认为:技术竞争情报是有关外部科技威胁、机会或发展,对企业竞争地位可能产生影响的商业敏感信息。[15] Pascal Savioz(2004)认为:技术情报是指对组织环境中有关技术事实与趋势(机会和威胁)的信息,进行及时的收集、分析和传播,从而支撑技术及综合管理决策的一系列活动。[16] 刘细文(2008)将技术竞争情报定义为:组织或机构为了获取技术竞争优势,对有关外部技术机会、威胁和发展的信息进行收集和分析,由此形成有关技术本身、技术竞争环境、竞争对手、竞争策略和战略的分析产品,并组织实施技术创新管理的过程。[17]

因此,分析企业技术竞争情报需求有两个关键点:第一,技术竞争情报范畴与市场情报、竞争情报相互关联,而非彼此完全独立。技术竞争情报侧重于关注给组织带来影响的技术相关因素,但绝非仅仅关注技术本身,对于影响技术发展的社会、经济、政策环境,技术应用领域市场竞争状况等各种潜在机会与威胁也同样关心。第二,技术竞争情报工作的目标是对企业战略决策、经营决策、技术及综合管理决策、技术创新管理活动等产生影响和提供支撑。

企业技术竞争情报活动的本质是情报用户(即决策者、研发人员)与情报人员之间的互动。一方面,情报用户通过"我想知道"(I want to know)向情报人员提出需求,他们的三个典型问题是[18]:(1)我们需要知道什么(What do we need to know)?(2)我们为什么需要知道(Why do we need to know it)?(3)如果我们知道,要做出何种决策或采取何种行动(What decision is to be made, or action taken, once we know it)?另一方面,情报人员以"你需要知道"(You need to know)找到合适的情报用户并提供相应情报,他们的三个典型问题是[19]:(1)谁需要知道(Who need to know)?(2)谁想要知道(Who want to know)?(3)谁应该知道(Who should know)?

W. Bradford Ashton 等(1994)认为[20],"需求"环节直接影响技术竞争情报的规划,识别潜在情报用户的关键需求和明确要调研的技术领域是规划阶段重点关注的两个层面。并且,不同技术竞争情报用户往往存在不同的需求侧重点(如表1所示)。

表1　　　　　　　　不同技术竞争情报用户的关键信息需求

信息用户	典型的关键信息需求
科学家/工程师	技术细节数据 ■ 研发的技术目标 ■ 研发方法——产品/流程设计 ■ 制造方法 ■ 研发结果或进展 ■ 技术联系人/研究者
技术经理	科技资助数据 ■ 技术领域的资助计划 ■ 研发或技术获取战略
市场人员	产品竞争性特点 ■ 产品销量 ■ 成本/价格数据
高层管理者	技术管理或商业方面的新闻 ■ 技术联系人/研究者
政策制定者/管理者	科技政策 ■ 国家的科学技术目标和资助 ■ 新的科学技术发展方向

(资料来源:W. Bradford Ashton, Anne H. Johnson, Gary S. Stacey. Monitoring Science and Technology for Competitive Advantage[J]. Competitive Intelligence Review, 1994, 5(1):5-16.)

C. I. V. Kerr 从"情报需求"与"情报提供"两个维度,划分出"挖掘(Mine)、搜罗(Trawl)、跟踪(Target)、扫描(Scan)"四种情报工作模式。[21]其中,"挖掘"与"跟踪"模式从本质上属于"被动型",主要针对组织意识到的、有价值的情报需求;"搜罗"与"扫描"模式则属于"主动型",在于捕获不可预知的、存在潜在影响的话题,所获得信息不确定是否有价值、会否满足情报需求。

美国佐治亚理工大学 Alan Porter 教授带领研究团队开发"技术挖掘"软件平台,对技术竞争情报需求展开调查,是有关技术竞争情报需求少有的、相对系统深入的研究。[22,23,24]

2.2 技术竞争情报对于企业技术创新的价值

金炬、梁战平(2006)总结美国技术竞争情报(CTI)在企业中的实践,指出技术竞争情报对企业五个方面的工作影响最大[25]:

(1)企业战略和技术战略。帮助企业确定技术在企业战略中的作用,是否进入新技术市场,是否需要保护关键技术的产权。企业依靠 CTI 了解竞争对手在科技方面的动向。

(2)技术获取。CTI 根据科技发展趋势和竞争对手的信息,帮助企业选择技术获取的方式,评价产品技术合作价值和工艺开发的价值。

(3)研究开发管理。CTI 帮助确定研究开发的重点、设计具体研发项目的技术路径,根据竞争对手的研发计划修正本公司的研发项目组合。

(4)技术配置。CTI 帮助公司确定哪些技术要上,哪些技术要下,即使目前还在赢利也要考虑过时技术如何退出的问题。

(5)生产过程。CTI 要了解公司生产的外部供应商和原料供应商方面的技术进步,以便维护正常生产,保护资本投资。除此之外,企业战略规划、生产营销、顾客服务等方面都可以受益于 CTI 产品。

Thomas F. Krol 等(1996)认为技术竞争情报在战略规划、业务发展、市场研究、商业情报等方面都存在重要价值。[26]

(1)在战略规划方面:为管理者的战略决策提供信息支撑,帮助决策者了解技术进展、竞争对手、未来情景,进行市场评估,识别更好的研发方法。

(2)在业务发展方面:识别和明确关键竞争对手在未来新产品推出可能产生的影响,识别研发改进方法,特定公司、产品以及对公司产生影响的竞争性产品,了解潜在技术突破及其时间,识别监测可选择技术对于未来市场的影响,研发绩效、研发风险预测,识别竞争对手技术的属性与特征,竞争对手产品战略,研发方向,识别潜在许可的项目或产品,新商业机会,新兴产品的技术特性。

(3)在市场研究方面:增加市场研究的技术专业性,识别处在销售或开发阶段的产品的关键问题,识别新产品推出的关键问题,产品的竞争地位,识别基于已有技术的类似产品,识别突破性技术对市场规模、地位与动态的影响。

(4)在商业情报方面:评估竞争产品的技术优点、属性和缺陷,产品技术特征,将专利技术数据与经营战略相联系,潜在收购对象评估。

Ashton 和 Klavans(1995)认为技术竞争情报应该能够帮助企业实现三个基本目标[27]:(1)提供可能对企业成功产生不利影响的外部科技发展与其他企业行动的早期预警信息;(2)识别科技环境变化带来的新产品、新工艺以及新的合作机会;(3)了解技术事件或变化趋势,以及相关的竞争环境,指出现有或未来产品、市场所存在的潜在威胁,为识别利用重大的新机会提供准备。

上述技术竞争情报可以发挥的作用与价值都是技术创新管理所迫切需要的,与技术创新管理的内涵和目标也十分一致。技术竞争情报的服务内涵和服务模式可以在企业技术创新过程中发挥核心作用。总体来看,技术竞争情报可以在三个层次上支撑企业的技术创新管理:(1)环境层。即关注企业外部环境中产业、技术、产品、市场、人才、资金等技术创新相关对象的发展变化趋势,发现利用机会,应对威胁挑战;(2)企业层。即从企业出发,整合利用组织内外相关资源,制定技术战略规划,实施研发活动,开展技术合作等;(3)项目层。即对 R&D 项目(如产品或工艺开发项目)的管理活动,具体包括创新构思、研发项目评估选择、试验开发、生产制造到商业化的一系列过程。

2.3 企业技术创新中竞争情报需求的阶段性

企业技术创新的各个阶段都存在着竞争情报需求。日本著名经济学家斋藤优将技术创新划分为设想、R&D、实用化、商品化四个阶段,并简要列举了四个阶段的信息需求(见表2)。[28]

可以看到,技术创新各阶段的信息需求主要包括研究信息、原材料和生产技术信息、市场有关信息、同行业其他企业信息、国外信息、需求与机会信息、一般技术信息、其他一般信息八大类。其中,前五类信息在 R&D、实用化、商品化阶段都有需要,只是重要性排序有所不同;设想阶段是技术创新的起始阶段,主要目标在于捕捉、把握和应对相应的机会与威胁,形成创新构想,因而信息关注面比较广泛,其信息需求为后三类信息。

表 2　　　　　　　　　　技术创新各阶段的信息需求

创新过程	设想阶段	R&D 阶段	实用化阶段	商品化阶段
信息（按重要性排序）	需求与机会信息	研究信息	原材料和生产技术信息	市场有关信息
	一般技术信息	同行业其他企业的信息	同行业其他企业的开发研究信息	同行业其他企业的开发研究信息
	其他一般信息	国外信息 原材料和生产技术信息 市场有关信息	研究信息 国外信息 市场有关信息	国外信息 原材料和生产技术信息 研究信息

（赵刚,汤世国,吴叶君等.技术创新与企业竞争[M].北京:华夏出版社,2003:232.）

柯贤能(2007)在其硕士论文中,通过理论归纳,从竞争对手、技术相关机构、技术本身与企业自身四个方面,总结出技术创新战略制定、技术创新计划制定、技术创新项目制定、技术创新总结各阶段的情报需求。[29]该需求分析已深入主题内容层次,重点关注了技术创新的技术竞争情报需求,但忽略了与技术创新有关的市场需求、竞争环境、行业供应商等相关方面。

技术竞争情报需求的阶段性,直接影响了关键情报课题的构成,是关键情报课题形成的因素之一,是关键情报课题构建的要素。

3　关键情报课题的组成要素与构建原则

3.1　两种典型关键情报课题体系的对比分析

J. P. Herring(1994)提出的关键情报课题方法论,在 Nutra Sweet、Southwestern Bell、Texas Instruments、Ford Motor Credit、Rockwel Automotive Design 等众多美国企业都取得了广泛而成功的应用,相关学者也继而开展了相应的研究,但关于关键情报课题内容体系构建的研究总结并不多。J. P. Herring 的关键情报课题体系和 Alan Porter 的技术管理课题体系是需求分析深入情报需求课题层次的典范,是少有的较为系统成型的关键情报课题体系。

(1) J. P. Herring 的 KIT 体系

J. P. Herring 将企业关键情报课题归为三类[30]:(1)战略决策和行动,包括战略计划和战略开发;(2)早期预警课题,包括竞争者的动机、技术上的新发现和政府行为;(3)对企业所处环境的关键参与者的描述,包括竞争者、客户、供应商、管制者和潜在的合作伙伴。三类关键情报课题之间相互关联,并不完全独立排斥,每类课题各包括12个关键情报课题(见表3)。

表 3　　　　　　　　　　　　Herring 关键情报课题体系

课题类型	编号	课题内容
战略决策与行动	HK 1-1	为企业的战略规划提供情报以创造"我们"未来的竞争环境
	HK 1-2	形成"我们"的全球竞争战略:评估竞争者在我们实现经营目标中的作用
	HK 1-3	行业的全球化:我们应该怎样/与谁一起前进?我们的竞争者在做什么?与谁一起?
	HK 1-4	亚洲/南美洲等市场发展情况:评估当前竞争态势,描述最为可能的未来态势
	HK 1-5	战略投资决策:识别和评估竞争环境的改变,包括: - 他人的关键行业投资 - 行业内其他公司的现金需求 - 投资机构的参与/角色 - 未来投资的可能渠道,包括联合、收购等
	HK 1-6	我们是该扩大目前的生产能力,还是该建立一个新工厂,采用更有成本效益的生产过程?
	HK 1-7	与关键竞争者相比,我们应当采取什么样的计划和行动来保持技术竞争力?
	HK 1-8	产品开发项目:识别和评估领先竞争者的项目,评估其他竞争性技术的态势
	HK 1-9	新产品开发与上市:竞争者什么时候、如何回应?它们怎样影响我们的计划?
	HK 1-10	行业、竞争者及分销商如何看待我们的分销/销售/营销策略?
	HK 1-11	对我们专有信息/技术的保护: - 竞争者为获取它所做出的努力? - 对之感兴趣的其他相关方?
	HK 1-12	人力资源问题:雇佣和留住重要员工

(续表)

早期预警	HK 2-1	对我们当前及未来竞争力可能产生显著影响的技术突破领域
	HK 2-2	影响生产能力或产品开发的技术进展,以及被竞争者相关方运用的情况
	HK 2-3	关键供应商的状况与绩效: - 他们的财务是否"健康" - 成本与质量问题 - 可能的收购/联盟
	HK 2-4	原油/部件等供应可能的中断
	HK 2-5	行业采购政策和流程的变动
	HK 2-6	客户或竞争者对我们及我们服务所持态度的变化
	HK 2-7	可能考虑进入我们行业或市场的公司或公司的联合
	HK 2-8	国际或国家政治、社会、经济或管理制度变化对我们竞争力可能造成的影响
	HK 2-9	监管问题:近期变动;长期趋势的偏离;其他影响目前监管制度的政府变动,如人或政策
	HK 2-10	有关竞争者、客户和供应商之间联合、收购和剥离的情报: - 导致变化的原因与驱动力 - 完成交易的目标与意图
	HK 2-11	主要竞争者的财务行动: - 当前财务战略的改变 - 联盟、收购与剥离行动等
	HK 2-12	其他相关方想要收购我们公司的兴趣和努力
市场主要参与者(竞争对手)	HK 3-1	提供主要竞争者的档案,包括他们的战略规划、竞争战略、财务与市场表现、组织和关键人员、研发、运营、销售与营销等信息
	HK 3-2	提供对主要竞争者的深入分析,包括: - 对于我们及我们的主要客户的竞争意图 - 战略规划与目标,包括国际目标 - 关键战略:财务、技术、生产、业务拓展、分销、营销 - 当前的运作与竞争能力
	HK 3-3	识别新的正在崛起的竞争者,特别是那些来自完全不同行业和业务领域的竞争者
	HK 3-4	描述与评估当前和未来的竞争环境,包括:客户和竞争者,市场和供应商,生产和产品技术,政治的和环境的,以及行业结构的变化与趋势
	HK 3-5	新客户,他们的需要和未来兴趣是什么? 竞争者是如何满足它们的?
	HK 3-6	行业与客户对我们的品牌、产品及服务价值所持的观点、态度和感受
	HK 3-7	识别和评估新的行业/市场参与者,包括考虑:供应商、主要分销商、客户,考虑进入我们业务领域的竞争者

(续表)

	HK 3-8	新技术/产品的开发者在行业竞争中的计划和战略是什么？
	HK 3-9	需要显著提高市场占有率与增长率方面的信息与数据,包括竞争者的
	HK 3-10	管理与运营需要更好的关于监管和环境活动的情报以进行规划和决策制定
	HK 3-11	投资/金融界对我们的业务、行业所持的观点与理解
	HK 3-12	不同供应商和行业观察家们对我们公司感兴趣的信息,及其搜集信息的目的

（资料来源:Jan P. Herring. *A Process to Identify and Define Intelligence Needs* [J]. *Competitive Intelligence Review*,1994,10(2):4-14.

注释:课题编号"HK m-n",HK 为 Herring KIT 的缩写,m 代表类型（取值范围为 1~3）,n 代表第几个课题（取值范围 1~12）

J. P. Herring 的关键情报课题体系是首个最为全面、详尽的情报需求课题列表。该体系主要侧重竞争情报应用,但在 HK 2-1、HK 2-2 等多处体现技术竞争情报需求,并且有许多课题都能加以转化至技术竞争情报、技术管理范畴。

(2) Alan Porter 的技术竞争情报 KIT 体系

Alan Porter（2005）在其专著 *Tech Mining*: *Exploiting New Technologies for Competitive Advantage* 中,对技术挖掘进行了系统论述,指出技术挖掘可以实现的目标包括[31]:

(1) 预测新兴技术可能的发展路径;

(2) 识别竞争者、合作者、新产品开发模糊前端;

(3) 识别你所拥有知识产权的潜在客户;

(4) 预测未来技术产品与服务的市场潜力;

(5) 利用他人的科学技术成果;

(6) 管理技术开发与实施过程的风险。

根据技术挖掘应用目标,Porter 提出技术管理课题体系。[32]包括 13 个技术管理主题（Technology Management Issues,TMI,如表 5）,39 个技术挖掘问题（Technology Mining Questions,TMQ,如表 4）,以及基于专利、科技数据库资源细分的 100 余个分析指标（Indicators）。Watt 与 Porter 将创新指标分为三类[33]:(1) 技术生命周期状况;(2) 创新环境接受能力;(3) 市场前景。

表 4　　Alan Porter 提出的技术挖掘问题

课题编号	课题内容
PT 1	有哪些新兴技术值得我们关注？
PT 2	该技术发展哪些部分是热点？
PT 3	该技术新的前沿动态是什么？（技术机会？）
PT 4	哪些组件技术最重要？有哪些重要的子技术？
PT 5	该技术的发展如何符合技术前景？
PT 6	什么驱动该技术的发展？
PT 7	有哪些关键竞争技术？
PT 8	该技术的发展前景如何？
PT 9	该技术可能的发展路径是如何？
PT 10	哪些组件技术最重要？有哪些重要的子技术？（同4）
PT 11	评估组件技术的成熟度。
PT 12	识别技术融合的潜力。
PT 13	我们是否应该应用该技术相关专利？应该怎样进行权利要求？
PT 14	开发技术－产品路线图。
PT 15	评估该技术应用系统的成熟度。
PT 16	该技术的哪方面符合我们的应用需求（兴趣）？
PT 17	新兴技术对我们有哪些机会？
PT 18	该技术及应用满足什么样的社会和市场需求？
PT 19	该技术哪些应用有前途？
PT 20	全球存在哪些机会？
PT 21	竞争环境下什么在改变？
PT 22	该技术是否有强的商业化前景？
PT 23	评估竞争环境。
PT 24	有哪些可获得的专家？
PT 25	哪些大学/研究实验室在该技术上领先（整体技术或特定方面）？
PT 26	我们的组织有哪些优势和劣势？
PT 27	哪些公司在该技术的特定方面（主要方面）领先？
PT 28	领先公司的研发队伍有多强大？
PT 29	该技术领先的公司有哪些？
PT 30	与我们相比，领先公司的发展有何不同侧重？

(续表)

课题编号	课题内容
PT 31	每个领先公司分别还有哪些技术优势?
PT 32	描述相关技术持有公司知识产权状况(竞争者分析,或合作者分析)
PT 33	哪些小公司或个人拥有具吸引力的相关技术知识产权?
PT 34	(竞争环境)存在哪些合作?
PT 35	竞争者介绍。
PT 36	哪些公司应该关注?
PT 37	有哪些可能给我们知识产权许可(或以某种方式合作)?
PT 38	企业处于怎样的竞争环境?
PT 39	评估每个主要竞争者。 – 评估竞争者技术战略(识别可能的目标、存在的不确定性) – 对竞争者进行 SWOT 评估 – 评价竞争者的产品定位 – 评价竞争者新产品或服务上市的可能时间 – 为每个主要竞争者构建一个技术路线图(用风险估计识别可能的障碍) – 与竞争者的对比

(资料来源:Alan Porter, Scott W. Cunningham. Tech Mining: Exploiting New Technologies for Competitive Advantage[M]. John Wiley & Sons Press, 2005: 255 – 266.

注释:课题编号"PT n",PT 为 Porter TMQ 的缩写,m 第几个课题(取值范围为 1~39)

如表 5 所示,Alan Porter 的技术管理课题体系中,13 个技术管理课题分别对应 39 个技术挖掘问题中不同的问题,将情报问题答案进行组合可解决相应的情报研究主题(课题或目标)。该对应关系巧妙地体现出"组合"、"拆分"与"复用"的思想,即一个技术管理课题对应于多个技术挖掘问题,回答一个技术挖掘问题能为多个技术管理课题提供部分答案。

表 5   Alan Porter 技术管理课题与技术挖掘问题的对应关系

技术管理课题	技术挖掘问题
研发组合选择	PT – 1,3,4,6,7,12,16,17,22,25,26
研发项目启动	PT – 2,5,6,7,8,11,12,15,17,22,23,25,26
工程项目启动	PT – 2,5,6,7,8,9,11,15,16,17,18,23,26
新产品开发	PT – 5,7,8,9,11,15,16,17,18,19,22,23,24,26,30,34
新市场开发	PT – 6,9,15,17,18,19,20,27,30,34,38

(续表)

技术管理课题	技术挖掘问题
合并	PT - 26,27,32,34
获得知识产权	PT - 2,7,9,11,15,16,22,23,26,27,28,29,32,33,39
开发利用自身知识产权	PT - 2,8,9,13,15,16,17,20,21,22,23,27,28,28,29,30,31,32,34,37,39
技术研发合作	PT - 2,5,7,8,11,12,15,16,25,27,28,29,30,31,32,33,34
识别并评估竞争性组织	PT - 1,12,21,23,24,27,28,29,30,31,32,34,35,36,38
跟踪和预测新兴或突破性技术（机会或威胁）	PT - 1,2,3,4,5,7,8,9,12,24
战略技术规划	PT - 2,4,5,7,8,9,12,17,18,22,24,29
技术路线图	PT - 1,4,5,7,11,14,15,16,18,26

Alan Porter 的技术管理课题体系尽管较为全面地体现出技术竞争情报的重点关注内容,但对于技术战略、风险控制、技术融资等相关管理决策缺少关注;另一大局限在于该体系主要基于专利与科技数据库资源,而没覆盖到商业信息、网络信息、报告、展会信息等其他来源渠道,有待进一步补充完善。

通过比较,可以看到两种体系存在差异,各有优缺(如表 6)。J. P. Herring 关键情报课题与管理决策联系十分紧密,能较好地体现管理目标、决策关注内容;但缺憾在于对情报任务指向稍显宽泛、不够明确。Alan Porter 技术管理课题体系的特点是一个问题有一个关注内容焦点,反映清晰明确的情报任务,其缺憾之处在于与管理决策联系不够紧密。这种差异一定程度上能体现管理思维与情报思维的考虑侧重角度的不同,而将两者结合起来,正好能优劣互补,形成更为完善的关键情报课题。

表6　J.P. Herring 的 KIT 体系与 Alan Porter 技术管理课题体系对比

比较	Herring – KIT	Porter – TMI
管理决策应用领域	商业管理领域,涵盖战略、市场、技术、产品、竞争者等	技术管理领域,侧重技术、产品、竞争者等
管理决策目标体现	管理决策目标与 KIT 课题紧密融合	目标与管理决策结合不够紧密
情报任务体现	情报任务指向稍显宽泛、不够明确	一个问题有一个关注内容焦点,反映清晰明确的情报任务
课题细分	举例阐释,分解成关键情报问题(Key Intelligence Question)	分解成技术挖掘问题(Technology Mining Question),创新指标 Innovation Indicators
课题与子课题对应关系	一对多,树形分解	多对多,组配复用
类型	三类: (1)战略决策和行动; (2)早期预警课题; (3)关键参与者	三类: (1)技术生命周期状况; (2)创新环境接受能力; (3)市场前景
数量	36 个 KIT	13 个 MOT,39 个 MOQ
详略	涵盖范围较广,相对宽泛	领域聚焦,具体
特点	- 与管理决策联系紧密 - 内容涵盖全面	- 子课题间组合、复用,支撑母课题 - 子课题具体,易于实施

3.2　关键情报课题的组成要素的选择

竞争情报活动的最终目标是支持战略、战术决策与行动。作为反映情报需求的关键情报课题,同样要体现战略、战术决策行动的目标,以及对决策的支撑作用。关键情报课题也是情报活动的"指南针",不同课题对应不同的情报实施活动,选择的信息源与分析方法、配备的人、财、物等资源也不相同。因此,关键情报课题一方面要反映管理决策目标和管理决策考虑因素,另一方面要明确情报任务、指导情报活动。

为了探究关键情报课题的组成要素,我们将较为体系化的 Herring – KIT 与 Porter – TMI 进行了要素分解(如表7、表8),寻找构建 KIT 的相关要素与模式。

表 7　　　　　　　　　　J. P. Herring 关键情报课题要素分解

Herring KIT	管理目标	决策关注内容	情报任务模块
HK 1-1	制定战略规划	未来竞争环境	战略规划竞争环境分析
HK 1-2	形成全球竞争战略	竞争者在实现经营目标中的作用	全球竞争者分析
HK 1-3	适应行业全球化趋势	与谁合作 竞争者的做法	行业全球化合作者识别,竞争者全球化合作调研
HK 1-4	开拓全球新兴市场	新兴市场发展情况 目前及未来的竞争态势	新兴市场发展前景分析,竞争态势分析
HK 1-5	战略投资决策	竞争环境改变,关键行业投资,行业现金需求,投资机构作用与投资渠道	关键行业投资跟踪,投资渠道分析,投资机构角色分析,行业现金需求分析
HK 1-6	扩大生产规模	扩大生产能力、建新工厂、改善生产工艺流程等方案的成本、收益、优劣比较	生产规模扩大建设方案选择评估
HK 1-7	保持技术竞争力、技术竞争优势	关键竞争者的计划和行动,我们如何应对	技术竞争力分析,竞争者技术竞争力行动计划调查
HK 1-8	选择产品开发项目	领先竞争者的项目 竞争性技术发展态势	产品开发项目评估,竞争性技术发展态势分析
HK 1-9	新产品开发与上市	竞争者新产品开发与上市动向,我们的计划	新产品开发、上市动态监测
HK 1-10	改进营销策略	行业、竞争者以及分销商看待我们分销/销售/营销策略的态度	营销策略调研
HK 1-11	保护专有信息/技术机密	需要保护的信息/技术 竞争者及相关方的兴趣	反情报
HK 1-12	雇佣和留住人才	人才,提高公司对人才的吸引力	人才资源发现,人力资源管理措施分析
HK 2-1	未来技术竞争力发展	对当前及未来竞争力可能产生显著影响的技术突破领域	关键竞争技术领域跟踪,突破性技术领域识别
HK 2-2	生产、研发技术改进与创新	影响竞争地位的新技术进展及应用(竞争者)	新技术进展分析(应用)
HK 2-3	选择关键供应商	供应商的财务、成本、质量、可能的收购/联盟	供应商选择评估

(续表)

Herring KIT	管理目标	决策关注内容	情报任务模块
HK 2-4	应对突发性供应中断	原油/部件等供应可能中断信号,应对措施	原材料供应突发事件预警
HK 2-5	应对行业采购政策变动	行业采购政策和流程变动信号,应对措施	采购政策或流程变动
HK 2-6	获得客户/竞争者态度变化反馈	客户或竞争者对我们及我们服务所持态度的变化	客户满意度调查,竞争者态度跟踪
HK 2-7	应对潜在竞争者	可能考虑进入我们行业或市场的公司或公司的联合	行业/市场动态分析
HK 2-8	利用或规避宏观管理制度对竞争力的影响	国际或国家政治、社会、经济或管理制度变化,对竞争力可能造成的影响	宏观管理政策分析
HK 2-9	了解监管近期变动和长期趋势	监管近期变动、长期趋势,以及影响监管制度的政府变动	监管政策跟踪分析
HK 2-10	了解行业竞争者、客户和供应商之间联合、收购和剥离计划与行动	行业参与者联合、收购和剥离行动的原因、驱动力、目标与意图	行业并购分析
HK 2-11	应对竞争者的财务行动	竞争者财务战略变化、联盟、收购、剥离行动	竞争者并购分析,竞争者财务战略分析
HK 2-12	应对潜在的被收购	潜在收购方的兴趣与努力	潜在收购方分析
HK 3-1	了解主要竞争者	主要竞争者的战略规划、竞争战略、财务与市场表现、组织和关键人员、研发、运营、销售与营销等信息	竞争者档案
HK 3-2	深入了解主要竞争者	主要竞争者对于我们及我们的主要客户的竞争意图、战略规划与目标、关键战略、当前的运作与竞争能力	竞争者档案
HK 3-3	提防新兴竞争者	新兴竞争者的相关信息	新进入竞争者识别
HK 3-4	了解当前及未来竞争环境的变化与趋势	客户和竞争者,市场和供应商,生产和产品技术,政治的和环境的,以及行业结构的变化与趋势	竞争环境分析
HK 3-5	争取新客户	新客户的需求与未来兴趣,竞争者争夺计划与行动	新客户需求调研

（续表）

Herring KIT	管理目标	决策关注内容	情报任务模块
HK 3-6	提升品牌、产品及服务的口碑	行业与客户对我们的品牌、产品及服务价值所持的观点、态度和感受	行业与客户口碑调研
HK 3-7	了解行业/市场新的参与者	新的供应商、主要分销商、客户,以及新进入竞争者的相关信息	行业/市场参与者评估
HK 3-8	了解新技术/产品动向	新技术/产品的计划与战略	新技术/产品的计划与战略跟踪
HK 3-9	了解市场竞争状况	市场份额、市场增长速度	行业市场分析
HK 3-10	了解监管政策情况	监管政策	监管政策跟踪分析
HK 3-11	了解投资/金融界对行业、业务的态度	投资/金融界对我们的业务、行业所持观点	行业研究
HK 3-12	反情报	供应商和行业观察家们对我们公司感兴趣的信息,及其搜集信息的目的	行业研究,反情报

表8　　　　　　　　　　Alan Porter 技术管理课题要素分解

Porter-TMI	管理目标	关注内容	情报任务模块
PT 1	N/A	新兴技术	新兴技术监测
PT 2	N/A	技术热点	技术热点识别
PT 3	N/A	技术前沿	技术前沿动态跟踪
PT 4	N/A	组件技术	关键组件技术识别与跟踪
PT 5	N/A	技术发展路线	技术发展前景评估
PT 6	N/A	技术发展驱动	技术发展驱动因素分析
PT 7	N/A	关键竞争技术	关键竞争技术识别
PT 8	N/A	技术发展前景	技术发展前景评估
PT 9	N/A	技术发展路线	技术发展路径预测
PT 10	N/A	组件技术	关键组件技术识别与跟踪
PT 11	N/A	技术成熟度	组件技术成熟度评估
PT 12	N/A	技术融合	技术融合潜力评估
PT 13	N/A	知识产权	专利战略,专利使用
PT 14	N/A	技术-产品路线	技术-产品路线图构建

(续表)

Porter – TMI	管理目标	关注内容	情报任务模块
PT 15	N/A	技术应用成熟度	技术系统成熟度评估
PT 16	N/A	技术机会	技术需求分析
PT 17	N/A	技术机会	新兴技术机会分析
PT 18	N/A	技术的市场机会	技术–市场需求分析
PT 19	N/A	技术应用前景	技术应用前景分析
PT 20	N/A	机会识别	全球技术机会分析
PT 21	N/A	竞争环境	竞争环境分析
PT 22	N/A	技术商业化前景	技术商业化前景分析
PT 23	N/A	竞争环境	竞争环境变化评估
PT 24	N/A	技术专家	领域专家识别
PT 25	N/A	技术研究机构	领先研究机构识别
PT 26	N/A	组织优劣	组织竞争优势与劣势分析
PT 27	N/A	技术领先	技术优势分析
PT 28	N/A	技术研发队伍	领先企业研发队伍调查
PT 29	N/A	技术领先企业	技术领先公司识别
PT 30	N/A	竞争对手	领先公司发展战略
PT 31	N/A	技术优势	领先公司技术优势分析
PT 32	N/A	知识产权	技术知识产权持有者分析(竞争者识别/合作者分析)
PT 33	N/A	知识产权	小公司或个人具有吸引力的技术知识产权识别
PT 34	N/A	合作	行业合作者分析
PT 35	N/A	竞争者	竞争者档案
PT 36	N/A	竞争对手识别	关注对象识别
PT 37	N/A	知识产权合作	技术获取可行性分析
PT 38	N/A	竞争环境	竞争环境分析
PT 39	N/A	竞争者	竞争者档案

(注释:N/A 指课题中没有体现该项内容)

综上所述,一个优化的关键情报课题的组成要素应包括:管理决策目标、管理决策关注内容和情报任务模块三个部分(如图1)。"管理决策目标"与管理决策活动相连;"管理决策关注内容"反映有价值的情报内容,与情报活动相连,是情报活动的关注目标;"情报任务模块"是根据"管理活动目标"与"管理决策关注内容"提炼得出的,用来确保情报工作模块化、目标定义清晰、易于执行和实施。

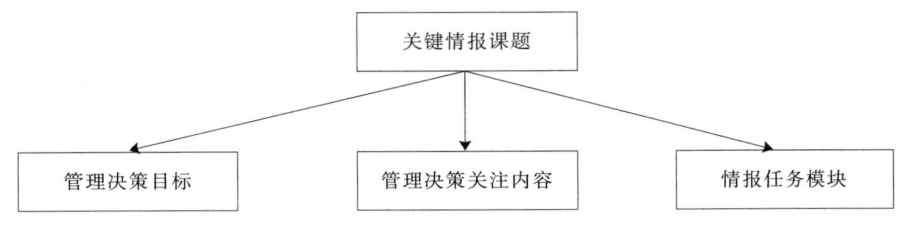

图 1　关键情报课题组成要素

每个关键情报课题要实现的"管理决策目标"相对独立;每个"管理决策目标"所对应的"关注内容"都不尽相同(尽管部分会有所重叠,但侧重点有所区别);每个"情报任务模块"对应一系列的关注内容,通常可服务于多个"管理决策目标"。例如,Herring – KIT 中 1 – 1、1 – 5 与 3 – 4 关键情报课题都有关注竞争环境,但 1 – 1 主要关注未来的宏观战略竞争环境,1 – 5 主要关注行业投资、资金环境,3 – 4 主要关注行业竞争环境。对于情报任务模块,1 – 1、1 – 5、3 – 4 可以归总为"竞争环境分析"模块,针对竞争环境不同方面开展分析。

3.3　关键情报课题的构建原则

构建"关键情报课题"并非易事,一些生成的关键情报课题往往容易出现以下问题:

(1) KIT 表述不够凝练,涵义模糊,指向不清;

(2) KIT 不面向管理决策需求,不清楚应用价值;

(3) KIT 过于笼统宽泛,涵盖范围过大,一个课题包含多个相互独立的问题,还很容易并值得细分;

(4) KIT 过于具体,数量过多难以控制;

(5) KIT 不能很好地指导情报活动执行,令情报人员无从下手;

(6) KIT 间出现明显重叠,合并成一个课题不影响对情报任务的理解,并且在情报活动执行过程中能更好地实现资源、工具共享,减少重复劳动;

(7) KIT 没有优先重要性评定,课题间缺乏逻辑关系,散乱地罗列;

(8)一些价值不大、不关键的 KIT,仅为搜集到某条具体的显性信息,而无需进行加工、分析等处理,这样对管理决策行动不会起到很好的支撑作用。

目前,研究者们尚未对关键情报课题提出一套统一的原则,只有 Herring 对 KIT 的涵义进行了较为集中的阐释和澄清。[34]通过与情报专家的交流,基于前述对 KIT 涵义的分析、常见问题的罗列,对 KIT 内容范例及其他类似需求课题[48],[49]的优劣分析,一个"好"的"关键情报课题"应当尽量满足"DFE - ASP"六大基本原则:

(1)面向管理决策(Decision - oriented)。表述凝练,涵义清晰,每个课题能够相对独立地辅助决策。

(2)目标性(Focus)。指意明确,以任务为导向,有比较明确的行动目标。

(3)课题可执行(Executable)。什么样的课题是"可执行"的呢?这不容易有一个确定的标准,但它至少应该是:

— 有明确的执行任务;

— 可以从公开或半公开信息来源渠道获得支撑数据或资料,常用的信息源包括:专利、科研论文、网络信息、会议、展览,以及专家(守门人)、主要客户、合作伙伴等人际信息源;

— 能够依靠一定的方法、工具、软件、专家或情报人员脑力来完成分析。

对于经验丰富的情报人员,他们对从事过的课题较有把握判断是否"可执行"、"易执行",而对陌生的课题则需要借助一定的直觉与经验进行判断。

(4)信息粒度适当(Appropriate)。所谓"粒度"(granularity),指的是信息单元的相对大小,用于表示信息的细化或综合程度。[35]细化程度越高,粒度级就越小;相反,细化程度越低,粒度级就越大。

关键情报课题应避免笼统宽泛,又不能过于细分致使单个课题无法有效地支撑管理决策。尽量使一个课题集中回答一类问题,而回答这个问题需要经过一定信息搜集、整理、分析,才能提供所需情报成果,该成果对管理决策有支撑作用。

通常,战略情报课题综合性、宏观性较强,形成的课题容易比较宽泛,此时应根据高效执行的原则划分情报任务模块,尽量进行适当细分,或列出子课题予以释义。而战术性课题往往比较具体,这时需要一定程度的合并,以便于形成模块化的情报任务。

(5)课题具有一定稳定性(Stability)。课题具有一定的稳定性,值得长期跟踪研究。

(6)课题存在一定的重要性优先级(Priority)。课题能反映支撑决策所需的关键信息,课题研究成果能起到辅助管理决策的作用,具有重要价值,并且课题间还存在一定的优先级,以便指导情报活动的协调与情报资源的分配。

因此,一个成功的关键情报课题体系则应满足以下条件:

(1)整个课题体系逻辑清晰,课题内容具有价值,能较为全面详细地反映组织情报需求,支撑组织管理决策活动,并与组织具备的情报资源与能力相适应。

(2)整体归为几类,各类型有不同侧重,同时又相互关联。

(3)每个具体课题相互独立,课题间不出现明显重叠,课题间存在一定的优先顺序。

值得注意的是:

第一,课题内容及优先顺序都是动态变化,不断更新完善的,绝非一劳永逸。例如,对某些情报课题执行过后,发现比较类似相近的课题可能合并,或发现比较复杂的课题也可能进一步细分;当组织竞争环境与发展策略发生变化,课题间的优先顺序也可能随之做出调整。

第二,对于一个组织而言,关键情报课题的数目与执行难度,都应与组织的情报资源与能力相适应。数目不宜过多,难度不能无法企及。

第三,对于新的、陌生的课题,应尽可能细分,或提供一些操作提示,以方便执行。

4 关键情报课题构建方法的选择

4.1 基于访谈的关键情报课题构建方法

J. P. Herring(1994)对关键情报课题的构建是通过与20多个行业的1000多名执行官员和管理人员开展访谈后归纳得出的。[36]该关键情报课题的构建流程是以访谈为主导,其核心是与公司关键决策者进行互动对话。黄英(2003)在其硕士论文中将以访谈为主导的关键情报课题识别流程划分为五个步骤(如

图2所示)。[37]

图 2　企业 KIT 流程步骤

(资料来源:黄英. 决策者需求分析——关键情报课题研究[D]. 北京大学硕士学位论文,2003.)

(1)确定与接近情报用户

情报用户通常为企业管理决策者,包括高层管理人员,战略规划、战略行动的负责人,业务部门、职能部门或项目的有关管理人员,以及需要情报支撑的基层业务人员等等。

情报人员需要与这些情报用户建立联系,以进一步开展直接、开放、深入、可信赖的交谈。对于情报意识尚比较缺乏的企业,需要先进行 KIT 教育,引导用户进入 KIT 访谈,让 KIT 进入用户的日常工作流程,以帮助用户形成对 KIT 的基本理解。在此基础上,定期召开 KIT 例会,在企业形成 KIT 交流的文化。

(2)访谈与明确决策需求

这一阶段,需要开展访谈调查来获得管理者的决策需求。采用访谈提纲、调查表能够保证采访过程地顺利开展,提高调查结果的一致性。

(3)挖掘与生成 KIT

在需求调查过程中,决策者可能提出各种各样的情报请求或问题,这些往往不能直接成为 KIT,有些可作为 KIQ 或 KIR(Key Intelligence Requests)。KIQ 或 KIR 需要经过进一步的筛选、处理、分析,从中挖掘形成真正的关键情报课题。

(4)推进 KIT 可操作化

初步形成 KIT 后,首先要将其分成几大类,将不同管理者、情报用户提出的共性课题进行合并,然后按照"重要性"、"紧急性"对课题进行优先级排序,并通过讨论进一步提炼和检验 KIT。

(5)评价与修正 KIT

在形成 KIT、按照 KIT 执行情报活动以及传递 KIT 情报成果的整个过程中,都可以接受管理决策者的反馈。通过交互,情报用户对 KITs 的理解不断加深,能对 KIT 内容以及情报活动、情报成果等提出更多意见和建议,并对 KIT 表达进行改进或调整。

基于访谈的关键情报课题构建流程需要情报人员与管理者进行密切的访谈交互,才可能达到较好的 KIT 识别效果。许多公司没有 KIT 流程,是因为以访谈为主导的 KIT 识别流程不容易实现。首先,大多数情报工作者难以获得如此多的与高层管理决策者进行沟通对话的机会,大多高层管理者工作繁忙,能进行访谈的时长、频次等都非常有限;第二,即使获得与高层管理者就需求进行沟通交流的机会,沟通过程也通常会出现许多障碍,例如,高层管理者对情报活动缺乏了解、对需求认识并不清晰,对需求表述比较模糊,或者反而需要情报人员告诉他们存在哪些需求,这样的境地令双方都感到尴尬。

4.2 非访谈为主导的关键情报课题识别方法

本研究采用一种非访谈为主导的 KIT 识别方法,构建一套关键情报课题内容体系。首先,通过文献调研、案例分析、逻辑分析方法,形成一个较为全面的 KIT 基本内容框架,这些情报课题与我们掌握的情报资源和能力基本适应;然后根据实际条件利用问卷调查或访谈调查方法与情报用户进行交互,可以将 KIT 基本内容框架递交给决策者,告诉决策者我们能做到这些,询问决策者您觉得哪些课题更重要、更优先,哪些课题不太必要,还有哪些课题应当补充。再结合调查对原 KIT 内容框架予以完善,形成最终的关键情报课题体系。这种方法更具可操作性,并能更好地激活决策者的需求思维,提高其表达需求的欲望与能力。该方法具体流程如下(见图3):

(1)范围界定。确定管理决策领域与情报活动范畴,使接下来的步骤更为聚焦。

(2)系统搜集相关文献与案例。文献、案例是 KIT 识别方法的"输入"、重要的"原料"。因此,需要在划定的管理决策领域、情报活动范畴内,系统搜集各种论文、案例、报告,并完成阅读、消化、吸收和逻辑分析,以熟悉相关背景知识,部分有价值的信息资料也可提供给决策者作为背景了解。

(3)构建管理要素模型,并分析得出管理要素相应的关注内容。针对管理问题目标,从文献中寻找相关的管理流程或模型,或分析其关键成功因素,构建一个合适的管理要素模型,使之能够基本全面地涵盖和反映管理决策相关的活动、业务、影响作用项等;在管理要素基础上,借助文献分析、逻辑分析得出管理要素相应的关注内容。

(4) 分析得出"管理目标、关注内容、情报任务"三大 KIT 组成要素的列表。以"管理目标、关注内容、情报任务"为焦点,在相关文献与案例中提炼、捕获这三方面的 KIT 要素。

(5) 三大 KIT 要素组合,形成初步情报课题。借助逻辑分析,对三大 KIT 要素进行有机组合,形成初步情报课题。

(6) 情报课题的合并、细分。按照 KIT 原则,对初步形成的情报课题进行合并、细分,初步形成关键情报课题的基本内容框架。

(7) 开展问卷或访谈调查,就初步的关键情报课题框架进行验证、修改和完善,并得出各关键情报课题的优先级。

(8) 最终形成关键情报课题体系。

非访谈为主导的关键情报课题识别方法最大的特点是易于执行,访谈调查研究的压力较小,对于尚未有情报意识、对情报活动了解不多的企业或管理者

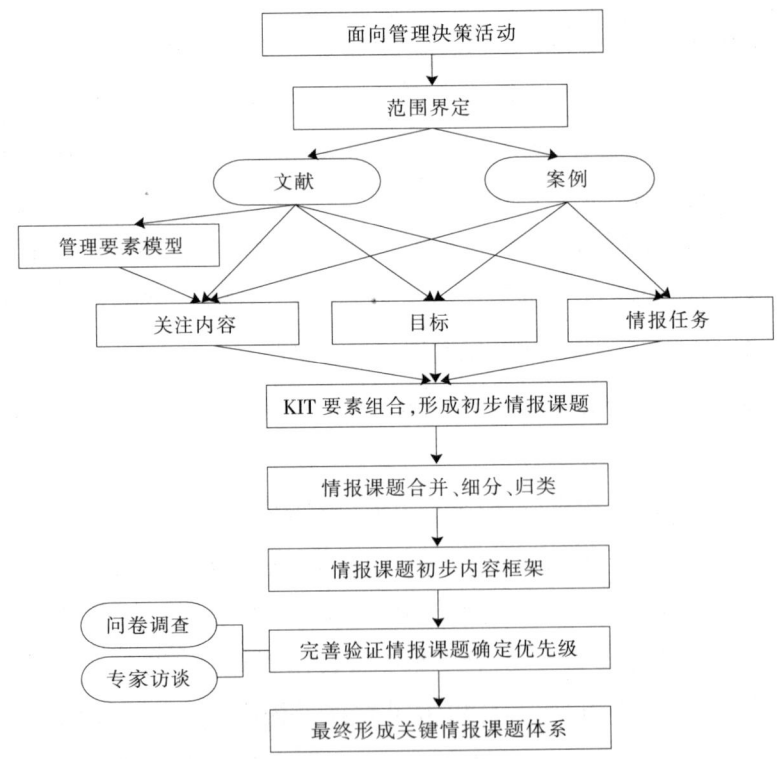

图 3　非访谈为主导的关键情报课题识别方法

尤为适用;能够有效帮助企业情报部门、情报服务机构、相关咨询机构等提供一个基本的关键情报课题框架,为进一步深入调查、访谈、挖掘情报需求,开展情报活动奠定良好的基础。即使具备需求访谈条件,情报人员也可使用该方法,在访谈前对决策者的情报需求形成一个基本的理解框架,或者给出一些历史案例、示例。

5 企业技术创新的关键情报课题构建

本研究选择企业技术创新领域作为应用切入点,基于非访谈式方法,构建基于企业技术创新的关键情报课题体系。通过广泛收集技术管理、技术竞争情报服务的相关文献[38,39,40,41,42],借助归纳综合、逻辑分析的方法,按照关键情报课题构建的原则,解析 KIT 的基本要素。同时,选择 Arthur D. Little 公司的 18 个最为典型的案例[43]作为基本分析源,按照 KIT 组成要素展开分析,将关键情报问题合并、细分、归类,形成符合标准的企业技术创新关键情报课题的基本内容框架。该内容框架包括"竞争环境、技术战略、技术创新过程、技术创新管理支持、行业相关参与者"六大类别,共有 58 个关键情报课题(见表9)。这些课题大多以"竞争情报服务目标"为逻辑基点,体现关注内容、情报任务职能。

表9　　企业技术创新的关键情报课题初步内容框架

类型	课题编号	课题内容
1 竞争环境	K - TIM 1 - 1	企业未来所处的技术环境:识别未来环境的不确定性因素,预见未来技术发展情景
	K - TIM 1 - 2	政治、经济、社会领域发生的对企业技术创新活动造成影响的突发事件,及其带来的潜在机会、威胁或改变
	K - TIM 1 - 3	企业所处国家地区的基本经济发展状况,包括经济发展态势、产业结构、进出口、人力成本等方面
	K - TIM 1 - 4	对企业与所在行业技术创新造成影响的政府政策、行业管制及许可规定有哪些?竞争对手如何应对?"我们"如何应对?
	K - TIM 1 - 5	环境保护、社会责任等方面给企业技术创新活动带来哪些潜在机会、威胁及风险?行业相关参与者采取了什么样的计划与行动?"我们"该如何做?
	K - TIM 1 - 6	对行业、企业技术创新活动造成影响的法律、法规(例如专利法、技术合同法、进出口国关税等)

(续表)

类型	课题编号	课题内容
	K-TIM 1-7	评估相关技术领域的发展趋势、应用前景及其对未来竞争力的影响,识别关键技术领域
	K-TIM 1-8	识别潜在的技术机会与威胁:关注对企业未来竞争可能产生影响的关键技术、新兴技术、突破性技术,以及相关行业有应用价值的技术成果或替代性技术
	K-TIM 1-9	识别市场机会:关注未来产品/业务增长前景良好、竞争对手不够重视的细分市场,以及新的商业模式带来的市场机会
	K-TIM 1-10	识别企业面临的威胁:关注产品、技术、市场方面具有威胁的新进入者和潜在替代者,跟踪其产品、技术、资金、优劣势及发展趋势
2 技术战略	K-TIM 2-1	开展关键基础研究,实现技术领先:识别对未来商业竞争地位造成影响的、具有潜力的基础研究领域,投入研发资源
	K-TIM 2-2	应用科技成果:识别监测对企业有潜在价值的新科学发现与技术成果,运用于产品/技术开发过程中
	K-TIM 2-3	打造核心技术竞争力:评估企业与竞争对手的技术竞争力、技术投入/产出情况,识别自身的竞争优势、劣势以及面临的机会、威胁(SWOT分析),调整技术战略
	K-TIM 2-4	全球化增长战略:关注全球范围内具有潜力的新兴市场及其竞争态势,开拓新市场,实现最大化增长
	K-TIM 2-5	专利申请战略:识别企业与竞争对手的核心专利,建立外围专利,形成专利技术保护圈,并选择合适的申请时机、申请国别和保护范围
	K-TIM 2-6	选择战略供应商:评估主要供应商的技术实力、技术发展规划能否适应企业未来的技术战略发展计划
	K-TIM 2-7	识别潜在合作对象:在大企业、小企业、大学、研究机构、政府、行业内参与者、行业外相关方等各类机构中,识别与企业技术研发方向相同或相近,或在技术、资源、市场方面与企业形成优劣互补的机构,建立评判标准,筛选出潜在合作对象
	K-TIM 2-8	建立潜在收购与投资对象的档案(技术、人才、市场、财务等状况),调查潜在收购与投资对象的意愿和条件,及其他的竞购方
	K-TIM 2-9	开展技术战略合作:建立潜在合作对象有关技术、人才、市场、财务等状况的档案,评估潜在合作对象的优势与劣势,选择符合双方目标的合作方式(项目合作、少数股权、生产采购等)
	K-TIM 2-10	识别具有吸引力的技术及其知识产权持有者(特别是个人或中小企业),采取技术购买或并购投资等相应策略
	K-TIM 2-11	专利技术获取:识别专利技术潜在的购买、引进、合作研发或出售对象

(续表)

类型	课题编号	课题内容
3 技术监测	K-TIM 3-1	跟踪监测相关科学技术领域的研究热点、最新进展、新突破和新发现
	K-TIM 3-2	专利分析:识别技术竞争热点、技术空白点、新兴技术领域
	K-TIM 3-3	专利分析:识别目标技术领域持有专利的主要公司、研究机构、研究团队、专家、专利持有人/所属机构
	K-TIM 3-4	专利分析:识别现有及潜在技术竞争对手
	K-TIM 3-5	专利分析:跟踪目标技术领域、目标机构的专利技术成果、研究进展、研究方向、技术发展变化趋势
	K-TIM 3-6	识别组件技术:存在哪些重要的组件技术?组件技术的研究进展与发展趋势如何?
	K-TIM 3-7	根据技术生命周期和专利申请时间序列,分析技术成熟度及所处发展阶段
	K-TIM 3-8	构建技术路线图:技术/产品发展的驱动力、发展路径、时间点等相关要素信息,清晰技术发展与研发活动、产业、基础设施、市场前景等不同层面条件的关系
	K-TIM 3-9	识别相关科学领域具有影响力的科研成果、专家、研究团队及其所在大学或研究机构,跟踪专家、团队、研究单位的研究方向和研究进展
	K-TIM 3-10	技术标准:调查相关领域的技术标准及其拥有机构,了解国际标准的制定、修改和协调,对技术标准贸易壁垒进行预警
4 技术创新过程	K-TIM 4-1	服务创新构想生成流程:捕捉利用新的发展趋势或理念,提出潜在的研发构想,建立研发构想的筛选和扫描标准(吸引力、适合性),对挑选出的构想进行市场评估(市场潜力与生存能力),获得最优先的创新构想
	K-TIM 4-2	把握领先客户需求:识别现有客户、合作伙伴中的领先客户,了解其需求特点、对技术/产品的构想,及其所在机构的(技术)战略计划
	K-TIM 4-3	研发项目选择:根据研发项目的价值、前景、可行性、风险性等因素,建立研发项目评估审核指标,辅助研发项目的支持/中止决策
	K-TIM 4-4	技术研发组合选择:关注评估技术研发组合的科学吸引力、商业吸引力、发展前景、政策支持及其对于现有和新市场的潜在战略影响,与行业领先者和主要竞争对手的研发组合与定位进行比较
	K-TIM 4-5	提高研发效率:根据研发机构的目标使命(基础研究、应用研究、试验开发),制定研发活动投入/产出绩效评估指标,衡量研发绩效
	K-TIM 4-6	提高生产制造效率,降低成本:分析产品生产制造流程环节,跟踪调查生产制造流程中的工作量、花费成本、产量、质量,不断改进生产制造效率

(续表)

类型	课题编号	课题内容
	K-TIM 4-7	扩大生产规模:选择是增加产量,还是建设新厂,或是采用更有成本效益的产品线设备与制造工艺
	K-TIM 4-8	了解客户需求,进行产品市场细分:调查分析个体客户的特点与偏好(地理位置、人群、个性、行为等方面)与企业客户的业务流程,按客户需求进行产品市场细分
	K-TIM 4-9	特定技术或产品领域的市场分析:特定技术或产品领域的市场规模、市场份额、市场潜力、主要竞争对手、竞争动态、市场战略意义
	K-TIM 4-10	围绕客户价值与体验开展创新:识别影响客户满意度的产品关键属性,分析畅销/滞销产品的优劣特性,调查客户对产品创新的评价反馈
	K-TIM 4-11	制定新产品上市策略:分析市场环境、竞争对手营销动向、目标客户购买行为及需求
	K-TIM 4-12	新产品推出风险控制:考虑市场管制、财务、竞争对手反应、潜在机会与威胁等不确定性因素,进行新产品推出的情景分析,识别不同情景下产品推出战略的可能结果与存在风险,制定相应策略
	K-TIM 4-13	提高新产品创新绩效:分析过去新产品项目的运营、研发、组织、绩效、市场营销情况,建立与评价关键绩效指标,评估新产品创新绩效
	K-TIM 4-14	选择品牌与市场营销策略:根据目标客户特点,选择合适的营销推广渠道,建立良好的品牌形象,并对营销策略效果予以评估
5 技术创新管理支持	K-TIM 5-1	为技术创新活动融资:比较风险投资、战略合作联盟、业务出售剥离等方式获得现金流的方案,对资金来源方进行评估,进行融资决策
	K-TIM 5-2	风险控制:对技术创新活动的高风险环节,包括研发可行性、商业化应用、产品市场竞争力、现金流、行业管制等方面,进行风险评估,制定应对策略
	K-TIM 5-3	跨国企业多元文化的差异化研发管理:对企业所在国家/地区的文化差异调研,包括研发人员的个性、特点、意愿、职业态度、最不能接受的管理方式、最受欢迎的管理方式等方面
	K-TIM 5-4	留住人才:主要竞争对手的薪资、福利、人才培训发展计划调研,制定人力资源管理策略
	K-TIM 5-5	员工培训发展计划:识别企业人才发展需求,调研行业技术创新人员培训计划方案,制定完善的培训计划
	K-TIM 5-6	满足技术创新需要的信息系统建设:行业内辅助技术创新活动的企业信息系统调研(如CAD,生产制造控制系统、ERP、知识管理平台等),竞争对手有关支持技术创新信息系统建设的计划与行动,调查分析企业技术创新、业务流程中的信息系统需求
	K-TIM 5-7	反情报:对方可能感兴趣的信息,保护核心技术、核心价值部分信息

(续表)

类型	课题编号	课题内容
6 行业相关参与者	K-TIM 6-1	关键竞争对手档案:包括研发领域、关键技术、技术平台、产品线、市场规模、技术战略及整体战略带来的优势与劣势、机会与威胁等
	K-TIM 6-2	跟踪关于竞争对手的专利、科技论文、科技新闻等公开信息,获得竞争对手新的研发投入、研究成果、新的研发方向等相关动态趋势
	K-TIM 6-3	跟踪竞争对手市场竞争动态,包括价格、营销策略、新产品推出、市场份额、客户满意度等
	K-TIM 6-4	识别行业相关方(特别是竞争对手)有关外部技术获取、技术合作、技术转让及并购投资的案例、计划与行动
	K-TIM 6-5	跟踪监测行业相关方(特别是竞争对手)的新产品推出情况,包括上市时间、优势/劣势、营销策略、市场反应等
	K-TIM 6-6	了解相关方(客户、供应商、当地政府、行业监管、员工等)对于企业及其相关计划行动的态度与期待

注释:什么是领先客户? 若一个产品/服务将在未来的市场上流行,现在就对其有强烈需求并能从中获益的厂商(用户)就是这个产品/服务的领先用户。[44] 换句话说,领先客户存在着尚未满足的需求,而这些需求一旦满足将使他们获益良多。

课题编号"K-TIM m-n",K-TIM 为"KIT toward Technology Innovation Management"的缩写,m 代表类型(取值范围为 1~6),n 代表第几个课题(最大取值为14)。

6 企业技术创新关键情报课题的实证研究

通过识别分析的企业技术创新关键情报课题框架,包括六大类、共 58 道关键情报课题。本研究通过问卷调查,分析评估 58 个关键情报课题的重要性、优先级别:(1)获得关键情报课题内容的重要性评估。让调查对象根据自身需求和经验,对识别形成的关键情报课题内容的重要性进判断,看是否对企业有价值,从而检验非访谈为主导 KIT 识别方法是否有效。(2)确定各个课题的优先级。根据各个课题的平均重要性程度,得出各个课题的优先级。(3)与部分调查对象开展交流访谈,获得其对关键情报课题的反馈意见。

本调查主要锁定的是技术竞争情报应用较广的电子信息通讯、生物医药、石油化工、汽车、航空航天五大技术密集型行业,目标调研单位主要是来自上述行业的技术型企业以及部分与企业有技术研发合作的科研机构。调查对象的职业类型则包括从事高层管理、基础研究、试验开发、生产制造以及市场销售等与技术创新管理环节有关的业务或管理人员。

问卷设计利用李克特量表方法,按重要性等级依次递减建立"非常重要,重要,一般,不重要,很不重要"的"五点"量表,由调查对象根据自身从事技术创新相关活动的经验与观察,对各个课题对于企业的价值和重要性程度做出判断。从"非常重要"到"非常不重要"分别赋予1、2、3、4、5的重要性等级。

共有17家技术型企业与科研机构参与了本调查,共发放问卷60份,回收问卷53份,其中有效问卷为47份。调查对象来自电子信息通讯、生物医药、石油化工、汽车、航空航天五大行业,它们的行业分布情况如图4所示,出于对调查对象信息的保护,具体企业名称不在文中列出。调查对象包括从事战略管理、基础研究、试验开发、生产制造以及市场销售等职业的相关业务和管理人员,具体职业类型分布(见图5)。

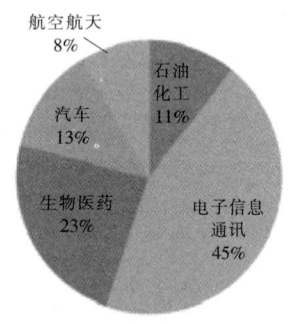
图4 调查对象行业类型分布

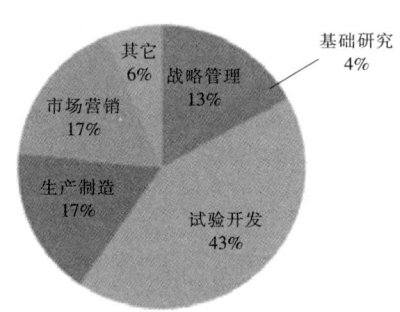
图5 调查对象职业类型分布

利用SPSS、Excel软件就调查所获数据展开分析,获得了相关结论。

第一,调查对象给予各KIT的重要等级评价较高。表11显示出"企业技术创新的KIT内容框架"中各KIT不同重要等级评价所占的比例、重要性等级均值及重要性等级均值标准差。可以看到,58个课题总体的重要性等级均值为1.85,处于"非常重要"与"重要"等级之间。其中,被评为"非常重要"的平均占34.6%,被评为"重要"的平均占48%,两者相加共占82.6%。所有KIT的重要等级均值都处于1.36至2.49之间,说明各KIT的平均重要性等级至少达到"一般重要"的评价。可见,本研究识别出的"企业技术创新的关键情报课题"是比较成功的,各KIT的价值、重要性受到从事技术创新管理活动相关人员的肯定。由此,表明非访谈为主导的关键情报课题识别方法可行、有效。

表 10　企业技术创新的 KIT 内容框架中各 KIT 重要性等级评判

课题编号	1 非常重要	2 重要	3 一般	4 不重要	5 非常不重要	重要性等级均值	重要性等级均值标准差
K－TIM 1－1	68.1%	25.5%	6.4%	0.0%	0.0%	1.38	0.610
K－TIM 1－2	36.2%	42.6%	17.0%	2.1%	2.1%	1.91	0.905
K－TIM 1－3	38.3%	51.1%	10.6%	0.0%	0.0%	1.72	0.649
K－TIM 1－4	55.3%	36.2%	8.5%	0.0%	0.0%	1.53	0.654
K－TIM 1－5	21.3%	44.7%	29.8%	4.3%	0.0%	2.17	0.816
K－TIM 1－6	31.9%	44.7%	23.4%	0.0%	0.0%	1.91	0.747
K－TIM 1－7	59.6%	34.0%	6.4%	0.0%	0.0%	1.47	0.620
K－TIM 1－8	53.2%	38.3%	6.4%	2.1%	0.0%	1.57	0.715
K－TIM 1－9	46.8%	44.7%	6.4%	2.1%	0.0%	1.64	0.705
K－TIM 1－10	42.6%	48.9%	6.4%	0.0%	0.0%	1.66	0.635
K－TIM 2－1	44.7%	44.7%	10.6%	0.0%	0.0%	1.66	0.668
K－TIM 2－2	44.7%	38.3%	8.5%	8.5%	0.0%	1.81	0.924
K－TIM 2－3	59.6%	40.4%	0.0%	0.0%	0.0%	1.40	0.496
K－TIM 2－4	31.9%	44.7%	23.4%	0.0%	0.0%	1.91	0.747
K－TIM 2－5	48.9%	40.4%	6.4%	4.3%	0.0%	1.66	0.788
K－TIM 2－6	21.3%	55.3%	23.4%	0.0%	0.0%	2.02	0.675
K－TIM 2－7	25.5%	46.8%	25.5%	2.1%	0.0%	2.04	0.779
K－TIM 2－8	6.4%	55.3%	21.3%	10.6%	2.1%	2.49	0.882
K－TIM 2－9	12.8%	63.8%	21.3%	2.1%	0.0%	2.13	0.647
K－TIM 2－10	14.9%	59.6%	23.4%	2.1%	0.0%	2.13	0.679
K－TIM 2－11	12.8%	59.6%	23.4%	4.3%	0.0%	2.19	0.711
K－TIM 3－1	27.7%	51.1%	21.3%	0.0%	0.0%	1.94	0.704
K－TIM 3－2	21.3%	48.9%	29.8%	0.0%	0.0%	2.09	0.717
K－TIM 3－3	21.3%	51.1%	23.4%	4.3%	0.0%	2.11	0.787
K－TIM 3－4	21.3%	53.2%	23.4%	0.0%	0.0%	2.02	0.683
K－TIM 3－5	29.8%	42.6%	23.4%	2.1%	0.0%	2.00	0.808
K－TIM 3－6	17.0%	48.9%	34.0%	0.0%	0.0%	2.17	0.702
K－TIM 3－7	21.3%	38.3%	31.9%	6.4%	0.0%	2.26	0.871
K－TIM 3－8	36.2%	42.6%	19.1%	0.0%	0.0%	1.85	0.751
K－TIM 3－9	27.7%	40.4%	29.8%	2.1%	0.0%	2.06	0.818
K－TIM 3－10	34.0%	46.8%	19.1%	0.0%	0.0%	1.85	0.722

(续表)

课题编号	1 非常重要	2 重要	3 一般	4 不重要	5 非常 不重要	重要性 等级均值	重要性 等级均值 标准差
K-TIM 4-1	44.7%	38.3%	14.9%	2.1%	0.0%	1.74	0.793
K-TIM 4-2	63.8%	36.2%	0.0%	0.0%	0.0%	1.36	0.486
K-TIM 4-3	44.7%	48.9%	6.4%	0.0%	0.0%	1.62	0.610
K-TIM 4-4	29.8%	59.6%	10.6%	0.0%	0.0%	1.81	0.613
K-TIM 4-5	44.7%	38.3%	14.9%	2.1%	0.0%	1.74	0.793
K-TIM 4-6	46.8%	42.6%	8.5%	0.0%	0.0%	1.64	0.673
K-TIM 4-7	25.5%	51.1%	17.0%	4.3%	0.0%	2.02	0.794
K-TIM 4-8	57.4%	36.2%	4.3%	0.0%	0.0%	1.49	0.621
K-TIM 4-9	42.6%	55.3%	2.1%	0.0%	0.0%	1.60	0.538
K-TIM 4-10	31.9%	51.1%	14.9%	0.0%	0.0%	1.85	0.691
K-TIM 4-11	29.8%	59.6%	8.5%	0.0%	0.0%	1.81	0.613
K-TIM 4-12	27.7%	53.2%	17.0%	0.0%	0.0%	1.91	0.686
K-TIM 4-13	25.5%	59.6%	10.6%	4.3%	0.0%	1.94	0.734
K-TIM 4-14	44.7%	42.6%	8.5%	4.3%	0.0%	1.72	0.800
K-TIM 5-1	25.5%	61.7%	12.8%	0.0%	0.0%	1.87	0.612
K-TIM 5-2	31.9%	55.3%	10.6%	2.1%	0.0%	1.83	0.702
K-TIM 5-3	21.3%	38.3%	31.9%	4.3%	2.1%	2.30	0.954
K-TIM 5-4	55.3%	40.4%	0.0%	4.3%	0.0%	1.53	0.718
K-TIM 5-5	40.4%	55.3%	2.1%	2.1%	0.0%	1.66	0.635
K-TIM 5-6	21.3%	66.0%	8.5%	2.1%	2.1%	1.98	0.766
K-TIM 5-7	31.9%	44.7%	17.0%	4.3%	0.0%	1.96	0.833
K-TIM 6-1	29.8%	61.7%	8.5%	0.0%	0.0%	1.79	0.587
K-TIM 6-2	27.7%	53.2%	17.0%	2.1%	0.0%	1.94	0.734
K-TIM 6-3	44.7%	51.1%	4.3%	0.0%	0.0%	1.60	0.577
K-TIM 6-4	10.6%	59.6%	25.5%	2.1%	0.0%	2.21	0.657
K-TIM 6-5	38.3%	53.2%	8.5%	0.0%	0.0%	1.70	0.623
K-TIM 6-6	34.0%	46.8%	14.9%	2.1%	0.0%	1.87	0.769
平均	34.6%	48.0%	14.9%	1.8%	0.1%	1.85	

第二，按照重要性等级依次递减，以四分位点值可将"技术创新关键情报课题"分为重要等级依次递减的核心区、重要区、次要区、普通区四个区间。如表

12 所示,其四分位点值分别为 1.66(25%)、1.85(50%)、2.02(75%)、2.49 (100%),均已在表中圈出。其中,核心区有 14 个课题,重要区有 14 个课题,次要区有 17 个课题,普通区有 13 个课题。

表 11　　　　　　　　课题重要性等级频率

重要性等级值	频率	百分比	累积百分比
1.36	1	1.7%	1.7%
1.38	1	1.7%	3.4%
1.40	1	1.7%	5.2%
1.47	1	1.7%	6.9%
1.49	1	1.7%	8.6%
1.53	2	3.4%	12.1%
1.57	1	1.7%	13.8%
1.60	2	3.4%	17.2%
1.62	1	1.7%	19.0%
1.64	2	3.4%	22.4%
1.66	4	6.9%	29.3%
1.70	1	1.7%	31.0%
1.72	2	3.4%	34.5%
1.74	2	3.4%	37.9%
1.79	1	1.7%	39.7%
1.81	3	5.2%	44.8%
1.83	1	1.7%	46.6%
1.85	3	5.2%	51.7%
1.87	2	3.4%	55.2%
1.91	4	6.9%	62.1%
1.94	3	5.2%	67.2%
1.96	1	1.7%	69.0%
1.98	1	1.7%	70.7%
2.00	1	1.7%	72.4%
2.02	3	5.2%	77.6%
2.04	1	1.7%	79.3%

重要性等级值	频率	百分比	累积百分比
2.06	1	1.7%	81.0%
2.09	1	1.7%	82.8%
2.11	1	1.7%	84.5%
2.13	2	3.4%	87.9%
2.17	2	3.4%	91.4%
2.19	1	1.7%	93.1%
2.21	1	1.7%	94.8%
2.26	1	1.7%	96.6%
2.30	1	1.7%	98.3%
2.49	1	1.7%	100.0%
合计	58	100.0%	

第三,竞争环境、技术创新管理过程类 KIT 集中分布在前三个区间,重要性级别相对更高;技术战略、技术监测类 KIT 集中分布在后三个区间,重要性级别相对低一些;技术创新管理支持、行业相关参与者类 KIT 则均匀分布在四个区间。各个区间包含的具体 KIT 及其相应重要性等级值(如图 6 所示)。

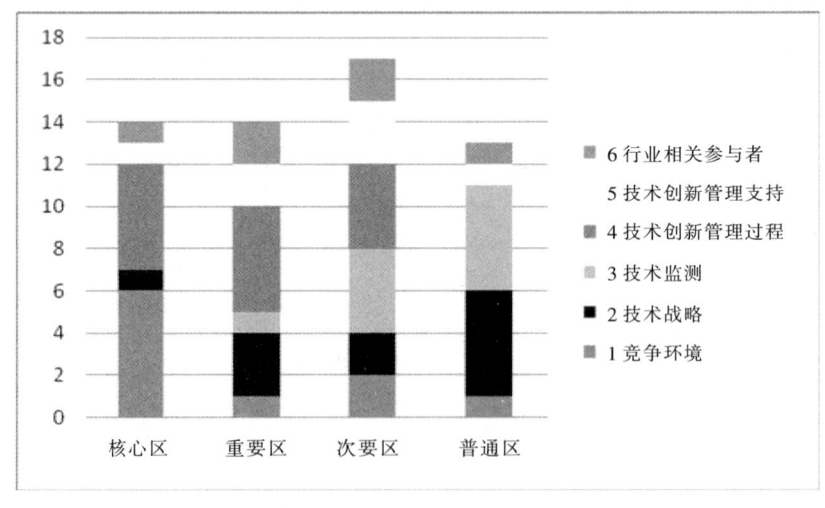

图 6　不同类型 KIT 在四个区间的分布

第四,各关键情报课题对应相对独立的情报任务模块。表13、表14、表15、表16 分别详细列举了核心区、重要区、次要区、普通区的 KIT,相应的情报任务模块以及 KIT 重要性等级均值,体现出针对情报需求课题开展情报工作的优先级。

表 12　　　　　　　　　　　　　核心区 KIT

课题编号	情报任务模块	重要性等级均值
K-TIM 1-1	未来技术发展情景分析	1.38
K-TIM 1-7	关键技术领域识别	1.47
K-TIM 1-4	行业监管政策调研	1.53
K-TIM 1-8	技术机会分析	1.57
K-TIM 1-9	市场机会分析	1.64
K-TIM 1-10	竞争威胁预警	1.66
K-TIM 2-3	技术竞争力 SWOT 分析	1.40
K-TIM4-2	领先客户识别,领先客户产品/技术需求调研	1.36
K-TIM 4-8	客户需求调研	1.49
K-TIM 4-9	目标技术/产品市场分析	1.60
K-TIM 4-3	研发项目评估	1.62
K-TIM 4-6	生产制造流程效率评估	1.64
K-TIM 5-4	竞争对手人力资源管理情况调研	1.53
K-TIM 6-3	竞争对手市场动态跟踪	1.60

表 13　　　　　　　　　　　　　重要区 KIT

课题编号	情报任务模块	重要性等级均值
K-TIM 1-3	宏观经济发展态势分析	1.72
K-TIM 2-1	基础研究重点领域识别	1.66
K-TIM 2-5	专利申请战略调研	1.66
K-TIM 2-2	具有应用潜力的科技成果识别	1.81
K-TIM 3-8	技术路线图构建	1.85
K-TIM 4-14	市场营销策略选择评估	1.72
K-TIM 4-1	创新构想评估	1.74
K-TIM 4-5	研发投入/产出绩效评估	1.74
K-TIM 4-4	行业领先者与竞争对手研发组合评估分析	1.81
K-TIM 4-11	新产品上市前调研	1.81
K-TIM 5-5	行业技术创新人员培训计划调研	1.66
K-TIM 5-2	技术创新风险控制	1.83
K-TIM 6-5	行业相关方新产品推出跟踪	1.70
K-TIM 6-1	关键竞争对手档案	1.79

表 14　　　　　　　　　　　　次要区 KIT

课题编号	情报任务模块	重要性等级均值
K–TIM 1–2	突发事件监测预警（政治、经济、社会）	1.91
K–TIM 1–6	行业相关法律法规调研	1.91
K–TIM 2–4	全球新兴市场分析	1.91
K–TIM 2–6	战略供应商评估	2.02
K–TIM 3–10	行业技术标准调研	1.85
K–TIM 3–1	科学研究进展跟踪,科技前沿热点识别	1.94
K–TIM 3–5	专利技术进展跟踪	2.00
K–TIM 3–4	技术竞争对手识别	2.02
K–TIM 4–10	产品关键属性调研,产品创新客户反馈调研	1.85
K–TIM 4–12	新产品推出风险评估	1.91
K–TIM 4–13	新产品创新绩效评估	1.94
K–TIM 4–7	生产规模扩大方案评估	2.02
K–TIM 5–1	技术创新融资渠道评估	1.87
K–TIM 5–7	反情报	1.96
K–TIM 5–6	行业技术创新信息系统支撑情况调研	1.98
K–TIM 6–6	行业相关方对企业的态度调研	1.87
K–TIM 6–2	竞争对手研究成果跟踪 竞争对手研发动向跟踪	1.94

表 15　　　　　　　　　　　　普通区 KIT

课题编号	情报任务模块	重要性等级均值
K–TIM 1–5	行业社会责任行动调研	2.17
K–TIM 2–7	潜在合作对象档案	2.04
K–TIM 2–9	潜在技术战略合作对象档案 技术战略合作对象选择评估	2.13
K–TIM 2–10	技术获取机会识别	2.13
K–TIM 2–11	专利技术获取/转让对象识别	2.19
K–TIM 2–8	潜在并购投资对象档案	2.49
K–TIM 3–9	研究专家/研究团队跟踪	2.06
K–TIM 3–2	目标专利技术领域识别	2.09
K–TIM 3–3	专利持有人/机构调研	2.11
K–TIM 3–6	关键组件技术识别与跟踪	2.17
K–TIM 3–7	技术成熟度分析	2.26
K–TIM 5–3	跨国企业文化差异调研	2.30
K–TIM 6–4	行业相关方技术战略行动计划调研	2.21

第五，关键情报课题情报任务模块可归纳为分析、评估、调研、档案、识别、跟踪、预警及其他八大类型、64个情报任务。各职能对应的情报任务模块按重要程度由高到低列于表17，能够对服务于技术创新管理的技术竞争情报工作模块划分提供参考。

表 16　企业技术创新的 KIT 体系对应情报职能与情报任务

情报职能	职能阐释	情报任务模块（按重要性排序）
分析	运用一定的分析方法对特定对象进行比较、预测	未来技术发展情景分析 技术竞争力 SWOT 分析 技术机会分析 目标技术/产品市场分析 市场机会分析 宏观经济发展态势分析 全球新兴市场分析 技术成熟度分析
评估	按照一定的指标对特定对象进行评价、比较和选择	研发项目评估 生产制造流程效率评估 市场营销策略选择评估 研发投入/产出绩效评估 创新构想评估 行业领先者与竞争对手研发组合评估 新产品推出风险评估 新产品创新绩效评估 战略供应商评估 生产规模扩大方案评估 技术创新融资渠道评估 技术战略合作对象选择评估
调研	系统全面地掌握特定对象相关情况	领先客户产品/技术需求调研 客户需求调研 行业监管政策调研 竞争对手人力资源管理情况调研 专利申请战略调研 行业技术创新人员培训计划调研 新产品上市前调研 产品创新客户反馈调研 行业技术标准调研 行业相关法律法规调研 产品关键属性调研 行业相关方对企业的态度调研 行业技术创新信息系统支撑情况调研

(续表)

情报职能	职能阐释	情报任务模块(按重要性排序)
		行业社会责任行动调研 专利持有人/机构调研 行业相关方技术战略行动计划调研 跨国企业文化差异调研
识别	在众多对象中寻找关注对象	关键技术领域识别 领先客户识别 基础研究重点领域识别 具有应用潜力的科技成果识别 科技前沿热点识别 技术竞争对手识别 技术获取机会识别 专利技术获取/转让对象识别 目标专利技术领域识别 关键组件技术识别
跟踪	持续关注特定对象的发展变化	竞争对手市场动态跟踪 行业相关方新产品推出跟踪 科学研究进展跟踪 专利技术进展跟踪 竞争对手研究成果跟踪 竞争对手研发动向跟踪 研究专家、研究团队跟踪 关键组件技术跟踪
档案	有关特定对象的、相对静态的背景资料,定期进行更新	关键竞争对手档案 潜在合作对象档案 潜在技术战略合作对象档案 潜在并购投资对象档案
预警	突发、威胁事件	竞争威胁预警 突发事件监测预警(政治、经济、社会等)
其他	其他	技术路线图构建 技术创新风险控制 反情报

7 总 结

本研究通过对关键情报课题涵义、内容范例的分析,得出关键情报课题包括管理目标、关注内容、情报任务三大要素。通过对比分析 Herring 和 Porter 的关键情报课题框架、关键技术创新管理框架的构建过程,指出了一个"好"的"关键情报课题"应当满足"面向管理决策(Decision-oriented)、目标性(Focus)、课题可执行(Executable)、信息粒度适当(Appropriate)、稳定性(Stability)、优先级(Priority)"六大原则。在此基础上,我们基于非访谈为主导的关键情报课题识别方法,以企业技术创新为切入点,建立"企业技术创新的关键情报课题内容框架";并通过进一步的实证调研,对其予以验证完善、确定各课题优先级;最后构建的企业技术创新的关键情报课题体系。该体系共包括竞争环境、技术战略、技术监测、技术创新流程、技术创新管理支撑、行业相关参与者六大类型、58个课题,并划分为核心区、重要区、次要区、普通区四个区间,形成分析、评估、调研、档案、识别、跟踪、预警及其他八大类型的情报任务模块、64个情报任务。

关键情报课题作为一种程序化的、正式的竞争情报需求识别与管理过程,是连接企业管理决策目标与情报任务执行的"桥梁",因此,构建关键情报课题体系成为开展竞争情报的非常重要的一环。明确关键情报课题的内涵、组成要素和构建原则,有助于关键情报课题体系的成功构建。当与高层访谈进行情报需求沟通的条件不够充分的情况下,结合情报人员的经验,采用非访谈为主导的关键情报课题识别方法,能够有效帮助企业情报部门、情报服务机构、相关咨询机构等提供一个基本的关键情报课题框架,这为下一步深入调查、访谈、挖掘情报需求,开展情报活动奠定良好的基础。基于关键情报课题框架,与管理决策者进行访谈、沟通和确认,则是进一步明确情报需求、确定情报需求优先级的重要环节,对于情报任务执行的优先性以及情报任务的模块化分解,它具有直接而明确的方向性指导作用。

参考文献

1 Jan P. Herring. *A Process to Identify and Define Intelligence Needs* [J]. Competitive Intelligence Review. 1994, 10(2):4–14.

2 Jan P. Herring. *Create CI programs for current and future needs* [J]. Competitive Intelligence Magazine. 2005, 8(5).

3 Jan P. Herring. *A Process to Identify and Define Intelligence Needs* [J]. Competitive Intelligence Review. 1994, 10(2):4–14.

4 李纲,李博. 论企业竞争情报的关键情报课题. 情报科学, 2005, 23(1):29–33.

5 David Francis, *Key Intelligence Topics:A Window on the Corporate Competitive Psyche* [J]. Competitive Intelligence Review, 1999, 10(4):10–19.

6 Hussey, D., Jenster, P.. *Competitor Intelligence*[M]. London: John Wiley & Sons, 1999.

7 戴侣红. 关键情报课题[J]. 情报理论与实践. 2000, 23(3):200-203.

8 黄英. 决策者需求分析——关键情报课题研究[D]. 北京大学硕士学位论文, 2003.

9 夏晨曦. 一种关键情报课题管理模型[J]. 图书情报工作. 2009,53(24):17-20.

10 Jan P. Herring. *KITs revisited: their use and problems*[EB/OL]. SCIP Online, http://www.imakenews.com/scip2/e_article000069099.cfm. [2010-3-3].

11 John Nolan. *CI Opportunity Number One in the Next Economy*[EB/OL]. SCIP Online, http://www.imakenews.com/scip2/e_article000069099.cfm. [2009-9-10].

12 C. Freeman. *The Economics of Industrial Innovation*[M]. The MIT Press, 2th ed. 1982.

13 S. Myers, D. G. Marquis. *Successful Industrial Innovations: A Study of Factors Underlying Innovation in Selected Firms*[M]. Washington, National Science Foundation, 1969.

14 傅家骥. 技术创新学[M]. 北京:清华大学出版社, 1998.

15 W. Bradford Ashton, Richard A. Klavans. *An Introduction to Technical Intelligence in Business. In: Keeping Abreast of Science and Technology: Technical Intelligence for Business*[C]. W. Bradford Ashton, Richard A. Klavans. Columbus, Ohio: Battelle Press, 1997:5-22.

16 Pascal Savioz. *Technology intelligence: concept design and implementation in technology – based SME'S*[M]. Basingstoke, Hampshire New York: Palgrave Macmillan, 2004:48.

17 刘细文. 技术竞争情报的演化与发展[J]. 图书情报工作, 2008,52(10):6-9.

18 Bernhardt, D. C. I want it fast, factual, actionable – Tailoring Competitive Intelligence to Executives Needs[J]. Long Range Planning, 1994, 27(1): 12-24.

19 Schultze, U. and Boland, R. J. Knowledge Management Technology and the Reproduction of Knowledge Work Practices[J]. *Journal of Strategic Information Systems*. 2000, 9(2): 193-212.

20 W. Bradford Ashton, Anne H. Johnson, Gary S. Stacey. *Monitoring Science and Technology for Competitive Advantage* [J]. Competitive Intelligence Review, 1994, 5(1): 5-16.

21 C. I. V. Kerr, L. Mortara, R. Phaal and etal. *A Conceptual Model for Technology Intelligence* [J]. Technology Intelligence and Planning, 2006, 2(1).

22 Alan Porter, Scott W. Cunningham. *Tech Mining: Exploiting New Technologies for Competitive Advantage* [M]. John Wiley & Sons Press, 2005: 249-266.

23 Alan L. Porter. *QTIP: Quick Technology Intelligence Processes*[J]. Technological Forecasting & Social Change, 2005, 72:1070-1081.

24 Cherie R. Courseault. *A Text Mining Framework Linking Technical Intelligence from Publication Databases to Strategic Technology Decisions*[D]. Georgia Institute of Technology, 2004:135-136.

25 金炬, 梁战平. 美国的竞争性技术情报及其对我国的启示[J]. 图书情报知识, 2006(4):72.

26 Thomas F. Krol, James C. Coleman, Patrick J. Bryant. *Competitive Technical Intelligence and Commercial Decision Making* [J]. *Competitive Intelligence Review*, 1996, 7(1): 28-37.

27 W. Bradford Ashton, Gary S. Stacey. *Technical Intelligence in Business: Understanding Technology Threats and Opportunities* [J]. *Technology Management*, 1995, 10(1): 79-104.

28 赵刚, 汤世国, 吴叶君等. 技术创新与企业竞争[M]. 北京: 华夏出版社, 2003: 232.

29 柯贤能. 基于创新过程的技术竞争情报分析方法框架构建[D]. 中国科学院研究生院硕士学位论文, 2007.

30 Jan P. Herring. *A Process to Identify and Define Intelligence Needs* [J]. *Competitive Intelligence Review*, 1994, 10(2): 4-14.

31 Alan Porter, Scott W. Cunningham. *Tech Mining: Exploiting New Technologies for Competitive Advantage* [M]. John Wiley & Sons Press, 2005: 249-266.

32 Alan Porter, Scott W. Cunningham. *Tech Mining: Exploiting New Technologies for Competitive Advantage* [M]. John Wiley & Sons Press, 2005: 249-266.

33 Watts, R. J., and Porter, A. L.. *Innovation Forecasting* [J]. *Technological Forecasting and Social Change*, 1997, 56, 25-47.

34 Jan P. Herring. *KITs revisited: their use and problems* [EB/OL]. SCIP Online, http://www.imakenews.com/scip2/e_article000069099.cfm. [2010-3-3].

35 粒度. 百度百科. http://baike.baidu.com/view/255840.htm. [2010-5-1].

36 Jan P. Herring. *A Process to Identify and Define Intelligence Needs* [J]. *Competitive Intelligence Review*. 1994, 10(2): 4-14.

37 黄英. 决策者需求分析——关键情报课题研究[D]. 北京大学硕士学位论文, 2003.

38 Mathias M. Coburn. *Competitive Technical Intelligence: A Guide to Design, Analysis, and Action* [M]. Oxford University Press, 1999.

39 W. Bradford Ashton, Richard A. Klavans. *Keeping Abreast of Science and Technology: Technical Intelligence for Business* [C]. Columbus, Ohio: Battelle Press, 1997.

40 Pascal Savioz. *Technology intelligence: concept design and implementation in technology-based SME'S* [M]. Basingstoke, Hampshire New York: Palgrave Macmillan, 2004.

41 Jan P. Herring. *A Process to Identify and Define Intelligence Needs* [J]. *Competitive Intelligence Review*, 1994, 10(2): 4-14.

42 Alan Porter, Scott W. Cunningham. *Tech Mining: Exploiting New Technologies for Competitive Advantage* [M]. John Wiley & Sons Press, 2005: 249-266.

43 Arthur D. Little 公司技术创新管理咨询案例[EB/OL]. http://www.adlittle.com/case-studies.html?&no_cache=1. [2010-9-1].

44 雍灏, 陈劲, 郭斌. 技术创新中的领先用户研究[J]. 科研管理, 1999, 20(3): 1-6.

Study on Signaling Theory and the Practice of High – Tech Information Exploring

Fumiyuki Takahashi①   Jiang Dianchun②   Xian Guoming③

Abstract

In this comprehensive study of market signals and Competitive Technical Intelligence on the basis of theoretical studies, combined with the characteristics of high – tech industries and Competitive Technical Intelligence practices in the enterprise were analyzed, sorted and summarized. This paper revealed the importance of technical information source selection and weak signals of information, while exploring information in high – tech industries. In addition, the effective usage of technical information sources was examined. Finally, we discussed multinational corporations with technological advantages in China, the competitive state and the impact of strengthened R&D investment, as well as technology spillover to Chinese enterprises. It provides a practical reference for Chinese enterprises looking for opportunities in emerging industries, exploring high – tech information in the fierce market competition to improve the international competitiveness.

Keywords

Market signal, Weak signal, Competitive Technical Intelligence, High – tech industry, Multinational Corporation, Foreign Direct Investment, Technology Spillover, Practice

---

① Fumiyuki Takahashi, Visiting Fellow, Center for Transnationals′ Studies of Nankai University.
② Jiang Dianchun, Professor, Deputy Director of the Centre for Transnationals′ Studies, Nankai University.
③ Xian Guoming, Professor, Director of the Centre for Transnationals′ Studies. President Assistant, Nankai University.

INTRODUCTION

Along with global information technology and the acceleration of world economic integration, market competition is getting intensifying. The use of Competitive Intelligence (CI) [1] to improve the identification and grasp of business opportunities, to provide an effective strategy decision support, and to secure the new competitive advantage, is a critical issue faced by modern enterprise.

Technology Competitive Intelligence (CTI) [2] or Technical Intelligence (TI) [3] is considered a subset of CI, the CI theory and methods in science and technology applications. CTI is specific information addressing scientific and technological aspects of the external competitive environment. [4] P. Savioz [5] defines CTI as collecting, analyzing and evaluating competitor's product or technology – related information, as well as timely delivery of technical facts and trends related to information technology management to support business decisions.

The whole process of implementation from a CTI viewpoint can be considered as the collection of information on technology, monitoring, analysis, forecast, prediction and early warning, to describe the process.

Gathering and analyzing timely and accurate information can understand technological changes and trends, also can provide early warning to avoid the technology change to be a threat to their business. As information technology continues to improve, and information visualization technology, intelligent retrieval, intelligent collection, data and text mining, information extraction, information filtering and other methods work in practice, CTI has been widely used.

However, this information must be based on reliable information sources. For public information gathering and analysis, the use of social network (Human Network or Social Network) to collect raw information in CI application is a trending topic. However, signal theory research has not been fully carried out in the CI research area, and there is a lack of practical application experience. Signal analysis method should become an important proposition in the fields of information science and competitive intelligence research. [7]

This paper is structured in 5 sections. Following this introduction, Section 2 elaborates on the literature review from market signal theory and information sources of CTI research. Section 3 presents an analysis of information exploration in high-tech industries by combining the characteristics of high-tech industries and practical experience of CTI. Then Section 4 discusses the multinational corporations (MNCs) with technological advantages and the existence of technology spillovers. Section 5 introduces the conclusion, and highlights areas for future research.

1 MARKET SIGNALS AND INFORMATION SOURCES

In the book "Competitive Strategy"[6], Michael Porter talks about the concept of market signals. Porter defines the market signal as any action by a competitor that provides a direct or indirect indication of its intentions, motives, goals or internal situation. The behavior of competitors provides signals in a myriad of ways. Some signals are bluffs, some are warnings, and some are earnest commitments to course of action. In the practice of CI activities, we collected information that includes some market signs to find early warning signs as an essential supplement to competitor analysis.

1.1 Classification and Selection of Information Sources

Source of information is the information source which involves generation, production, storage, processing, and dissemination of information. Sources of information can be classified according to the different ways, such as the chronological order of information, forms of communication, information processing level. In the CI field, it can be classified by hierarchie and structure (ex: fact, process, result, and trend); classified by the department or staff who acquired the information; classified according to information content and by the carrier, and format. This paper focuses on the analysis of the information sources in high-tech industries by the information contents.

Market signals appear in many forms. There is a need to correct the logic in identifying and distinguishing between true and false signals. The selection of reliable sources of information is necessary. It must be independent of information from multiple sources to gather information, control, compare and analyze to verify its accuracy. After long – term verification, a more reliable source of information can be caught.

1.2 Weak Signals and Signal Analysis

According to the amount of information revealing trends, the signals can be divided into strong signals and weak signals to the market. Day and Schoemaker [8] point out that the weak signals are often vague, irrelevant, uncertain, and mixed with a lot of "noise". Many weak signals are often hidden in phenomena, data, text and conversation, and mostly due to lack of convincing empirical data and logic, weak signals have been ignored. Though it is difficult to discover, weak signals are important in CI practices.

Moreover, the weak signals maybe not develop into the main or even correct information in the follow – up market. However, if ignored, these signals may cause the loss of a market, loss of development chance or loss of the optimum time to solve the problem. Therefore, information collation and analysis has become necessary. Accurately capturing these weak signals and taking action at the right time is not an easy task. To support tracing and finding more detail and related information to clarify its meaning will become extremely important. Schoemaker and Day propose an evaluation framework from weak signals into decision support on new business strategy exploring. [9] It is worth further empirical testing. These practices will promote more activity of prediction and early warning.

For any business, getting and giving any signal can help to understand their competitive environment or their predominance, also be able to take appropriate actions against to their competitor. On the other hand, if there is a lack of signal identification and evaluation methods, it will reduce the accuracy of forecasting and early warning. Regard to weak signal analysis, especially for the high – tech industries information gathering and analysis, such as technology foresight in the various "signs", "clues" and other weak signal analysis, it is worth further consideration and study. The exploration of high-tech industries information in CTI activity, there is valuable practical significance to find various "clues", "sign" and signal analysis.

1.3 Technology Information Sources

Regarding information sources research, there are many researches on human relationships.[10, 11] Finding information in social networking service (SNS) have received extensive attention recently.[12] Toni Wilson[13] discusses the sources of economic intelligence and competitive intelligence.[14] However, the research for the sources of information on technical intelligence, and how to obtain technology information from a reliable source is still not cover.

When Merrill S. Brenner[15] talks about technology intelligence and technology scouting, he expresses the relationship between technical information sources and signal strength of the relationship along the new product introduction time line from development till go to market (Ref. Figure 1). The first signals often appear in scientific and technical discussions, following signals include scientific publications, research cooperation, R&D alliances, joint ventures or partnerships are shown. These signals might be weak, but gathering, assessing, and communicating this information are crucial objectives to uncover and anticipate new technology trends or commercial developments. Later, patents will begin to issue, which is usually applied three to four years earlier before development. Next, process development efforts on the new technology might be rumored. Finally, near the end of the development cycle, the strongest signals occur, perhaps involving a product release or competitive product sales. Merrill S. Brenner re-emphasized the importance of gathering the information signal in the early stage in the case studies on aerospace products.[16]

It can be possible to gather technology information in industry or competitors, to provide technological innovation strategy support by detailed technical analysis,

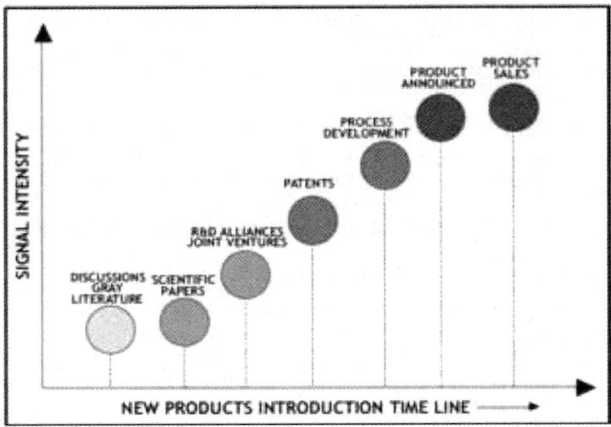

Figure 1. Technology Signals

Source: Merrill S. Brenner, Technology intelligence and technology scouting

based on scientific literature and research and development trends analysis, as well as patent information which is the core information. However, in order to provide the product to the market as soon as possible, enterprises in high – tech industries sometimes start product development before patent applications. Therefore, during product planning, it becomes essential to understand early weak signal dynamic information such as scientific literature, research and development information etc.

2 HIGH – TECH INDUSTRY INFORMATION EXPLORING

The first source information, which is obtained from suppliers, distributors, customers and employees, can increase the strength of competitive intelligence for businesses. However, it is quite difficult to gather this information which impacts on decision making from the public ones. In particular high – tech information is grasped by a few MNCs and other industry – leading technology companies. Gathering weak signal information, strengthening the information and early warning analysis and other analytical methods have become increasingly urgent.

2.1 The Characteristics of High – tech Industry

High tech is a technology that is at the cutting edge. High – tech industry is knowledge and technology intensive industries considered having the latest and most advanced technology. The high-tech sector of the economy develops or uses the most advanced technology known, and as such is often seen as having the most potential for future growth. However, there is no specific class of technology that is high-tech. The definition shifts over time. For example in the 1960s, as 'high-tech' color TV would now be considered obsolete. It has been replaced by the new television technology.

As each country focuses on different areas, the definition for high-tech industry is different. For example, in foreign countries it has generally been accepted to use research intensity such as the number of engineers, R&D expenditure ratio, and the number of patents etc. as industry classification indicators.

High-tech enterprise in China is to support the national key high-tech areas, ongoing research and development and technological achievements, to form core independent intellectual property rights, and as a basis to carry out business activities of enterprises.[17] Even the production of electronic information, bioengineering and other high-tech products of the enterprise, if not their core technology, in fact, cannot be called high-tech enterprises. Although the high-tech industries have different definitions, but as shown in Figure 2, there are always three characteristics of with the market uncertainty, technology uncertainty, and competitive factors uncertainty.[18] This paper will focus on the enterprises in high-tech industries with these characteristics for further study.

2.2 Management Information System in Enterprise

When discussing the high-tech industry information, firstly we must review the development progress of the management information system and data processing.

The concept of supporting corporate decision making from a large number of internal and external data came in the mainframe era. In the 70s, MIS (Management Information System), and in the 80s, DSS (Decision Support System) provided the information needed to support decision making. In the 90s, DWH (Data Warehouse), OLAP (Online Analytical Processing), DM (Data Mining) and other data

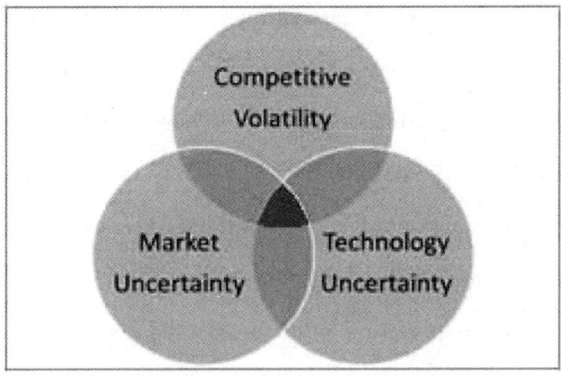

Figure 2. Characteristics of High – tech Industries

processing techniques have been developed. However, even data mining and OLAP still need some expertise or technical staffs to extract and process data. Since the beginning of 2000, with the development of information technology makes information more visual and higher efficiency. BI (Business Intelligence) is used as the company's management information system, so that data savings, collection, analysis can support business decisions. BI is used to analyze internal data and business processes, while CI gathers and analyzes information with a topical focus on company competitors. Industry information, product information, technical information, is all necessary competition information in order to make a management decision. This paper mainly focuses on exploring high – tech industries information.

2.3 High – tech Information Sources

The general technology information needed for R&D is new technology trends, technical standards, competing technologies and alternative technologies etc. essential information. It is an extremely important position to improve the development and competitiveness of the industries in every country. The government takes the initiative in actively providing information services to enhance the international competitiveness of industry. For example, in Japan, science policy and industrial development plan is settled on by the central government, and the detail technical roadmap and implementation plan is created by the independent administrative organizations, such as Japan Science and Technology Agency (JST), Japan's New Energy and Industrial Technology Development Organization (NEDO). They also have long – term responsibility for tracking, monitoring, collection and analysis of the technical development to simulate those key industries growth. These government agencies report includes a large number of technology trends related to the important information. Based on government publications, you can understand national policy, activities, achievements of scientific and technology and so on.

Scientific literature, papers and other academic research are also one valuable source of technical information. Those contents are highly technical, high quality, and they reflect the academic standards of professional disciplines, research developments and trends. Through exploring the scientific literature and journal articles, we can understand the industry the level of basic research and results, and be able to grasp the direction of future technology development. Generally the company will encourage employees to apply patents for protecting its intellectual property rights. Therefore, the analysis of patent information can help companies understand the situation of patent applications and technology developments. But for high – tech products, in order to prevent leakage of product development projects, and to provide the new product into the market before competitors, patent application is often delayed or abandoned. Therefore, it has become more important to predict the trend of a competitor's product development depending on scientific literature and publications to dig out industry and competitors' basic research strength.

We can find some certain correlation without reliance on human experience and intuition, by using such statistics, data mining, artificial intelligence and other methods. Through the patent literature and meta – analysis of scientific literature, we can glimpse the whole picture from embryonic research to product development, then to commercialization. As mentioned above, sources of information in accordance with the technical content of the signal intensity can be summarized and shown in Figure 3.

In fact, the enterprise employees in the various functional departments hold more valuable technical information, especially, the technical report, technical standards, product surveys, technical documents, test reports, manuals, newspapers, and company meetings, etc. Most of Japanese companies pay attention to internal corporate information. According to the Japanese Ministry of Science and Technology Policy Research's innovation survey report in September 2010, the main source of technical information is from internal group, suppliers and customers. The ratio that takes the scientific literature and patent information as an important source of information is still real small. [19] Obtaining information from enterprise internal group is a significant characteristic of Japanese companies, as a lot of outside information has been converted into the enterprise's internal information. As technical information requires professional, reliable and useful information, it is critical how to determine the reliability of the technology information.

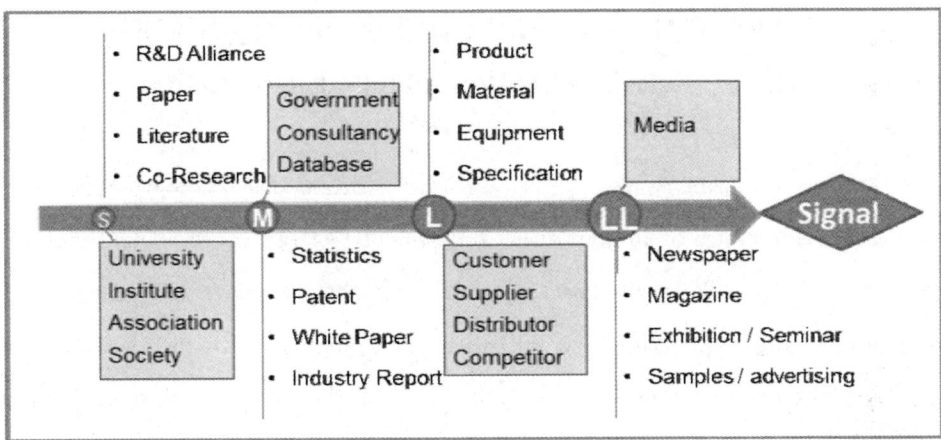

Figure 3. High - tech Information Sources and Signals Intensity

2.4 Capture Reliable Technical Information Source

With the growth of network technology, the information by a quick search often has to rule out the noise firstly, because their definitions and sources of information are not clear. The specific method is: the first, be sure to confirm the number of different sources of information, instead of depending on a single source; the second, to check out the time of the data. If only single message, it is difficult to convey the truth. But by comparing with other sources of information, the noise can be noticed. The third is to analyze the relevance to other information sources. If some inconsistencies are found, validation information from a third party is necessary.

The Ansoff matrix [20] is one of the most widely used marketing analysis tools that help businesses decide their product and market growth strategy. It takes product and market as two basic element, shows the difference of four product / market portfolio (existing products - existing markets, existing products - new markets, new products - existing markets, new products - new markets) and corresponding marketing strategies require different technology information. Also, according to the strategic direction and product development life cycle in different situations, the key of information collection, analysis is also different.

3 TECHNOLOGY SPILLOVER OF MNCS AND HIGH - TECH INFORMATION EXPLORING

MNCs are the primary inventor of the world's advanced technology. When MNCs invest in a host country by foreign direct investment (FDI), it is assumed that a part of their technology spills to the host country firms. [21-23] Kokko [24] indicated the occurrence of technology spillovers from two aspects: one is from the demonstration, imitation and communication; and the other is from the competition. Demonstration by MNCs and imitation by domestic firms is probably the most evident spillover channel. FDI spillovers can occur through five main channels: demonstration, imitation, labor mobility, exports, competition and backward and forward linkages with domestic firms.

Due to overall downturn in the global economy environment, China's rapid economic growth has been given much attention. Foreign investment is still flowing into China. FDI technology spillover impact on China's economy is growing. Since the 1990s, MNCs in China continue to increase investment to the establishment of more and more R&D center. But on the technology spillover effects of FDI in China R&D center, scholars have different views. Xian Guoming etc. [25, 26] discuss the spillover effects of FDI on innovation capability in China by using provincial data, through overflow channel of demonstration, linkages between industries, and human resource flows. The empirical results show that FDI host country's innovation activities can have positive effects. Jiang Dianchun's research found that spillover effects do exist, and are subject to market structure and characteristics of the technology gap and other industries[27]. Then he followed by analysis using panel data models within the Chinese high-tech industry FDI on the domestic impact of technological innovation and pathways. Our previous research result [28] shows that the competitive effect of FDI is not conducive to the growth of domestic innovation capabilities, but through the demonstration effect and the effect of the flow of scientific and technical people and other activities, it can promote the development of domestic enterprises.

With the further improvement of China's economic opening, competition has become increasingly fierce. Enterprises not only face competition from domestic counterparts, but also have to deal with MNCs squeeze and challenges. In the fierce competition to capture market opportunities, gain the initiative in development, competitive intelligence has become one of an important factor in the survival and development. With the intensification of global competition, intellectual property competition has been a serious concern. Currently, MNCs through patent invention, licensing and transfer, etc. in the world market have an enormous economic benefit, and maintain their technological advantage. MNCs with the high-tech industry technology in China should be the targets of technology scouting, technology scanning and technical monitoring. Local Chinese firms can accelerate technological innovation and realize to catch up the competitors, through learning, digestion and absorption of advance technological knowledge.

4 SUMMARY

With the accelerating process of globalization, how to get macro-economic trends, how to predict future developments, how to looking for opportunities of emerging industries, all become crucial issues for enterprise development to win the market in keen competition. Technological innovation and technology strategic management decision-making is supported by Competitive Technical Intelligence. By looking the initial weak signals of the information, observing and predicting possible future changes, appropriate measures will be possible.

High-tech industry plays an important economic growth leading role. In this paper, the importance of the technical information source selection and weak signals of information was described through the review of the characteristics of high-tech business and competitive intelligence application, while exploring high-tech industries information. As the weak signals are often vague, irrelevant, uncertain, and mixed in a lot of "noise", obtaining accurate technical information seems even more difficult. In this paper, noise exclusion and the effectiveness of technical information sources analysis was further studied. MNCs from developed countries are the protagonists of the global technology competition and technological innovation, globalization, and the most influential driving force. Finally, the paper discussed the strengthen R&D investment in China by MNCs, and analyzed the impact of FDI technology spillovers to Chinese enterprises. As the result, we suggest strengthening the Competitive Technical Intelligence to MNCs while exploring high-tech industries information, in order to improve the technological competitiveness. Access to technology information is just the first stage of CTI. It is necessary to analyze and associate with a variety of information. Future research will focus on the combination of a weak signal data analysis and early warning analysis in empirical research.

REFERENCES

[1] Prescott, J. and Miller, S. H. 2001. *Proven strategies in competitive intelligence lesson from the trenches*, Society of Competitive Intelligence Professionals (SCIP), John Wiley & Sons, Inc.

[2] Coburn, M. M. 1999. *Competitive Technical Intelligence, A Guide to Design, Analysis and Action*, Oxford University Press.

[3] Lichtenthaler, E. 2003. *Third generation management of technology intelligence processes*, *R&D Management*, Vol. 33, No. 4, pp. 361-375.

[4] W. Bradford Ashton. 2009. *Competitive Technical Intelligence: Past and Future*, Vol. 12, No. 4, pp10-12, July/Aug.

[5] Savioz, P. 2004. *Technology Intelligence: Concept Design and Implementation in Technology based SMEs*, Hampshire, UK: Palgrave Macmillan.

［6］Porter, M. E. 1985. *Competitive Advantage: Creating and Sustaining Superior Performance*, New York: The Free Press.

［7］Shen Guchao. 2009. *Signal Analysis: An Important Area for Studying Competitive Intelligence – A Brief Survey. Proceedings of International Forum on Technological Innovation and Competitive Technical Intelligence* 2008: 148 – 154. Peking Univ. Press.

［8］George S. Day, Paul J. H. 2006. *Schoemaker, Peripheral vision: Detecting the weak signals that will make or break your company.* Boston' HBS Press, pp. 4 – 6.

［9］Paul J. H. Schoemaker and George S. Day. 2009. *How to Make Sense of Weak Signals*, MIT Sloan Management Review, Spring Vol. 50, No. 3, pp. 81 – 89.

［10］Kent Potter. 2005. *Finding Human Sources: Beastly Metaphors for Research Planning*, Vol. 8, No. 2, 57 – 59.

［11］David Carpe. 2005. *Understanding Human Sources*, Competitive Intelligence Magazine, Vol. 8, No. 4, 49 – 51.

［12］August Jackson. 2009. Web 2.0 Changes Everything, Competitive Intelligence Magazine, Vol. 12, No. 2, 8 – 15.

［13］Toni Wilson. 2008. *Information Sources for a Global Economy*, Competitive Intelligence Magazine, Vol. 11, No. 3, 49 – 50.

［14］Toni Wilson, Christine Wunderlin. 2006. *Uses of Publicly Available Sources for Effective CI Collection*, Vol. 9, No. 5, 28 – 33.

［15］Merrill S. Brenner. 1996. *Technology intelligence and technology scouting*, Competitive Intelligence Review, Vol. 7, No. 3, 20 – 27.

［16］Merrill S. Brenner. 2005. *Technology Intelligence at Air Products*, Competitive Intelligence Magazine, Vol. 8, No. 3, 6 – 19.

［17］Notice of the Ministry of Science and Technology, Ministry of Finance and State Administration of Taxation. The Administrative Measures for Determination of High and New Tech Enterprises, No. 172, 2008.

［18］Jakki J. Mohr, Sanjit Sengupta, *Stanley Slater.* 2010. *Marketing of High – Technology Products and Innovations*, Third Edition, Prentice Hall.

［19］Ministry of Education, Culture, Sports, Science and Technology Japan, National Institute of Science and Technology Policy. Japanese National Innovation Survey, 2010.

［20］Ansoff, H. I. 1957. *Strategies for diversification*, Harvard Business Review, Vol. 35, No. 5, 113 – 124.

［21］MACDOUGALL G. D. A. 1960. *The Benefits and Costs of Private Investment from Abroad: A Theoretical Approach*, Economic Record, Vol. 36, 13 – 35.

[22] CORDEN W. M. 1967. Protection and Foreign Investment, Economic Record, Vol. 43, 209 – 232.

[23] CAVES R. E. 1971. International Corporations: The Industrial Economics of Foreign Investment, Economica, Vol. 38, 1 – 27.

[24] Kokko A. 1992. Foreign Direct Investment, Host Country Characteristics and Spillovers, the Economic Research Institute, Stockholm.

[25] Xian Guoming, Yan Bing. 2005. The Spill – over Effect of FDI on China's Innovation Capacity, World Economy.

[26] Xian Guoming, Bo Wenguang. 2005. The Impact of FDI on China Firm's Technology Innovation: Analysis from the Industry Aspect. World Economy Study, (6): 16 – 23.

[27] Jiang Dianchun, Zhang Yu. 2006. Industrial Characteristics and Technology Spillover of FDI: The Empirical Evidence of Chinese High – Tech Industries. World Economy, (10):21 – 29.

[28] Jiang Dianchun, Xia Liangke. 2005. The Empirical Study of the Function of FDI on Innovation in China's High – Tech Industries, World Economy, (8): 3 – 10.

The applications of Method and Technology of Competitive Intelligence

WHEN CHINESE ECONOMY, TERRITORY AND SOCIETY MIGHT PROVE BOTH EFFICIENT AND SUSTAINABLE

Jean – Marie Rousseau[①]　Wen Hongjian[②]
(Translations by LIU Qin Louise[③])

Abstract

China has been responsible for fostering more prosperity than any other economy in the past 30 years. Nowadays, after enjoying a decades – long economic boom built on cheap labour and the intensive use of energy, China is attempting to diversify the sources of its economic growth. But the risk of a "double – dip recession" occurring in the US and in Europe, not only is a specific economic concern, but also could turn into a societal problem for the whole world, including China.

Due to these US' and Europe's falls in recession – China's largest trade partners – export and investment growth is expected to continue to fall in the near future and force it to focus on SMEs' tech – absorptive capacity and domestic consumption. China should now manage the transition from a mercantilist model of growth, driven by exports, to a model that respects environmental and social issues, and then consider evolving towards a sustainable development, without sacrificing the previous evidence of

---

①　Jean – Marie ROUSSEAU, TAO – ITINeRIS, BRUXELLES, BELGIUM, Jeanmarie. a. rousseau@ gmail. com

②　WEN Hongjian, CAPITAL UNIVERSITY OF ECONOMICS AND BUSINESS, BEIJING, CHINA, hjwen55@ hotmail. com

③　Translations from English to Chinese and from Chinese to English for the abstract below, as well as some footnotes, have been done and/or checked with accuracy and a high level of competency by LIU Qin Louise, qin. louise. liu@ gmail. com *efficiency. For such an evolution, three steps of grown – up strategies sound essential, if not crucial, and are hereby explored as*: TAO – SHANZHAI – YI JING.

Keywords

Innovation, Territorial intelligence, Strategy, SMEs, Domestic consumption, TAO methodology, Shanzhai innovation, Yi Jing, Competitiveness, Resilience, Sustainability

INTRODUCTION

The US and the European debt crisis is still far from resolved, and could be set to continue slowing down and enter recession regions in the coming months. The risk of a "double – dip recession" occurring in the US and in Europe, not only is a specific economic concern, but also could turn into a societal problem for the whole world. Many economic experts and analysts are pessimistic about G20 leaders' ability to improve the global economy. Currently the US, the EU and China all have different problems. There may be a lot of bickering at the G20 and it is hard to say if G20 leaders can come up with a cohesive plan at all. Indeed, the objective should be to put new initiatives that seek to prevent Europe's sovereign debt crisis from triggering a global slump. The OECD just reduced its forecast for the United States' economic growth next year, suggesting it likely to be 1.8 percent it had previously predicted. The OECD's report also stated that China is likely to say farewell between 2011 and 2013 with two – digit economic growth (likely to grow by 8.6 percent next year).

China has been responsible for fostering more prosperity than any other economy in the past 30 years. Nowadays, after enjoying a decades – long economic boom built on cheap labour and the intensive use of energy, China is making an attempt to diversify the sources of its economic growth, which are now mainly in trade and domestic investment. However, China could be quite satisfied with its reputation of "*World's Workshop*", but eventually realises that this could not be a credible and long – run strategy. The Chinese central government thus yet attempted to accelerate a second stage process by massive investments in R&D and a series of measures aiming at easing the country to access the position of the "*World's Lab*"... As the other advanced countries, China is now accessing to global markets with a rapid pace of technological changes. Even in terms of "overseas direct investment" (ODI), China might take a new policy from seeking markets and natural resources to acquiring strategic assets for research and development, proprietary technology, design facilities and brands, which are abundant in Western economies.

Since China plans to increase domestic consumption, its market will become much more of an export destination for the US and European goods and services in the coming decade. Due to these US' and Europe's falls in recession – China's largest trade partners – and as a result, export and investment growth are expected to continue to fall in the near future.

This threshold paper aims a demonstrating that China is not only a country in transformation, but essentially a country of transformations, and then attempts to reflect the commitment whereby China is meeting as follows: After catching – up developed countries at a tremendous speedy pace [1. *"A fast sort of country in a moving world*], China needs to balance its economy and society; [2. *Rebalancing the wealth of China*], and then consider evolving towards a sustainable development, without sacrificing the previous evidence of efficiency, for the coming decades; [3. *Competitiveness and cohesion for sustainable development*]. Three steps of grown – up strategies sound essential, if not crucial and are explored as: *TAO – SHANZHAI – YI JING*.

1 "A FAST SORT OF COUNTRY" IN A MOVING WORLD

China's economic success over the past three decades has been widely regarded as the result of its ability to produce manufactured goods at low cost, building on the availability of cheap labour and scale economies, while relying on existing technologies of production. More recently, however, there has been increasing evidence to support the argument that China is catching – up fast in terms of scientific and technological innovation.

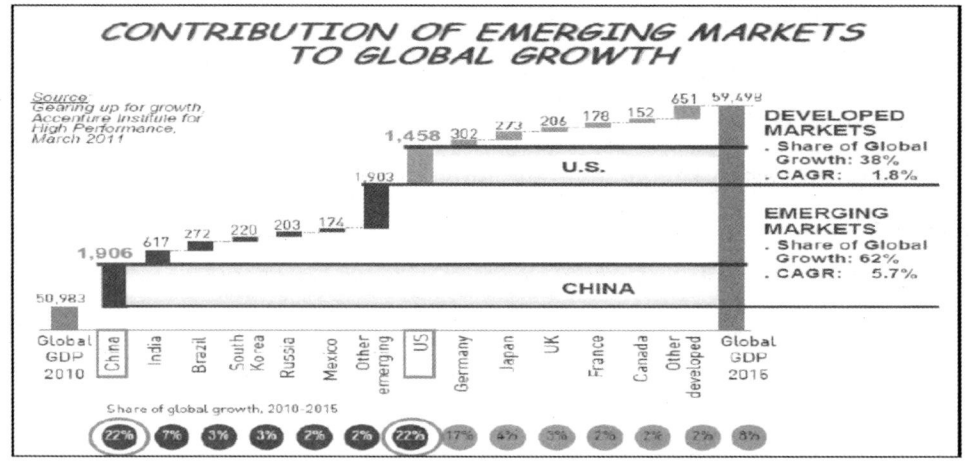

Figure1. Contribution of emerging markets to global growth

Meanwhile, the number of domestic invention patents has increased with the Chinese patent office, during the period 1999 – 2006 at an average annual rate of 35% from 15,600 to over 122,000. The number of full time equivalent R&D workers has tripled between 1998 and 2008 reaching almost 2 million, and everything suggests that this trend remained if not expanded and accelerated. China is really catching – up faster than expected the other advanced countries in terms of S&T and innovation.

This section intends to stress the ability of China to accelerate the process of catching – up and even, to a certain extent, the re – enforcement of its technology – edge: [1.1. *Soaring China vs. Sluggish West*], as well as its concern about achieving an independent innovation and improving a progressive re – orientation of its economy; [1.2. *Hi – tech absorptive capacity of SMEs + enhancement of internal consumption*].

1.1 Soaring China vs. Sluggish West

China comes back on the world theatre ... China's reintegration in the world community has been welcome by Europe as much as by America or Japan, which all adopted and promoted an engagement policy towards China. However, as China yet was becoming more powerful and more influential, Western countries have been further and further concerned by a "China threat syndrome", at least a "China problem" or the idea that China may now become a source of problems including economic and research issues.

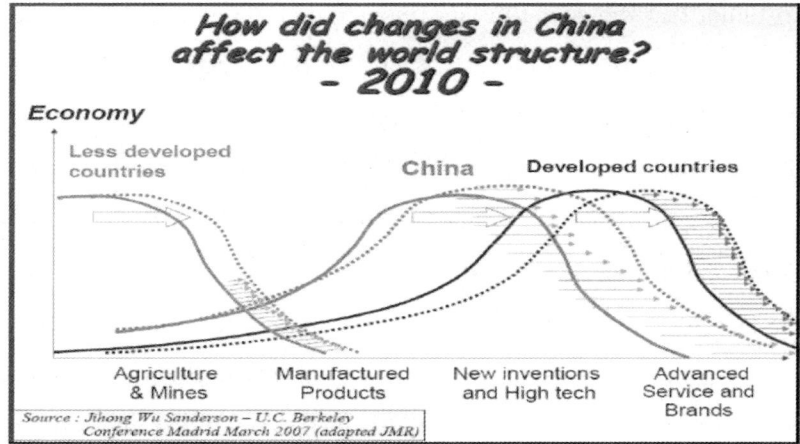

Figure 2. How did changes in China affect the world structure?

Today in fact, China is facing a golden opportunity to achieve S&T catch – up with the West, despite its relatively backward condition just 25 years ago. China is already second only to the USA in terms of R&D personnel and one of the world leaders in high – techs such as nanotechnologies, new materials and genetic engineering. Contrary to what general wisdom may suggest at first sight, regional concentration of R&D activities in China could not be found to be particularly stark.

Nevertheless, everybody knows that the Chinese invented practically everything hundreds of years ago. It is clear, for instance, that printing, the magnetic compass and gunpowder weapons were all Chinese in origin, despite the puzzlement that Francis Bacon had expressed over their beginnings when in the seventeenth century he pointed to "*the force and virtue and consequences of discoveries*". But, it is only in the early 1950s that Joseph Needham[1], the so – called *Erasmus of the 20th century*, through his massive work on *Science and Civilisation in China* series, made the western countries discover the great part China played in sciences and technologies. The

---

[1] Joseph Needham (1901 – 1995); far beyond the professional domains of sinology, and the history of Chinese science and technology, there are few works with an impact comparable to his monumental *Science and Civilisation in China* (Cambridge 1954). Seventeen large volumes published, and still being continued) and many minor studies have been produced as a spin – off of that large project, of which he was the founding father.

main question Joseph Needham raised was about the reasons it had been in Europe and not in China that the scientific and industrial revolutions occurred, despite the immense achievements of traditional China. In 2008, Simon Winchester's book, *Bomb, Book and Compass*, reminded the world of this achievement, but there is also a great library① that I recently visited within the *Needham Research Institute*, and which has its origin in the collections assembled from 1937 onwards from sources both in China and the Western world.

In the late 90s, China's R&D intensity (around 0.8%) was relatively unremarkable, just above countries at a similar level of development but certainly not an outlier. Since 2007, the picture substantially changed > R&D intensity: 1.5%. In 1999, around half the R&D expenditure in China was accounted for by business enterprises, putting it toward the bottom, alongside with Turkey, Argentina and

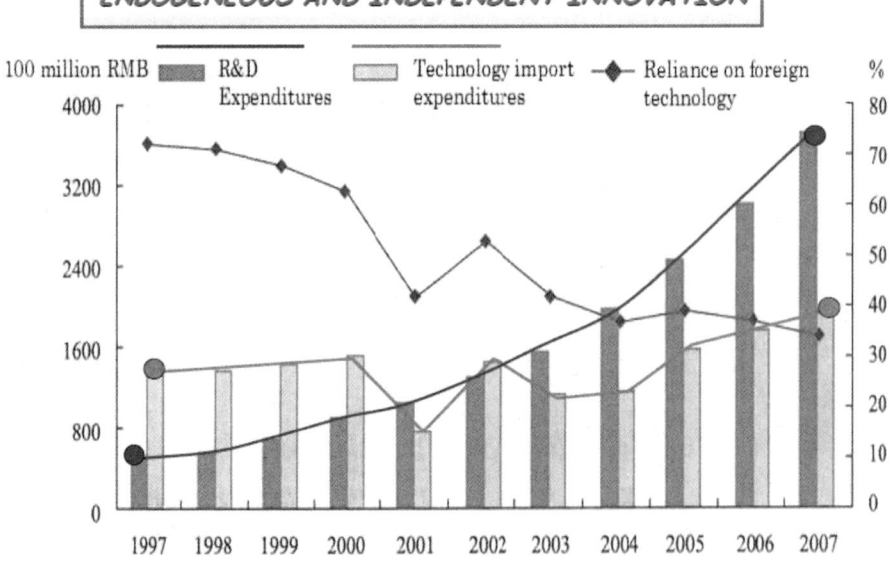

Figure 3. **Endogenous and independent innovation**

---

① The Library now holds nearly 30,000 titles, focusing on the history of Chinese and East Asian traditional science, technology and medicine. These include three major collectaneous Chinese works: *the Siku Quanshu* 四库全书, *Daozang* 道藏 (Daoist Canon), and *Dazangjing* 大藏经 (Tripitika). It was originally intended for the furtherance of the researches on which the *Science and Civilisation in China* project is based.

Mexico. By 2007, the business share had risen to over 70%, thus placing China firmly in the line with top OECD innovators such as Japan, Korea, the US or Germany. Yet, in terms of R&D expenditure by sector, the late 1990s became a game – changer for Chinese innovation effort: in 1997, 42.7% of the R&D expenditure was spent by enterprises, this share rose to 44.7% (1998), 49.7 (1999) and 60.2% (2000), reaching 69.1% by 2006 and probably up to 74% by 2011.

But *Breznitz & Murphee* (2011)① argue that the successful process and logistics innovation has equipped China, while we often wrongly think that it could be due to "*the fabled creature of true [novel product] innovation*" of the last decades, with "*ultra mass – flexibility production*" capabilities, and thus put it into a uniquely strong position within the global network that represents manufacturing production today. At first sight, most innovation in China sounds of merely incremental nature as the corresponding patents protect "*small inventive steps*" rather than substantive new technologies.

> "*A slow sort of country!*" said the Red Queen. "*Now, here, you see, it takes all the running you can do to keep in the same place. If you want to get somewhere else, you must run at least twice as fast as that!*" Through the Looking Glass (Alice in Wonderland), Lewis Carroll.

The 11*th National People's Congress* which was held on last March gave place to a very important report on *China's Economic and Social Development Plan* (March 15, 2011) which deserves to be hereby commented, specifically for the part related to the *National Development and Reform Commission*. ② It is obvious that the main target of this "Plan" that actually proved a real strategy, aiming to increase the China's capacity for independent innovation. Good progress was made in implementing 16 key – state – S&T programmes together with the March 1997 Program for Basic Research, the *March 1986 High – Tech Program* and the *National Key Technology*

---

① *The Red Queen Run*, Breznitz & Murphee (2011).

② Report on the implementation of the 2010 *Plan for National Economic and Social Development* and the 2011 *Draft Plan for National Economic and Social Development* (Fourth Session of the eleventh National People's Congress, March 5, 2011 – *National Development and Reform Commission*, NDRC.

R&D Programme. According to the NDRC's reporter, "*smooth progress was made in carrying out major projects such as building* 50 *national engineering centres*, 32 *national engineering laboratories and* 56 *key national laboratories seated in enterprises in areas such as digital television and next – generation.* [...] *An additional* 93 *enterprise technology centres received state recognition*, 550 *enterprises were now included in the national pilot program to support innovative enterprises*, *and the national pilot projects for innovation – oriented cities were carried out in* 45 *cities. The calculating speed of the high performance Tianhe – 1 supercomputer*, *which was developed independently*, *is ranked first in the world.*" Priority is now given to funding of key ongoing projects, and the construction on the major projects in *the Twelfth Five – Year Plan*. At the same time, healthy development of nongovernmental investment should be further encouraged and guided. The appropriation for science and technology spending is 194.413 billion yuan, that is, an increase of 12.5%. The figure above consists of 190.159 billion yuan of central government spending and 4.254 billion yuan in transfer payments to local governments, while appropriating 43.5 billion yuans, up 44%, to speed up the implementation of major national science and technology projects ... demonstrating evidence for a more balanced country, not only in terms of economy, but also in terms of S&T issues.

While science is becoming increasingly globalised, China is particularly building up its own scientific capabilities rapidly and in a targeted way. This is provoking concern within advanced economies that they might be losing their advantage in the scientific domains that can be part of the foundation for new areas of growth. The so – called *INNOVATION* 2010 BCG's survey[①] recently revealed that, after a moderate retrenchment in 2009, companies have recommitted to pursuing innovation during the 2010s, including in China. The report also postulates that a new world order in innovation is taking hold, that is one world in which the so – called *Rapidly Developing Economies*, led by China, will increasingly assume more prominent positions,

---

[①] *INNOVATION* 2010 – *A return to Prominence – and the Emergence of New World Order* – April 2010 – The *Boston Consulting Group* (James P. Andrew, Joe Manget, David C. Michael, Andrew Taylor, Hadi Zablit) bcg.com.

while the western mature economies continue to play major roles but gradually become less dominant.

China doesn't stop going further and further ... After other Asian nations such as Japan, South Korea and Taiwan, China successfully adopted the so – called "*Flight of wild geese*①" development model. For industrialised and advanced economies, challenging China now consists of facing its huge and powerful human resources. On the other hand, the evolution of the global economy since the world crisis raises questions about future growth in export markets which pushes China to transform itself. The future will not be a mere extrapolation of the past decades' trends ...

In the first phase of globalisation, only the old industrial and low added – value activities had been affected in China, as Japan's competition in the 80s, and then the "new industrialised countries" in the 90s. But now, the whole Chinese industry, with the service sector as well, is more or less directly completed by the companies of emerging economies: not only steel, shipbuilding and electronics, but also, more recently, automotive, telecoms, railways, aeronautics, nuclear power... In all sectors, a few decades – should we say "a few years"? – are required for the Chinese regions to compete with the flagship of the old Europe.

China doesn't intent to let its place in the international division of labour only defined by low – cost labour. The so – called "*wild – geese –flying*" model is a concrete development strategy, fully embedded in the continuous changing principle, moving towards a high added – value and up – scaled production. China is now preparing itself to compete with the most advanced economies in high – tech production sectors: high – speed trains, telecom equipments, satellites, and, probably in the

---

① A "*wild – geese –flying pattern*" is the image that the Japanese economist Akamatsu in 1961 used to describe the model by which development might be disseminated in Asia, whereby new techniques spread for gradually catching up to advanced and industrialised economies. These Asian newcomers developed their specialisation in traditional industries and later moved to the new technology sector and the wild – geese – flying model is related to a certain extent to the interdependence in Asia between emerging economies and advanced ones. Both were linked by strong inter – sectoral complementarities and technology transfer processes.

near future, aerospace, nuclear, space... Compared with observations of the previous Asian experimentations in terms of technological catch – up, the size of the Chinese economy and its vast reserves of manpower introduce a new factor: the capacity and ability to play on all fronts, with a gradation of production according to their technological intensity of coastal areas to hinterlands and the deep inland.

One should however recognise that the success of the recovery plan is essentially due to the administrative and political structure of the country. The Prime Minister recalled in the same sentence he would pursue the path of reform towards a market – oriented economy while continuing to make the *"best use of advantages of the socialist system which is able to efficiently decide, rigorously organising production and concentrating resources to carrying out great actions and projects"*.

1.2 Hi – tech absorptive capacity of SMEs & enhancement of internal consumption

Nevertheless, four concrete facts and behaviours, which yet proved themselves and were successfully verified on the spot of innovation, prove to facilitate the transfer of science and technology to innovation, that is, "the four aces of innovation": the inter – disciplinarity or cross – fertilisation, the related variety, the serendipity, and then the technological irrigation of technology performances combined with the improvement of the absorptive capacities of local SMEs.

1. Edgar Morin[①] stresses the significance of "trans – disciplinarity", "inter – disciplinarity", and/or "poly – disciplinarity" as the merging of different sets of knowledge (*"rencontre des savoirs"*) according to the exchanges between scientific and innovative disciplines. Besides the split between hard sciences and humanities, barriers and boulders to knowledge's exchanges, particularly in Europe, are of several kinds: institutional and personal, through a tendency to hyper – specialisation.

---

① In his latest book, "*La Voie – Pour l'avenir de l'humanité*" (Ed. Fayard, 2011), Edgar Morin shows that the stage of globalisation began with the collapse of the Soviet society and the so – called economy of 'widespread capitalism', while coinciding with the time of access to immediate telecommunication – fax Internet, television, mobile – that is, when the globe could be fully merged.

Sometimes, within the scientific disciplines, problems of fragmentation of knowledge emerge. The harmful nature of the specialisation of scientific disciplines is that it cuts a continuum in many separated fragments. To put it right, we have to seek the best way to link these separated parts, connect the knowledge, or "*to spin together*" – from the Latin '*complexare*' – and thus face the *complexity* of our world. ①

2. Related variety② is expected to have a positive effect on regional development, because knowledge is likely to spill over between complementary sectors. When constructing regional advantage a policy framework, based on a related variety approach may be highly relevant, since the risk of selecting wrong activities is reduced when the region – specific context is taken as a point of departure. This would mean that regional competences are sued as building blocks for the purpose of broadening the economic base of a region. By contrast with any specialisation concept, whatever smart or updated, constructing regional advantage based on related variety may dampen the risk of sector – specific shocks. The knowledge creation and innovation processes have become increasingly complex, there is a larger variety of knowledge sources and inputs and there is more interdependence and division of labour among actors such as individuals, companies and other organisations. This does not mean however that R&D and the level of technological complexity are the only indicators of knowledge intensity and innovativeness ...

3. One specific aspect of serendipity③ is linking together apparently innocuous facts to come to a valuable conclusion. It also could be regarded as a chance to unexpected, incidental and fortunate effects. But, as told Louis Pasteur: "*In the fields of observation chance favours only the prepared mind.*" Michael Porter picked up on the

---

① *La Méthode*, Edgar Morin, Ed. *Le Seuil*; this encyclopaedic book entailing 6 volumes all written from 1977 to 2004.

② Since Jane Jacobs diversity's concept in regional economies is regarded as one of the driving forces of economic growth, stimulating creativity and reducing the risk for a sector specific shock harming the whole of local economies.

③ The first noted use of the word "serendipity" was by Horace Walpole (1717 – 1792) since he formed it from the Persian fairy tale, known as *The Three Princes of Serendip* (*Serendip is currently Sri Lanka*).

theme and created the term "blind spots" to refer to conventional wisdom which no longer holds true, but which still guides business strategy. An alternative technique is known among competitive intelligence professionals as "*strategy's reverse engineering*" which looks for the underlying assumptions which can rationalise existing strategy. It is also possible to consider this alternative technique as an art of finding the right product by cross – fertilisation and poly – disciplinarity we just stated above with Edgar Morin. Chinese, for instance are able to find these "blind spots" by adapting new technologies from abroad for low – cost products which in addition prove much more domestically marketable. It is often due to the foreign competitors' groundless and misreading of the local habits and behavioural facts, while local entrepreneurs and/or researchers are able to do so.

4. Successful technology transfer and knowledge transfer depend on a double way of exchange and cooperation since they are related to the will of irrigation of the knowledge and technology's sources and the capacity of the beneficiaries in absorbing and efficiently exploiting this knowledge, tackling other boulders and then conquering new markets. Effective knowledge absorption capabilities are of vital importance in the facilitation of innovation effectiveness. As inefficiency in production exists and depends upon the level of human capital of the regions' workforce, evidence that the amount of R&D in industry undertakes is also important when less robust. The impacts of the ability of firms to use external knowledge sources were inquired especially for external knowledge stemming from scientific research. Absorptive capacity plays a key role in determining firms' capability – and, by extension, the whole territory they are implemented in – to access and make use of external knowledge. European firms in the manufacturing industry with in – house absorptive capacities and a high relevance of scientific knowledge are characterised by higher sales shares of new and improved products and higher probabilities of competitiveness of the local firms and their whole territory. Thus, insufficient levels of territorial capital should hamper the capability of regions to grasp and fully exploit new knowledge. A lower regional absorptive capacity increases knowledge spill – overs towards surrounding territories. Moreover, if European regions turn their focus away from manu-

facturing, they risk losing the opportunity to profit from the process innovations that take more often on assembly lines and in manufacturing facilities than in labs. Building a bridge between education and the economy for all workers is critical in a labour market defined by an increasing demand for workers with job churn requiring new skills with new companies more often than ever before. Aligning regional economic development initiatives with national priorities such as energy efficiency, advanced manufacturing, and new technologies turns essential when administering this matching – grants programme.

In this respect, the overall influence of SMEs at the macro level appears to be barely noticeable to local governors. The fundamental problem is that local authorities have never developed a correct view of SMEs. It is known to all that SMEs have played an indispensable role in increasing jobs, promoting economic growth, scientific and technological innovation, as well as social stability and harmony. What local authorities want is political achievements and taxation of which big enterprises, both State and private, are the major sources. So, it is no surprise that local officials offer preferential policies to big enterprises, and it is significant that most SMEs in China have faced these last months greater difficulties than during the financial crisis in 2008. There are too many opportunities for speculative profits of various kinds in society, which leads to a lack of resources and impetus promoting long – term start – up and innovation.

However, these last months, economic indicators in China started weakening and still sound to deteriorate, pushing the Chinese government to consider easing current monetary policy and giving more priority to maintaining economic growth. Actually, the *Consumer Price Index* (CPI), a main gauge of inflation, slipped to 6.1 percent in September from 6.2 in August and the more – than – three – year high of 6.5 percent in July. Inflation could be on track to ease, which might provide leeway for Beijing to fine – tune policy to strike a better balance between growth and inflation priorities. With the current regimen of credit austerity, imposed to contain economic overheating and inflationary pressure, making conditions for SMEs worse, while the whole financial sector risks affecting the country's economic and social dynamism.

Only about 10 percent of Chinese SMEs' finance comes from banks. The main impediment in China proves to be local governments which compete with SMEs for bank loans and inevitably push them out from the formal banking sector. Meanwhile, local governments rely on bank credit to invest in infrastructure and real estate development and one-third of the country's total outstanding loans, 14 trillion yuan was owned by local governments. In the last few years, 30 – 40 percent of bank credit therefore went to government infrastructure projects. Another impediment is the dominance of large banks, as the four largest banks in China accounts for 60 percent of the country's total bank lending. Large banks tend to lend to large companies in order to save costs. In this context, technology – edge SMEs are often considered synonymous with high risk by financial institutions. They are frequently refused loans, but IP – collateralized loans that combine intangible assets with financial capital for innovation in economic growth, are welcome as an effective financing option for SMEs. But, as a matter of fact, though the ZhongGuanCun national innovation park has heavy support from the central government, its 17,000 smaller tech companies often still need significant financing to turn their concepts into reality. To help them raise capital, in 2006 park officials implemented the nation's first pilot project that uses intellectual property (IP) as collateral to borrow money from banks.

With most capital being diverted to the stock market, property market, precious metal and even underground illegal banks, industry bosses are finding themselves with a critical lack of capital. Many small and medium – sized enterprises even face bankruptcy. Therefore, the key to re – attracting private capital lies in letting industry have higher profits. China's manufacturing activity fell short of expectations in October, spreading jittery sentiments across the market, which had not long before cheered over a renewed expansion in manufacturing according to a preliminary report of the HSBC PMI. The official PMI surveying mostly large – and medium – sized State enterprises, moderated to 50 – 4 in October from 51 – 2 in September, hitting a low since February last year, the China Federation of Logistics and Purchasing announced yesterday. The previous market consensus was at 51.8 for the PMI reading for October. This falling PMI indicates that the economy is still facing a downward pressure, but it also sends a positive signal that the economic growth is becoming more sustainable, shifting to self – initiated growth from the expansion generated by government policies.

With the increasing cost of labour and harsher restrictions on resources, SMEs need the central and local governments to create a nurturing business environment and provide easier access to financing.

For similar reasons, the investment – driven economic development model should be changed to focus more on internal consumption, which still represents only 40% in China while it is more or less 70% of the GDP in the advanced economies is healthier and sustainable. A second downgrade – either from Moody Investor's services – would follow *Standard & Poor's* downgrade on US concerns about budget deficit and rising debt burden. A second loss of the US's top credit rating would be an additional blow to the sluggish US economy. European services and manufacturing outputs contract at the fastest pace in more than two years, adding to signs the region's economy is edging toward a recession. Nouriel Roubini (*Roubini Global Economics LLC*) said that there is a 50% risk the US, the UK & the Eurozone will slip into a recession in the next 12 months. Western countries as a whole are still slumping low and consumer sentiment is also drastically weakening...

In 1990, Chinese income per capita was 30 per cent lower than the average for Sub – Saharan Africa. Today, it is three times greater, over $4,000. By 2030, China might reach a per capita income of $16,000, and therefore the effect on the world economy would be equivalent to adding 15 of today's South Koreas. But, as that expansion is rather accommodated within an export and investment – led growth model, China now might urge needing rebalance through boosting domestic demand, lowering savings and then increasing consumption.

2 REBALANCING THE WEALTH OF CHINA

Keystones provide flexibility and adaptability enough to what is likely to endure in new contexts, new markets, and new business realities. What really matters is which "*knowledge ecosystem*" is more likely to endure in the face of shocks and transitions, which embodies a greater capacity for integration and resilience. For several decades, too many territories continued to deny making a genuine effort to foster R&D and innovation to be combined with a clearly defined vision of the future, based on the value of its citizens, should be backed by strong political systems.

As a matter of fact, this future is not only to be constructed on the spot of the territories [2.1. *Construction of a territorial advantage in differentiated Chinese economies*], but also would lead to run an innovation policy market – oriented in terms of exports and conquest of a potentially huge domestic consumerism [2.2. *Shanzhai innovation for affordable and marketable new techs*].

2.1 Construction of a territorial advantage in differentiated Chinese economies

Social and societal dimensions of the territories are less considered than technology and the name of *Silicon Valley* is only resonant with echoes of physical endowment, heavy infrastructures and successful technological champions. The true goal of the economy should be "*the full development of the resources of resources, i.e. people*". This at least was the policy recommended by the economist François Perroux, often against and in resistance to the ideologies of the last century. The "Knowledge ecosystem" which could result from the local organisation of a given territory in order to construct a regional advantage that roughly speaking could be summarised with three axial processes: 1/ the *KIT – Tool* – *K*nowledge, *I*ntelligence and *T*echnology – as a top – down initiative for a knowledge dissemination (irrigation) to put into motion learning organisations, validation of new ideas which help face scepticism and any resistance to innovation; 2/ the *HUMUS* – *HU*man resources, *M*obilisation of local actors and *US*ages – by motivation of the local actors and sharing of strategies in terms of common values and common projects; 3/ *NET* – *N*etworks and *E*xchange of *T*alents – with cross – fertilisation between disciplines and among research centres within open – innovation processes, *Triple Helix* agreements, as well as inter – personal relationships and public – private partnerships ...

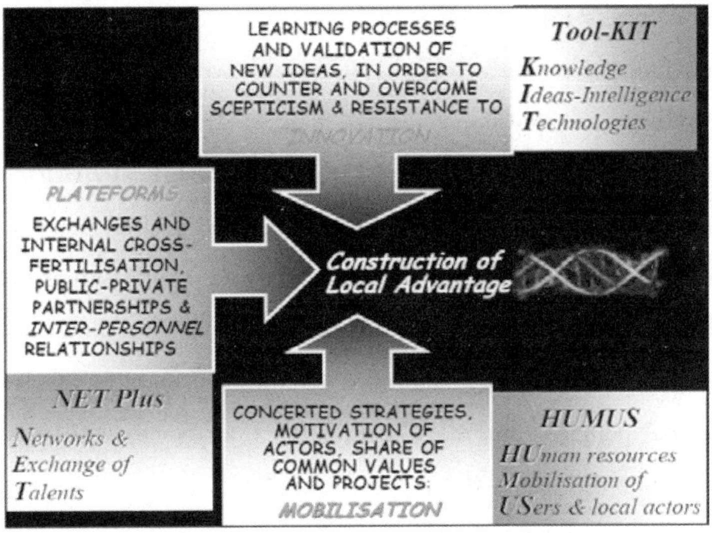

Figure 4. Construction of local advantage

While manufacturing remains crucial in China, it will not be sufficient to carry this country through the next stage in its development. China first opened its markets and industries to *Foreign Direct Investments*, initially to boost exports, although laying the foundation for industrial & technological upgrading that facilitates its technological catch up. Thus, China could turn the "World's workshop" into the "World's Lab", while according to the UNDP 2007 report, the incidence of absolute poverty plunged from 31% to just 2.8%... But the race for "Xiao Kang" – 小康 – which contributes to create a harmonious wealth is still a long way ... We therefore should wonder whether some innovation policies and new differentiated competitive advantages are taking place within some Chinese provinces.

It is nevertheless worthy wondering whether China considered orientating its economy too late, in terms of industrial and technological sectors, as well as in terms of economical balance and differentiated regional developments. Today, 83 (56 up to 2010, plus 27 in 2011) *National New & High – tech Industry Development Zones* have been created with the implementation of *TORCH Program* (http://www.ctp.gov.cn), which is a guideline programme launched by 1988 to promote the development of new and high – tech industries in China, and then enhancing R&D investments for an open window to the future …

Although China's high – tech parks have changed enormously in recent years by focusing on innovation, attracting more foreign investment, and producing more high – tech products, the question remained as to whether this transformation has addressed the fundamental problems of how to churn out the next *Hewlett – Packard* or *Intel*, and how to make Chinese High – Tech Parks and ETDZs more or less similar to their model of a "*China's Silicon Valley*". Past experiences represent the background which policy makers tried to work with in order to find their own regional solution, rather than the exact replication or "cloning" of more or less successful examples of regional policies from elsewhere, often from places with very different economies and socio – institutional environments.

China still sounds not to have integrated such concrete assets. Copying of best practices is almost impossible when it comes to intangible regional assets – such as particular knowledge bases or institutional settings – that are the results of long histories in particular contents. Policy makers should therefore reflect on this and be wary to simply imitate successful models. Unfortunately for China, *ZhongGuanCun*, the huge ETDZ in Beijing and n°1 in China, was dubbed "*China's Silicon Valley*" when it was established … Doubts still exist about the appropriateness of the label. *ZhongGuanCun*, in following the example of *Silicon Valley* instead of mirroring its success, is but a poor shadow of its role model: many S&T firms, spin – offs from state – owned institutions of research and education – training, used those institutions' funding, staff, facilities, and most important research achievements, denying the full range of entrepreneurial risks for start – ups.

Eventually, there is a general need in China for a more innovation – based economy. There are new and differentiated competitiveness policies which lead to benchmark the main knowledge economies all over China. It proved useful to improve the innovation policies, according not only to the "human" and "social" capitals' assessments, but also with respect to the three axes of the so – called *TAO* methodology [韬] survey① that is, the "*Technology edge*" of the territories, the "*Attractiveness of talents*" and an "*Open – minded and entrepreneurship climate*" within the local policies ... This *TAO* methodology, already experimented in China in 2005, enabled observing the potential of four internal cities, Nanjing, Wuhan, Chongqing and Chengdu, by benchmarking with two high level Chinese cities in terms of competitiveness: Shanghai and Beijing.

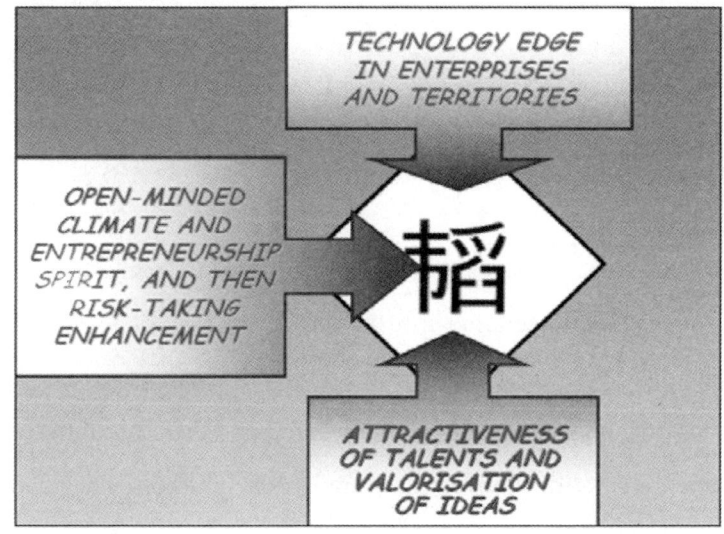

Figure 5. The three axes of the TAO methodology

By contrast with the usual sense which claims that "*the more we go inland, the more the assets will be tricky and critical*", internal cities witness and demonstrate aptitudes to play a central rather than peripheral role, and a huge capacity to rebalancing a Chinese knowledge economy for the construction of local advantages in the near future ...

Such an innovation policy mapping first consisted of tracking two key criteria:

---

① Mission TAO – Yangzi, – Mission cartographique innovation – Axe du Yangzi – Jean – Marie Rousseau, Ambassade de France en Chine (Service pour la Science et la Technologie, novembre – décembre 2008.

Partie 1: En remontant l'axe du Yangzi (http://www.bulletins – electroniques.com/rapports/somm09_013.htm).

Partie 2: L'innovation aux sources de la compétitivité (http://www.bulletins – electroniques.com/rapports/somm09_014.htm).

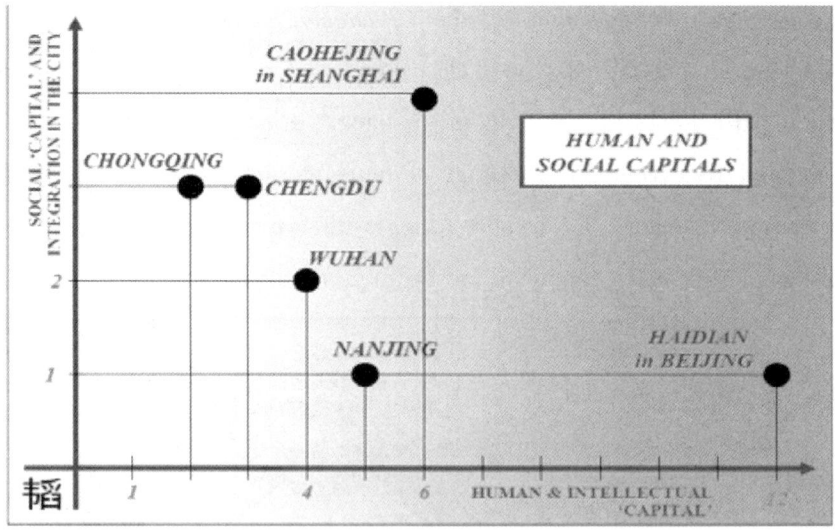

Figure 6. Human and Social Capitals in six Chinese cities

1) the measurement of integration rate of the innovation in terms of citizenship; 2) the apprehension concerning the human and intellectual resources. As for the latter criterion, Beijing unquestionably is in a leading position, while the universities of the *Yangzi Axis* hold a still relatively honourable place. Thus, considering the level of the "material" and "immaterial" infrastructures of R&D and education, Beijing with 12 points serves as calibration, whereas Shanghai maintains its place of second with 6 points, whereas Nanjing follows with 5 points, Wuhan with 4 points, Chengdu with 3 points, and then Chongqing with 2 points. However, this advocates neither the superiority of Beijing in terms of innovation policy, nor the promising position of

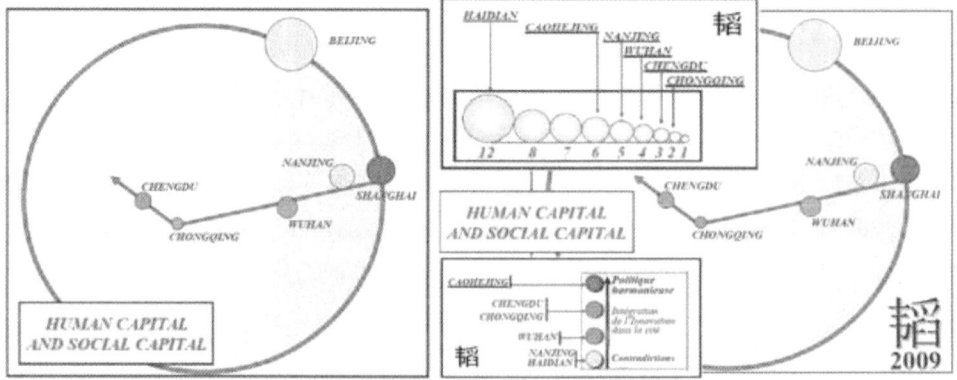

Figure 7. Mapping Human and Social Capitals

the other Chinese sites. By contrast, the *TAO* survey demonstrated the interest to reflect on three relevant and convergent strengths: 1) the technology edge of the companies and supported by the local knowledge centres; 2) the valuation of territories in order to attract qualified workforces and talents; 3) the formation of a entrepreneurial "atmosphere" with an open – up entrepreneurship policy at a local level. And as a matter of fact, it occurs that the order established by the *Yangzi River* course is completely upset by the *TAO* mapping.

Chengdu, at the very end of the *Yangzi Axis*, with its high degree of S&T integration within the city, as well as with its organisation of exchanges on Innovation Platforms, shows surprising capacities in this respect for a relevant growth approach and the construction of local advantages to the future.

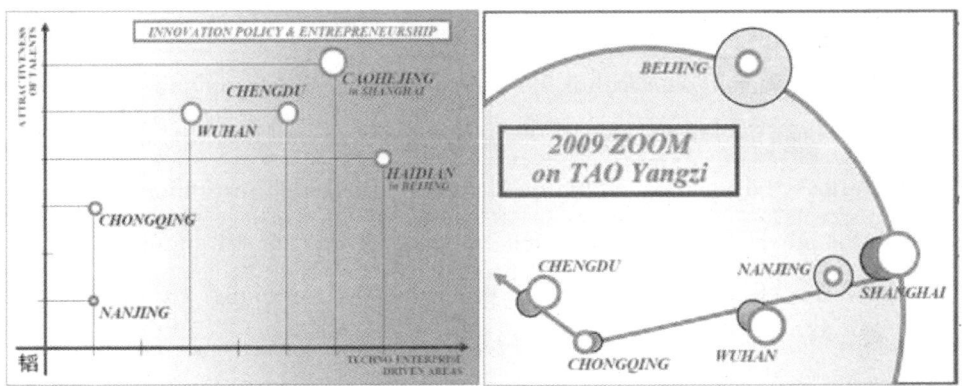

Figure 8. Mapping and Zooming on the TAO Yangzi Landscape

That, however, does not mean that the sites which are emphasized in this analysis, *Beijing* and *Nanjing*, will be denying new opportunities for successfully entering the competitive economy of the next decades. These two sites, with their most past creative assets of growth and employment, still could be able to continue to find the occasion and time for a policy of proactive innovation. It is highly relevant to observe China as a diversified series of landscapes, although we also have to be aware of a generalised need for a more innovation – based economy. Thus, it sounds interesting to adopt a methodology which may help analyse new and differentiated competitiveness policies which lead to adding distinctive values. This improvement of the innovation policy at local levels, accordingly to the human and the social capitals, has also to be complemented by an assessment of the three additional axes of the *TAO* methodology, that is, *Technology edge*, Attractiveness and *Open – up entrepreneurship*. As a result and by contrast with the usual sense which claims that the more we go inland, the more the assets will be tricky and critical, internal cities witness and demonstrate aptitudes to play a central rather than a peripheral role, and a huge capacity to rebalancing a Chinese knowledge economy for the construction of local advantages in the near future ...

Innovation policies can be implemented only by the best articulation around regional synergies. They must consider at the same time new forms of business support and knowledge bodies or institutions (universities, research centres ...) that could participate together to promote the territories.

The *Pole – Chengdu* 2010 study[①] did not aim at a comprehensive collection of industrial and academic data within the site of Chengdu. By an enquiry based on local polls, it consisted essentially of measuring the actual and potential ability of partnerships between businesses, on the one hand, and research institutions and universities, on the other. In this investigation, although it was not still optimised in terms of performances, Chengdu proved very promising – especially with the different "*Technology Platforms*" or "*Technical Platforms*", and sometimes even "*Multidisciplinary Platforms*" ... Initiated by the municipal government and managed by the CDHT, these ones might usefully turn into "*Innovation Platforms*".

Conceived for bringing a contribution to a mutual local knowledge and intelligence, these platforms enable companies to recruit their staff and improve the skills of young talents and graduates from the university. Education systems, continuing training, vocational training and lifelong education aim to provide people better career options and new opportunities for personal advancement. Through these *Platforms*, there is a real pooling of interests between local companies researching talents

---

① Mission Pôle Chengdu, Ambassade de France en Chine), Jean – Marie Rousseau, Ambassade de France en Chine (Service pour la Science et la Technologie), février – mars 2010, Stratégie régionale d'innovation et valorisation des territoires en Chine (http://www.bulletins – electroniques.com/rapports/somm10_010.htm).

and enhancing skills and practices of their employees, and universities eager to find outlets for their students, as well as public local authorities willing to enhance the attractiveness of the region, that is to say, the resilience and competitiveness of their whole territory. Thus, since these *Platforms* help strengthen regional capacity for innovation, the socio – economic rebalancing of China could pass through a similar commitment of local actors around this major and specific asset of Chengdu. It should however be adapted to the context of international competitiveness by directing them not only towards the promotion of research, but also by the technological irrigation of SMEs and start – ups on a real industrial basis, as well as strengthening the knowledge absorption capacity of the territory. Through all these initiatives, we can observe that Chengdu is already positioned as a major centre in the heart of China, and then is ready to assume commitments in terms of innovation policy and international competitiveness.

The organisation of changes in the territories must aim to sustainable development for the community's advantages including actors and citizens living and working there. This dynamics requires the mobilisation of economic and societal partners, as well as collection and processing of knowledge and information related to a process going from territorial engineering to territorial intelligence. In turn, this process par-

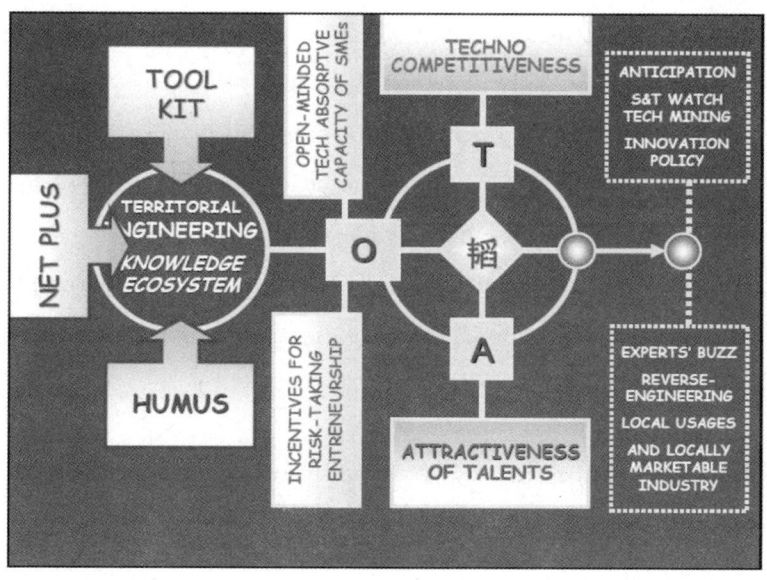

Figure 9. From Territorial Engineering towards TAO Strategy

ticipates in practices allowing ownership and involvement of local communities, but also should imply the commitment with a top – down process of public authorities as facilitator and further more decision – makers, at local and international levels.

As a result, further progress was made in relocating industries to the central and western regions. One of the main projects is about the new capacity to reinforce the optimisation and the balance of the regional development, while the unavoidable raise of the level of urbanisation: *"We will steadfastly give priority to thoroughly implementing the strategy of large – scale development of the western region in the master strategy for regional development, carry out the major tasks and policies for developing the western region in the new decade, and formulate the twelfth five – year plan for large – scale development of the western region."* Considerable progress has yet been achieved to this respect and a series of industries in the western region have been encouraged by the government, with a greater support to the development of infrastructure and ecological and environmental conservation.

Nonetheless the results suggest that the current regional pattern of distribution of S&T activities in certain fields harbours potential to develop local linkages in the future. Moreover, while high – tech activities may still be concentrated on a number of key locations, activities in the medium – tech sectors are far more distributed.

Therefore, it is nowadays admitted that regions should create local and regional knowledge synergies by providing incentives for interaction between small business and educational institutions and resources. It should also sponsor research into the processes involved in teaching creativity, inventiveness and commercialisation in technical environments. Universities, and the academic sphere as a whole, should promote an innovation – oriented culture while maintaining a commitment to creating new knowledge at the frontiers of research. This culture should seed traditional technical studies with new exposure to methods for creative thinking and translating ideas into commercial applications.

2.2 Shanzhai Innovations for affordable and marketable new technologies

By 1986, to meet the global challenges of new technology competition, four

Chinese scientists[1] jointly proposed to boost China's high-tech development. With strategic vision and resolution, DENG Xiaoping personally approved the *National High-tech R&D* Programme, namely the 863 *Programme*, which aimed to achieve, through the *Five-year Plans*, breakthroughs in key technical fields that concern the national economic lifeline and national security. From such "leap-frog" developments in key high-tech fields, China enjoyed relative advantages. It should take strategic positions in order to provide high-tech support to fulfil strategic objectives in the implementation of the third step of the modernisation process. The *National Basic Research Program - 973 Programme* - is China's on-going national keystone basic research programme, approved by the Chinese government in June 1997 and implemented by *MOST*, on the basis of existing R&D activities and deployment made by the *National Nature Science Foundation*, for basic research to meet the nation's major strategic needs. The 973 has gathered together strong expertise to launch innovation studies of major scientific issues related to sustainable development such as: agriculture, energy, information, resources and environment, population, health and materials. It also aims at deploying relevant and explorative forefront basic researches; nurturing a number of outstanding personnel with high scientific qualification; building a group of high-level scientific and technological assignments, thus constituting some interdisciplinary scientific research centres. The *Key Technologies R&D Programme* is the 1st national program aiming at addressing major S&T issues in national economic construction and social development, with remarkable contributions to upgrading traditional industries and forming new industries. It focuses on promoting technical restructuring of industries, and tackling major technical issues concerning public welfare.

China's ability to upgrade its technology-base and its moving up the value-chain has been widely regarded as hampered by weak intellectual property rights enforcement. More recently, however, there has been increasing evidence to support the argument that China is catching-up fast in terms of scientific and technological

---

[1] *WANG Daheng, WANG Ganchang, YANG Jiachi and CHEN Fangyun.*

innovation. The number of domestic invention patents filings with the Chinese patent office has increased at an average annual rate of 35% from around 15,600 to over 122,000 during the period 1999 – 2006. This catching – up process is paired with strengthened statutory intellectual property rights protection and an increased interest by policymakers in the role of intellectual property in fuelling domestic innovation by increasing foreign technology transfer and providing domestic forms with incentives to invest in R&D. At the same time, there is evidence to suggest that most of the innovation in China is of merely incremental nature and hence the corresponding patents protect "small inventive steps" rather than substantive new technologies. While such incremental innovation may still be valuable and in fact account in large part for China's growth success, the concern is that the recent strong increase in domestic patent applications is produced overwhelming by low quality inventions which are driven by the incentives put in place by the Chinese government to encourage patenting directly rather than indirectly through the promotion of innovation.

The next challenge for China now seems occurring from the imitation stage to the true innovation one with a significant capacity of regions and cities to develop indigenous innovation. Thus, it is interesting to point out some of the signs that collectively can lead to these abnormal conditions, characterised by lack of both indigenous innovative capability, and capacity to turn discoveries into profitable products, as well as unclear ownership rights, and other issues.

Leading – edge innovation of sophisticated high – tech products is neither sufficient nor necessary for sustained economic growth. To this respect, China's secret could lie in its skill in a new way of innovation, making things in new and better ways, rather than inventing better things. As the *Red Queen*, Chinese firms run as fast as they can stay in the same spot right at the global technology frontier, without actually advancing it. Chinese firms offer 80% of global best quality, at half the cost. Apple engineers design the iPhone in America. Within three weeks, Chinese engineers know how to make it in China: *Faster*! *Cheaper*! *Better*!

Breakthrough Innovations refer to radically new products/services, and require top scientists and engineers, who work at the frontier of basic and applied research.

Such tech breakthroughs are only the tip of the iceberg, as innovation essentially aims to meet the needs of the society and create an edge, if not playing a critical role in manufacturing, and then constructing a territorial advantage.

Incremental Innovations do not require substantial inputs for science, but they do require considerable skills and ingenuity to introduce continuous improvements to an existing product or process, often through *"reverse" engineering of foreign technologies*: Reverse engineering techniques consist of analysing these technologies in details in order to redesign and improve them.

Logistical Innovations use existing component technologies but change the way they work together, with a capacity to leverage deep understanding of market and users' requirements in order to break new ground in product development: *iPhone, iPad ...* In contrast to radical innovations, they need less science inputs and investments, but require strong system integration and strategic marketing capabilities and skills ...

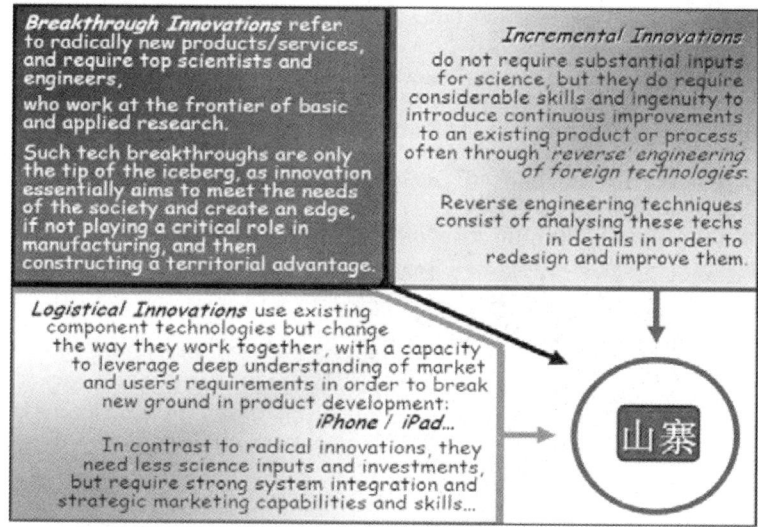

Figure10. From Three Usual Types of Innovation towards an Emerging Shanzhai Innovation

Shanzhai literally means "mountain fortress" and implies banditry and lack of state control, while referring to China's vast array of name – brand knockoffs. Chinese authorities appear to regard Shanzhai warily, especially when it comes to intellectual property issues. "*The Shanzhai culture as a celebration of the DIY [Do – it –*

yourself] spirit or as a parody to mainstream culture can add fun to our daily lives", said one recent editorial in an official state newspaper. A second area where the Chinese excel is in "bandit" or "guerrilla" innovation, known as *Shanzhai*. The original bandits lived in isolated villages and carried out raids on upright citizens. Today's bandits live at the margins of official society but are much in evidence: in Shanghai's People's Square you will be offered a cheap watch or phone at every step. These "bandits" are parasites who profit from China's weak property rights, but they are also talented innovators, quickly producing copies of high-tech gadgets that are cheap enough for migrant workers to be able to afford them but also fashionable enough for young professionals to covet them. In their own way the "bandits" may deploy as much innovation and ingenuity as their legitimate counterparts. However, *Shanzhai Innovations*, 山寨, offer the radical territorial advantage of local firms by claiming prior art more quickly than any "foreign" competitors, who just can rely on formal invention patents. Such locally adapted innovations, both mixing logistical, incremental and even, sometimes, breakthrough innovations, are not copycat, but fully fit the consumers' needs, while being affordable for local populations and further markets abroad. Originally considered as local counterfeit and fake and pirate products, the concept of Shanzhai gradually evolved towards a more acceptable scanning knowledge and creating new ideas, and even a fully tailored and

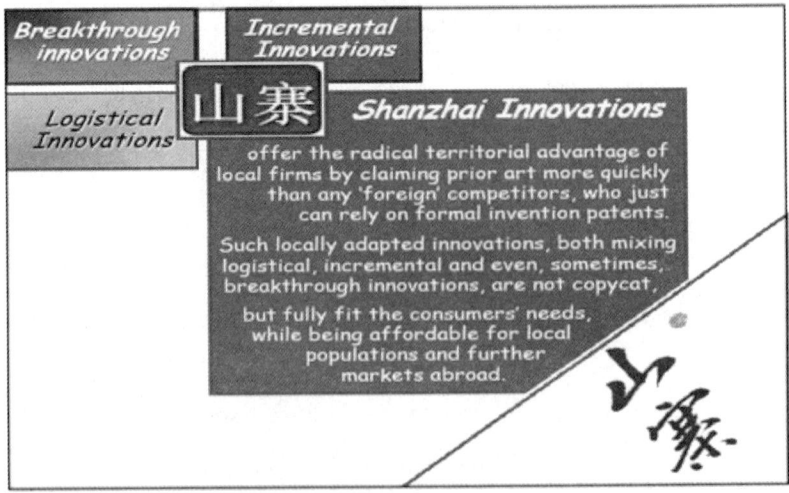

Figure 11. Shanzhai Innovation

bespoke science and technology to make the foreign hi-techs products, locally affordable and turn them into domestic marketable technologies.

The proposed changes are generally opposed by patent agents and attorneys, manufacturing companies, biotechnology companies, and independent inventors. They are concerned that the rule changes fail to consider the difficulties commonly encountered in getting a patent, and that the changes would result in inventors failing to get the full range of patent protection to which they are entitled. The groups also maintain that the rule changes are not consistent with the current regulations on continuations.

> 实 事 求 是
> Seeking truth from practice[①]

Contrary to a genuine "*Red – Queen Run*", a number of Chinese companies appear to be truly innovative, potentially even pushing the technology frontier beyond China. At the same time, there are very few such companies, and some of the most active among them are foreign-invested. Most companies are thus likely to concentrate on incremental process innovation rather than the generation of "new-to-the-world" innovation.

What is the likely impact of the patent explosion? It points to China becoming an economy that competes not only on cheap labour and sheer scale, but also in terms of innovation. Concepts of innovation and of domestic marketable products both offer a synergy which fully meets the commitments and the realisation of innovation. Shanzhai couldn't be considered as mere pirating and counterfeiting foreign high-technologies: in contrast, it should be admitted as a real new sort of efficient economy which fits the need of China for reinforcing the balance of the country by making

---

① Wang Fuzhi (1619 – 1692) also named Wang Chuanshan, born in Hengyang city, Hunan Province, actually lived in the Shichuan Mountains where he wrote his masterpieces, including *Du Tong Jian Lun* and *Song Lun*. These masterpieces were comprehensively printed in Nanjing city and made him very popular by promoting pragmatism against dogmatism.

these technologies affordable and more adapted to the middle – class Chinese consumer.

By its process of imitation and reverse engineering, Shanzhai must be regarded as a new form of knowledge acquisition, constantly growing and being improved, with codifications that would always lag behind even if it was feasible or affordable. At the highest level of adaptation and unpredictability lie actions which are almost wholly situation specific, and/or whose outcomes rely to a great extent on serendipity. Considering creativity and innovation as social and connected phenomena, today more than ever, Shanzhai innovations must be incorporated into increasingly intricate social, economic and technological systems, and reciprocally, those systems have to be adapted to facilitate innovations and penetration of a domestic market for a reinforced domestic consumption.

3 COMPETITIVENESS AND COHESION FOR SUSTAINABLE DEVELOPMENT

To a certain extent, we also measure the efficiency of the previous *TAO* methodology and *Shanzhai* concept as a causal effect of "*Stigmergy*"[①] and a mechanism of natural coordination between agents or actions in a process of development or construction, since the trace left in the environment by an action stimulates the performance of a next action in a collective intelligence. In that way, subsequent actions tend to reinforce and build on each other, leading to the spontaneous emergence of coherent, apparently systematic activity, without need for any planning, control, or even direct communication between the actors.

As a result, China is obviously attempting to successfully manage the transition

---

① The term "stigmergy" was introduced by French biologist Pierre – Paul Grassé in 1959 to refer to termite behaviour, as: "*Stimulation of workers by the performance they have achieved.*" It is derived from the Greek words στγμα *stigma* "mark, sign" and ργον *ergon* "work, action", and captures the notion that an agent's actions leave signs in the environment, for determining and inciting their subsequent actions.

from a mercantilist model of growth, driven by investment and exports to a growth model that respects environmental issues and induces more balanced relations with its neighbours. China in 2011 could rank first in the world in terms of industrial production, passing the US, according to the influential American analytical services of *HIS Global Insights*. Optimists say that the latest figures show China's manufacturing sector is stabilising despite being squeezed by Beijing's inflation – fighting measures, and a decline in demand for Chinese exports.

At the same time, Chinese firms might face increased pressures from rising labour costs, higher interest rates and a firmer yuan. As a result, policies should be prudent to avoid harming the real economy. But there is growing pressure to embrace more deep – rooted structural reforms. The head of the *World Bank*, Robert Zoellick, recently (October 2011) stated that China's leaders realise the country's existing growth model is "unsustainable". For the past 30 years, China has enjoyed average annual growth of about 10 per cent: "*In* 1990, *its income per capita was* 30 *per cent lower than the average for Sub – Saharan Africa – today, it is three times greater, over* $4,000. *By* 2030, *if China reaches a per capita income of* $16,000 – *a reasonable possibility – the effect on the world economy would be equivalent to adding* 15 *of today's South Koreas.*" Could we therefore conclude with him that: "*it is hard to see how that expansion could be accommodated within an export and investment – led growth model, so China will need to rebalance through boosting domestic demand, lowering savings and increasing consumption?*" Without fundamental structural changes, Zoellick warns, "*China is in danger of becoming caught in a 'middle income trap' – exacerbating the world's growth problems.*"

New driving forces, including the destruction of old path dependencies and emergence of new trajectories, actually look forward to seeing the emergence of a new position within a new world. This last section thus is a tentative assessment of potential futures of China, in order to observe its capacity to compensate immediate efficiency by measures of prevention for achieving resilience and insuring sustainable development [3.1. *Resilience as a counterpart and complementarity of immediate efficiency*], and then elaborate a comprehensive approach of territorial intelligence for the whole society and economy [3.2. *Territorial intelligence for innovation strategies*].

3.1 Resilience as a counterpart and complementarity of immediate efficiency

The Chinese influence is felt everywhere and about any issues. The amazing efficiency that China has yet been demonstrating since three decades is far not exhausted. The changing face of the scientific world shows how many its government has come to view science and technology as an integral component of its economic growth, and has consequently taken steps to develop the science and technology infrastructures, not only in the main spots of the country, but also with an interest for easing these infrastructures and human capital all over the country. In its twelfth *Five - Year Plan* (2011 - 2015), China lists the promotion of scientific and technological progress and innovation as a major tool for supporting strategic economic restructuring, while aiming to be the world's scientific leader by 2050.

But China still faces obstacles to becoming a more creative and innovative society, although these are more related to the continued institutional deficiencies due to the China's transition from a planned economy rather than some endemic cultural barriers. In sum, it is realistic to keep a cautious optimism regarding China's future as a technological power. China also faces challenges in generating a technology workforce of sufficient quality, as well as problems in utilising these workers effectively and efficiently. Between the brain drain, the generation gap created by the *Cultural Revolution*, continued quality problems in education and training, and the looming greying of China's population, the country will do face at least qualitative constraints on the supply side of competencies. The numbers are for human resources in S&T, "rencai" (人才: human talent), and other representative categories in terms of overlapping knowledge workforce. Too many of the data sources focus on personnel in state organisations and thus present a severe limit on assessing the contribution of S&T workers on the economy.

Beyond simple industrial considerations, China's decision marks the dawn of a new era in the history of international relations, that could consist of less and less access to resources the major industrialised countries need, whatever the price they are willing to pay.

In addition, there is an idolatrous ideology of progress that China could unfortunately adopt ... With one of the most important books, Jacques Ellul①, *The Technological Bluff*, dispelled the stereotypical idea of technological progress by means of a binding cascade of truth, wisdom, and foresight of the foreseeable future. The book progressively leads us from the concept of *Uncertainty* to a well relevant and well structured *Discourse*, but after a series of versatile trajectories of thoughts, eventually completes *The Triumph of the Absurd*, as a cardinal bifurcation that therefore turns into techniques and technologies issues. Outlined in Ellul's terminology, technique and technology drive the folly of this economic "progress", shaping the individual into a mere automaton of this system. He believed that "technology tyranny", represented by the increasing encroachment of modern technology into our private lives, posed a threat to the human freedom. Jacques Ellul, who is now classified as the most important thoughtful sceptical philosopher who worries about the negative impact of technology on the human condition, can help us interpret and translate the message Erasmus delivered five centuries ago. *The Praise of Folly*② has long been famous as the best – known work of the greatest of the *Renaissance* humanists, Erasmus of Rotterdam, although this started off as a learned frivolity. It eventually proved the finest example of a new form of *Renaissance* satire, whereby *Folly* is character whom Erasmus uses for projecting his view through her mouth. So, *Folly* comes down to

---

① Jacques Ellul (1912 – 1994), true pioneer of political ecology, carried out an inspired critique of modern society and committed himself in the events of the century by nourishing a considerable amount or writing (a thousand of articles or so books translated into more than twelve languages. The *Technological Society*, the first of his trilogy on the technological subject, appeared in France in 1954, and was promoted by Aldous Huxley, but the book he was proudest of was *Hope in Time of Abandonment*. *The Technological Society* is an important continuation from his previous titles, *Propaganda*: *The Formation of Men's Attitudes*, and The Technological Society.

② This book might be written within a week as Erasmus claimed, while staying with Thomas More and waiting for his books to turn up, but it was certainly revised before publication in 1511, and this was supposed to be considerably augmented and rewritten.

earth "as Homer does", and discoursed on her role in human affairs, relationships and wars, while nowadays we also essentially argue on progress and high – tech performances and energy efficiency.

In fact, we always have been and still are influenced by permanent mutations in a world of continuous transformations. But, could we then consider the obligation of imitation of the visible assets of innovation? It will be understood that the concepts of "*Innovation Cluster*" can not gain consistency as in – and by – the immaterial. They may not lead to harmony as through the entanglement of interconnections as well as tensions between different components of the environment. The regional advantage whose speaks AnnaLee Saxenian can only be built in concrete terms based on intangibility. The Cluster will become more visible on the condition of transparency of the institutions which it consists of.

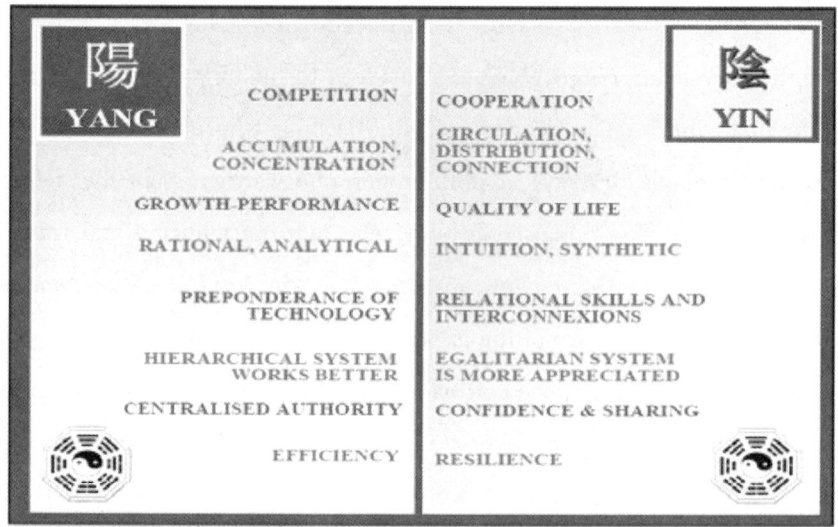

Figure 12. Yin and Yang implications in Territorial Intelligence

We call the continuity which delivers things from their lethargy and set in motion. We could call "change" which gives the things different forms by adjusting them to each other. As for what exalts them in order to make them accessible to everyone on earth, this is called the field of action. By opposing "*consistency*" to "*immateriality*", "*harmony*" to "*entanglements*", "*construction*" to "*intangibility*" and "*transparency*" to "*visibility*", we may find an echo in the conception of the world that many common assumptions with the Chinese, through the *Yin* – 阴 – and *Yang* – 阳 – and even more by the knowledge of the *Yi Jing* (易经) – Book of Changes.

In a society constantly changing in a world not only in processing, but in a world of transformations, it is expected of scientific research it produces new ideas, but also it sets up new means capable lead to products and services of tomorrow. Indeed, these intangibles that build competitive advantages of the territories are linked to key factors such as: corporate culture and risk – taking, anticipation of new needs, institutional participation, critical mass of resources, both financial funds that talents, and on the wider part of the territory for diverse strata of population, an explosion of creativity.

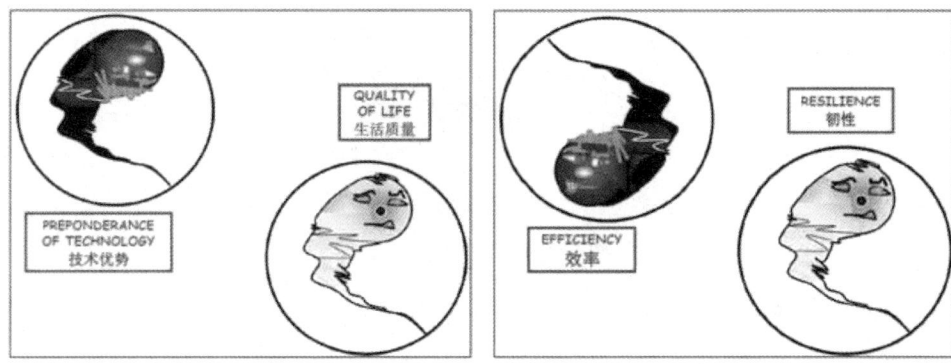

Figure 13. Quality of Life vs. Preponderance of Technology and Efficiency vs. Resilience

"*Resilience*" might be one of the key words for explaining the concept China should be aware of for the near future. In "*Physics*", "resilience" consists of ability to resist to external pressures and resuming its original structure, while about "*Computer's practice*", it is about insensitiveness of a system to elements' lapses; in the field of "*Sustainable development*", this refers to the capacity to resist to extremely severe and continuous chocks in order to escape disasters, and in terms of "*Psychology*", to capacity to successfully face risks and setbacks of the life. As for "*Territorial intelligence*", "*Resilience*" could be considered both as a resistance to centrifuge socio – economical forces, such as: brain – drain, capital – drain, industrial disinvestment, *students' disaffection, and as an* ability to resume a new socio – economical vitality and launch an internal dynamic, with an inner strength, capable to turn risks into opportunities.

It seems useful to ensure the competitiveness of the most efficient territories, while ambitioning to bridge the gap of the less developed neighbouring areas, and taking these concepts to reconcile non – prejudicial or contradictory objectives. In fact, it should refer to the "*Book of Changes*" – *Yi Jing* 易经 – step by step, concept by concept, to act positively on complementarities rather than to come up against opposition. Thus, "*competition*" can rhyme with "*cooperation*", leading to the notion of "*Coopetition*". Similarly, efficiency is necessarily compatible in long – term with resilience.

Figure 14. Coopetition

3.2 Territorial Intelligence for innovation strategies

The future we are fighting for is not as the world's largest importer, consuming products made elsewhere, but as the world's largest manufacturer of ideas and goods sold around the world. That is maybe a truism but also the mere and strong truth. To compete in the 21st century, regional policy makers must implement a far – sighted competitiveness strategy that links policies across many different fields and agencies, and innovation must be at the centre for that strategy. The critical question is not whether we can compete, but whether we have the leadership and vision to take the steps necessary to do so. China is now developing a coherent alternative energies' policy: solar panels, wind energy, investments in hybrid or electric cars, and capitalisation and/or monopolisation of mineral resources of rare earths and other metals are at the heart of the low – carbon economy.

However, we easily understand that these territorial organisation and animation of social capital can't exist and expand in isolation as they need external links and reflect the international context. Territorial intelligence is to know, from a local level, what the world wants next. For constructing a local or regional advantage, it is necessary to build it in accordance to rising technologies which prevail everywhere and also the emergent knowledge markets.

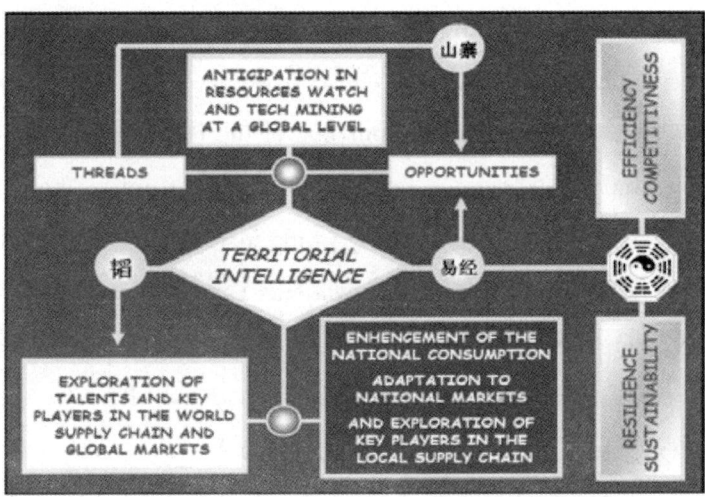

Figure 15. From Territorial Intelligence towards Yi Jing

A major question that previously was essentially arose about the competitiveness of coastal provinces, is now likely to extend to the hinterland and the provinces often regarded as peripheral. This question is of course not limited to China, as it is worthwhile balancing such huge territories whatever the country. In 2007, the OECD's edition on the *Chinese National Innovation System*[1] in collaboration with the Chinese Ministry of Science and Technology, MOST, ranked the fundamental as-

---

[1] OECD Review of Innovation Policy: China, published in September 2008. *A Review of China's National Innovation System: Domestic Reform and Global Integration* conference was organised by OECD and Chinese Ministry of Science and Technology (MOST) in Beijing, 27 August 2007, for launching the preliminary synthesis report of the first OECD review on *Chinese National Innovation System (NIS)*.

sets of innovation as follows:

☞ role of science, technology and innovation in building an effective system of market – based innovation;

☞ assessment of the Chinese R&D and innovation characteristics and improvements in terms of entrepreneurial environment, public research centres, universities and interfaces between science and industry;

☞ analysis of China's policy in terms of science, technology and innovation, including public governance and national innovation system.

This comprehensive study, referring to the *National Innovation System*[①](NIS) , proves very useful about the Chinese Central Government's policy and its mechanisms for R&D, but lacks a practical approach of the differentiated provincial innovation policies in innovation policies and their results in China. The *National Innovation System* concept, formally adopted by China in 1998, has led public authorities to strengthen national competitiveness innovation. The problem that the 2008 OECD study could not overcome is related to the lack of innovative entrepreneurs and the low absorptive capacity of domestic firms. These national characteristics of China's innovation system sound symptomatic offbeat approaches as regards the reality while disconnected from the real actors of development and the innovation. Similarly, all the technology transfers from university, the management of incubators and the spin – offs as well, are always reported at a national level within a very theoretical and monolithic national R&D – driven approach. These issues simply do not ease understanding relationships among universities, businesses and local governments.

The constantly improvement of its knowledge becomes a critical determinant for international competitiveness. China's provinces and cities are keen to contribute to the drive towards innovation and several of China's companies have emerged as able innovators, but we still can wonder whether China yet became a nation of innovators. While its government hopes so and has a plan to make itself an innovative society by 2020, increased innovation sounds now vital to move up the technological ladder,

---

① OECD Review of Innovation Policy: China, published in September 2008.

and then produce high – value products and position Chinese companies competitively in the global market and a sustainable society, through diversified but stigmergic innovation strategies.

图书在版编目(CIP)数据

竞争情报进展. 2012/谢新洲主编. ――北京:华夏出版社,2016.5
ISBN 978－7－5080－8789－4

Ⅰ.①竞⋯　Ⅱ.①谢⋯　Ⅲ.①企业竞争－竞争情报－文集　Ⅳ.①F274－53

中国版本图书馆 CIP 数据核字(2016)第 072869 号

竞争情报进展. 2012

主　　编	谢新洲
责任编辑	田红梅
出版发行	华夏出版社
经　　销	新华书店
印　　刷	三河市少明印务有限公司
装　　订	三河市少明印务有限公司
版　　次	2016 年 5 月北京第 1 版 2016 年 5 月北京第 1 次印刷
开　　本	787×1092　1/16 开
印　　张	18.75
字　　数	550 千字
定　　价	116.00 元

华夏出版社　网址:www.hxph.com.cn　地址:北京市东直门外香河园北里 4 号　邮编:100028
若发现本版图书有印装质量问题,请与我社营销中心联系调换。电话:(010)64663331(转)